FAMILIES AND CHILDREN LIVING

IN POVERTY

Families and Children Living in Poverty

Monica Miller-Smith

Central Michigan University

Bassim Hamadeh, CEO and Publisher
Amy Smith, Senior Project Editor
Alia Bales, Production Editor
Emily Villavicencio, Senior Graphic Designer
Stephanie Kohl, Licensing Coordinator
Natalie Piccotti, Director of Marketing
Kassie Graves, Vice President of Editorial
Jamie Giganti, Director of Academic Publishing

3970 Sorrento Valley Blvd., Ste. 500, San Diego, CA 92121

Brief Contents

Contents

Preface

This text explores the exogenous factors that contribute to the existence of poverty. Throughout the text, there are different poverty-related topics, concepts, and perspectives explored. Various theoretical frameworks are used to examine the social, developmental, and environmental effects of poverty. Small- and large-scale studies, case studies, historical occurrences, and everyday happenings are discussed to explore poverty and its connections to topics such as adverse childhood experiences, lack of a living wage, health disparities, social exclusion, homelessness, intervention programs, and community empowerment.

How the Text Is Organized

The text is divided into four sections:

- Part I: Poverty and Social Class Inequality
- Part II: Health Disparities
- Part III: Housing Instability, Homelessness, and Social Exclusion
- Part IV: Supportive Resources and Creating Change in Communities

The text mainly discusses poverty in the United States; however, the text also presents concepts, topics, and ideas that are connected to global poverty. The global poverty section expands the discussion of poverty by describing the relationship between poverty and global social, health, and environmental challenges. The text also explores approaches that are being utilized to address the multifaceted issues of U.S. and global poverty. The book provides a comprehensive look at what poverty is;

how it affects people and communities; why poverty continues to persist; and how poverty is being addressed in countries, states, cities, towns, and communities within America and across the globe.

Textbook Features

This text includes features that support the teaching and learning process. The following features are included in each chapter:

Thought questions promote critical thinking as you review the content presented in each chapter.

Key terms are identified in bold and defined to help the reader understand the concepts, theories, and information that is discussed in the text.

End-of-chapter activities are included at the end of each chapter. There are discussion questions, individual and group assignments, and service-learning activities.

The **discussion questions** are a learning tool that encourage students to engage in group discussion with their peers so that they can review information, practice critical thinking, and exchange ideas.

The **individual and group assignments** provide students with the opportunity to apply their learning and expand their knowledge on the topics that are discussed in each chapter. These assignments often include the use of technology.

The **service-learning activities** provide students with an opportunity to work in the community and apply course materials to real-life experiences. **Service learning** is a teaching framework that fulfills a community need, provides students an opportunity to perform community service, and promotes civic engagement. Students can examine their experiences through reflective journal assignments. The service-learning activities are categorized as direct service, indirect service, research-based service learning, or advocacy-based service learning.

- Direct service occurs when people perform face-to-face service. People can directly address a community need and receive instant feedback from the service that is performed, for example tutoring students at an after-school program.

- Indirect service does not involve face-to-face contact. People identify a problem and gather resources to channel toward the need, for example hosting a back-to-school backpack drive. People would donate supplies and volunteer to pack backpacks with school supplies.

- Advocacy involves bringing awareness to a public interest issue. People speak out on the issue and organize activities to increase public awareness, for example organizing a community meeting to discuss the need for pedestrian crosswalks and crossing guards near the local elementary school.

- Community-based research occurs when students, faculty, and community partners engage in collaborative research that addresses a community problem. The research helps in learning more about the issue and often helps guide social change, for example conducting research on food insecurity and lack of quality grocery stores in a neighborhood.

Author's Note

Thank you for using this text to guide your learning on families and children living in poverty. I hope that the information in the chapters, along with the end-of-chapter activities, help you to understand why poverty persists and how the multidimensional issue is being addressed in communities in America and throughout the world. For additional teaching and learning resources, visit the textbook companion site.

Acknowledgments

Thank you to Jim Brace Thompson for contacting me about the project. Also, thank you to the editors that I worked with at Cognella Publishing: Jim Brace Thompson, Laura Pasquale, Leah Sheets, and Amy Smith. I appreciate your patience and guidance through each stage of the editing process. I would also like to thank the production editor, Alia Bales, the copyeditor, Michele Mitchell, and proofreader, Laura Mcgowan, for helping with the final editing details, and the graphic designer, Emely Villavicencio, for designing the cover of the textbook.

Thank you to my colleagues and friends that shared articles, Web links, and information for nonprofit and community-based organizations with me. This information helped me to highlight individuals, organizations, and communities throughout the textbook. Also, thank you to the people and organizations that took the time to meet with me, give me tours of their organizations (and communities), and speak with me about the work that they do each day. Thank you for all that you do in your communities.

I would also like to thank my husband, Greg, and daughters, Ava and Sky. I am so happy that I get to share this experience with you. Thank you for your support and understanding throughout my writing journey.

PART I

POVERTY AND SOCIAL CLASS INEQUALITY

1

Poverty

THOUGHT QUESTIONS

As you read this chapter, consider the following:

- How is poverty measured in the United States?
- How does the Multidimensional Poverty Index differ from the other poverty measures?
- Why does poverty persist?
- Do the federal minimum wage or state minimum wage provide a living wage that allows people to provide basic needs and sustain over long periods of time?
- What is "the American dream," and is it easy for most immigrants to achieve after they emigrate to America?

Introduction

Poverty is a multidimensional concept. It affects individuals, families, communities, and society. Poverty is often described using the terms *absolute* and *relative*. When people live in **absolute poverty**, they are unable to meet basic needs such as shelter, food, and clothing. Absolute poverty does not consider people's social and cultural needs; the focus is solely on the ability to provide basic needs (United Nations Educational, Scientific and Cultural Organization (UNESCO), n.d.), on whether the person can survive on his or her own. With **relative poverty**, poverty levels are determined based on the living standards of the environment. When people are poor in comparison to those in their society, they are living in relative poverty. Relative poverty views poverty in connection to the economic standing of other people in society (UNESCO, n.d.). There are three perspectives that broaden the definition of relative poverty:

1. Income perspective: If a person's income is below the country's poverty threshold, they identify as poor. In the United States, this measure is based on food consumption, the income level to provide a specific amount of food. This will be discussed more later in the chapter.

2. Basic needs perspective: This perspective focuses not only on income; it also considers that people need basic necessities to survive, and individuals need access to preventative social services that will help keep them from entering poverty.

3. Capability (or empowerment) perspective: Poverty-stricken individuals lacks some type of basic capability to function. (UNESCO, n.d.)

There are different poverty measures used to categorize those who live in poverty. This chapter explores the poverty measures that are used in the United States—the poverty thresholds and poverty guidelines. The chapter also includes a discussion on the persistence of poverty, as it relates to social marginalization and inequality in American society. This discussion is followed by an overview on several causes of poverty, including generational poverty, limited economic opportunity, and lack of a living wage. The last section of the chapter describes the vision of economic opportunity that America provides for many people who come to the country. People emigrate to America for different reasons, but many come with the desire to achieve their version of the "American dream." For anyone who lives in America, the quest to succeed is often filled with challenges and triumphs. However, the effects of living in poverty can create additional obstacles for people to overcome as they progress through life and work toward achieving their goals.

How Is Poverty Measured in the United States?

In this section, the discussion will focus on the poverty measures that are used in in the United States. According to economic terms, an individual experiences income poverty when the family's income level falls below an established federal threshold; these thresholds vary across countries. In the United States, the official poverty measure is known as the **poverty thresholds**. To determine if an individual or family is considered living in poverty, the individual or family's annual income is compared to the corresponding poverty threshold level. The threshold amounts vary by the number of family members living in the household and age of family members. The pre-tax annual income is used to determine poverty status. If the income falls below the identified threshold, the individual or family is considered to live in poverty (Glassman, 2019).

The Census Bureau updates the poverty thresholds annually, and they are used primarily for long-range planning and statistical purposes. The poverty guidelines are another type of poverty measure that are issued annually by the Department of Health and Human Services. The guidelines are a simplified version of the poverty thresholds and used for administrative reasons (e.g., determining eligibility for federal programs) (U.S. Census Bureau, n.d.). Table 1.1 lists the United States poverty thresholds and **poverty guidelines** from 2010 to 2020 for a family of four. Alaska and Hawaii use different sets of poverty guidelines. For a current and complete list of all the poverty thresholds, visit the United States Census Bureau. For the poverty guidelines, visit the U.S. Department of Health and Human Services.

TABLE 1.1 Poverty Thresholds and Poverty Guidelines

Poverty Thresholds 2010–2020, U.S. Census Bureau (weighted average thresholds)		Poverty Guidelines 2010–2020, U.S. Department of Health and Human Services	
Year	Family of four	Year	Family of four
2020	Not available	2020	$26,200
2019	$26,017	2019	$25,750
2018	$25,554	2018	$25,100
2017	$25,094	2017	$24,600
2016	$24,563	2016	$24,300
2015	$24,257	2015	$24,250
2014	$24,230	2014	$23,850
2013	$23,834	2013	$23,550
2012	$23,492	2012	$23,050
2011	$23,021	2011	$22,350
2010	$22,314	2010	$22,050

Sources: U.S. Census Bureau, n.d.; U.S. Department of Health and Human Services, n.d.a.

The History of the Poverty Thresholds

Mollie Orshansky, a family and food economist, developed the thresholds in 1965 when she worked for the Social Security Administration (SSA). Prior to working at the SSA, Orshansky was a family economist at the United States Department of Agriculture (USDA) from 1945 to 1951. Orshansky and her coworkers were responsible for responding to publics inquiries, preparing food budgets based on income levels, and distributing information on food plans and meal planning using food budgets. She conducted research on family lifestyles and consumption across social classes. As a food economist, Orshansky continued to study food consumption in American households (Fisher, 2008). She was a contributor to the 1955 Household Food Consumption Survey that was published by the USDA. In 1958, Orshansky began working as a research analyst at the Social Security Administration. Her area of focus was social sciences, and she continued to conduct research on food consumption, family budgets, and elderly food budgets. In 1963, she was given the task of researching childhood poverty. Before starting her research, she needed to develop a poverty measure. She utilized the USDA's food plans to develop the official poverty measure (Fisher, 2008). These plans described sample meal planning, nutritional information, and food estimates. There were four diets, and Orshansky used the lowest plan (also referred to as the "economy plan"). The plan she chose was a temporary diet for when people had limited income; it was more of an emergency diet plan rather than an average daily use diet (U.S. Department of Health and Human Services, n.d.b.).

She also used information reported in the 1955 USDA Household Food Consumption Survey. The survey revealed that families with three or more people used a third of their post-tax income on food. At the time, this was a current finding, and Orshansky used it to configure the poverty thresholds. She took this information and created food estimates. She considered the average family's income (Fisher, 2008) and estimated that the hypothetical family would use a third of its income on food and the remaining two-thirds on non-food items. She assumed that the family's spending formula would remain constant at any income level. She used this approach and reduced the family's budget until the food figures matched that of the "economy plan." She only calculated the food category on the family's budget. She used this "one-third approach" to develop poverty thresholds for families of different sizes. She calculated the threshold figures by taking "the economy food plan" estimate for each size family and multiplying it by three. She used this "one-third approach to create a mathematical matrix system that displayed threshold levels by family size, gender of head of household, number of children, farm/non-farm status, and aged/non-aged classification" (U.S. Department of Health & Human Services, n.d.b.).

Orshansky's first set of poverty measures focused solely on households with children, and the information was published in an article, "Children of the Poor." After the 1963 article, the President's Economic Advisory Council developed a set of poverty measures, which Orshansky reviewed. After her review and analysis, Mollie Orshansky developed a set of poverty measures for the entire population. In 1965, these measures became known as the poverty thresholds. Since 1965, the poverty thresholds have been used for statistical, budget, and program purposes (Fisher, 2008).

While the poverty measures are a much needed item, they are outdated and have limitations that need to be addressed. Orshansky did not consider a family's standard budget for living; costs such as housing, clothing, health care, transportation, and childcare were not included in her calculations. The price of gas, produce, and household expenses vary from state to state; however, the thresholds do not consider these variations. The thresholds are adjusted annually for inflation based on the Consumer Price Index (CPI), which is distributed by the Bureau of Labor Statistics. The CPI presents the cost fluctuation over time for common household goods, such as housing, food, utility costs, and medical care (Bureau of Labor Statistics, n.d.b.). However, the approach to calculating the initial poverty measures has not changed since 1965 (Fisher, 1992). Our world has changed greatly since 1965, and the tool to measure poverty should reflect the changes in our society. The thresholds are not an accurate measure of poverty because the approach to how the thresholds were developed was limited to focusing on food costs. The poverty formula needs to be changed, and the poverty thresholds, poverty guidelines, and other figures that are calculated using the thresholds and guidelines need to take into account the true cost of housing, providing living and sustainable needs, and income levels across states, cities, and towns throughout America.

The Supplemental Poverty Measure

In 2009, the U.S. government established an interagency technical working group to provide recommendations on developing a

supplemental poverty measure (SPM). The group was comprised of individuals from the Office of Management and Budget, Census Bureau, Bureau of Labor Statistics, Council of Economic Advisers, Economics and Statistics Administration, and Department of Health and Human Services. The SPM does not replace the poverty thresholds or guidelines; it is an experimental measure that considers more information than the original poverty measure. The measure is used to provide additional information on economic conditions in the United States and understanding on policy outcomes. Table 1.2 highlights the differences between the original poverty measure and the SPM (Fox, 2018).

Unlike the OPM, the SPM is a poverty measure that is not unidimensional. The measure is multidimensional and updated with information from the Bureau of Labor Statistics. It considers expenditures for shelter, clothing, food, and utilities. Additionally, it also considers noncash benefits and taxes. Based on data from the U.S.

TABLE 1.2 Poverty Measure Concepts: Official and Supplemental

	Official Poverty Measure	Supplemental Poverty Measure
Measurement units	Families (individuals related by birth, marriage, or adoption) or unrelated individuals	Resource units (official family definition plus any co-resident unrelated children, foster children, and unmarried partners and their relatives) or unrelated individuals (who are not otherwise included in the family definition)
Poverty threshold	Three times the cost of a minimum food diet in 1963	Based on expenditures of food, clothing, shelter, and utilities (FCSU)
Threshold adjustments	Vary by family size, composition, and age of householder	Vary by family size and composition, as well as geographic adjustments for differences in housing costs by tenure
Updating thresholds	Consumer Price Index: All items	Five-year moving average of expenditures on FCSU
Resource measure	Gross before-tax cash income	Sum of cash income, plus noncash benefits that resource units can use to meet their FCSU needs, minus taxes (or plus tax credits), work expenses, medical expenses, and child support paid to another household

Source: Fox, 2018

Census Bureau, the 2017 SPM rate was 13.9%, which is slightly higher than the official poverty rate of 12.3%. Since the development of the SPM in 2009, the SPM rates were consistently higher over 9 years (2009–2017) than the official poverty rate. The supplemental poverty measure provides an additional perspective on how to measure poverty (Fox, 2018).

Multidimensional Poverty Index

When measuring poverty, it is important to consider factors outside of income; the **Multidimensional Deprivation Index** (MDI) is a valuable tool because the estimates include people who experience monetary and non-monetary hardships. For example, people who possess income security may experience deprivations in other areas, such as access to health care. The MDI does exclude some individuals who have low-incomes and who do not experience any deprivations (Glassman, 2019). The focus of this poverty measure is the deprivations that the individual experiences.

The MDI is not intended to replace the other poverty measures; however, it complements the other measures and helps expand the discussion on how poverty is measured. The MDI uses the Alkire–Foster method to construct a poverty index (Glassman, 2019). Dr. Sabina Alkire and Professor James Foster, from the Oxford Poverty and Human Development Initiative at the University of Oxford, developed the methodology. The method considers the various areas of deprivation that individuals experience within the same period of time, such as lack of education or living in suboptimal housing. This information is used to determine who lives in poverty, and the deprivation information is used to develop an MDI (University of Oxford, n.d.).

To create a MDI in the United States, researchers have used information from the following sources: the National Health Interview Survey, the Current Population Survey Annual Social and Economic Supplement, the American Community Survey (ACS) 1-year sample, the Survey of Income and Program Participation, the Panel Study of Income Dynamics, and the General Social Survey. In *Multidimensional Deprivation in the United States: 2017, America Community Survey Report*, the index evaluates six dimensions: standard of living, education, health, economic security, housing quality, and neighborhood quality (Glassman, 2019). Table 1.3 describes each of the dimensions from the index.

TABLE 1.3 The Multidimensional Deprivation Index Defined

The Multidimensional Deprivation Index Defined	
Dimensions	How dimensions are measured
Standard of living	In poverty according to the official poverty measure
Education	Aged 19 or older and without a high school diploma or GED; based on the household educational attainment for those under the age of 19
Health	Predicted health status is poor. Based on cutoff value of 3 for people under the age of 65 and 3.5 for people aged 65 and over
Economic security	At least two of the following conditions: Lacked health insurance Unemployed all the prior 12 months Cumulative hours worked per week for the household was less than 35 hours and no retirement or Social Security income in the household
Housing quality	At least two of the following conditions: Lacked complete kitchen Lacked complete plumbing Overcrowded housing unit High-cost burden
Neighborhood quality	Lived in a county with at least two of the following: High crime Poor air quality Poor food environment

Source: Glassman, 2019

The 2017 report primarily uses data from the ACS and County Health Rankings and Roadmaps datasets to generate the MDI data. The American Community Survey is administered across the nation, and it gathers housing, social, and economic data. This demographical data is used by counties, states, congressional districts, and other places. The ACS annual sample size is 3.5 million households in the United States and Puerto Rico. The University of Wisconsin Population Health Institute and Robert Wood Johnson Foundation produce the County Health Rankings and Roadmaps datasets each year. This data provides information on air pollution, violence in neighborhoods, and availability of healthy foods in communities. Using these datasets, the 2017 report generated the MDI data that is in Tables 1.4 and 1.5. The tables provide information for the 50 states; the U.S. territories are not included in the data.

In 2017, based on data comparisons between the official poverty measures and the Multidimensional Index, there was a significant

TABLE 1.4 Percentage of People Deprived in Individual Dimensions: 2016 and 2017

Dimension	2016	2017
Standard of living	14%	13.4%
Education	12.3%	11.8%
Health	6.3%	5.6%
Economic security	9.6%	9.2%
Housing quality	11.6%	11.2%
Neighborhood quality	11.1%	9.7%

Source: Glassman, 2019

TABLE 1.5 Percentage Deprived in Different Numbers of Dimensions: 2016 and 2017

Number of Dimensions	2016	2017
One or more dimensions	39.1%	37.1%
Two or more dimensions	16.4%	15.4%
Three or more dimensions	7.0%	6.4%
Four or more dimensions	2.0%	1.8%
Five or more dimensions	0.3%	0.3%

Source: Glassman, 2019

correlation between an increase in deprivation rates and an increase in poverty rates. The precise correlation rate between the OPM and MDI was 70.6%. The MDI is an important poverty measure because it considers more than income; it also evaluates other ways that people are affected by poverty. It is important to identify inequities in access to health care, substandard housing, and neighborhood violence. Even if individuals can provide basic needs, they may still experience these types of deprivations. Deprivations can negatively affect developing children, adults, families, and communities. Since the MDI includes deprivations, it broadens how poverty is measured. As previously mentioned, the MDI does not replace the OPM but helps to supplement it by generating additional poverty-related information.

The Persistence of Poverty

There are many reasons why poverty persists in the United States and across the globe. In this section, there are six poverty-related topics presented to begin the discussion on the persistence of poverty in the United States. While this chapter only focuses on poverty in the United States, many of the presented topics are related to why poverty persists in other countries too. These topics are **social marginalization, generational poverty, lack of a living wage**, single-parent families, limited economic opportunity, and emigrating to a new country.

Social Marginalization

On August 23, 1963, Martin Luther King, Jr. delivered his famous "I Have a Dream" speech at the Lincoln Memorial in Washington, DC. His speech was a statement of hope for an America that would embrace all citizens equally, regardless of race, religion, or social class. "I have a dream that one day this nation will rise up and live out the true meaning of its creed: 'We hold these truths to be self-evident; that all men are created equal'" (King, 1963). Fifty-seven years have passed since Dr. King's speech, and his vision for America has yet to be fully achieved.

Today, there are many marginalized populations that are socially excluded from society. Marginalized populations are relegated from social, cultural, economic, and political life. People may experience marginalization due to race, ethnicity, gender, religion, sexual orientation, age, ability/disability, and social class. Other types of marginalization are often related to social conditions such as social exclusion and homelessness.

Our society constructs definitions of social categories (see marginalization list) and generalizes entire populations without considering their innate qualities (Cook, 2008). Many people accept, internalize, and perpetuate social constructs, and they are used to organize our society into dominant and subordinate groups. Once a population of people is identified as inferior, the superior class can then label the group as defective and/or substandard. The dominant group then defines acceptable social roles for the subordinates, which are the less valued roles in society. When people who are labeled as subordinates display characteristics such as having initiative or intelligence, there are often limited resources for them to cultivate these characteristics (Miller, 1986). Lack of access to resources and supportive services can often impede people's ability to rise out of poverty.

Dr. King, along with numerous other civil rights leaders, fought tirelessly to end segregation and provide equality, but many of the

struggles from that era still persist in our society. For example. there
is a high incidence of minorities in the juvenile justice and prison
systems, which is directly correlated with the inequality that is seen
in low-income minority neighborhoods and school districts across
America. Inequalities such as exposure to violence, crime, and drugs,
decaying neighborhoods, schools with limited educational resources,
and minimal access to quality grocery stores can potentially have
vast developmental effects on children and adults, which can lead to
negative health and life outcomes.

The cost of marginalization is not borne by the individual alone.
The documentary *Waiting for Superman* (2010) discussed the high
number of high school dropouts who eventually end up in the prison
system. John Wetzel, the state secretary of corrections in Pennsylvania, stated that 50% of Pennsylvania inmates, about 25,000 inmates,
do not have a high school diploma (Baldridge, 2017). Over the last
40 years, there has been a decrease in the Pennsylvania prison population. However, the numbers are still high, and the cost of running
prisons across America is exorbitant. A Federal Notice by the Bureau
of Prisons reports that the 2017 annual average cost of each inmate
was $36,299.25 ($99.45 per day) (Bureau of Prisons, 2018).

If an inmate has a 5-year sentence in California, the cost would be
$75,560 per year, totaling $377,800 (Associated Press, 2017). California
is one of the states that spends over $40,000 annually on inmates. In
one of the "average inmate cost states," the cost would be $181,496 for
a 5-year sentence. The average cost of private school is $10,000 per
year. Consider what this means in economic terms: *The cost to send an
inmate to private school for 12 years would be $120,000, which is $257,800
less than the cost of 5 years of incarceration in California and $61,496 less
in a prison that spends the average per prisoner amount.*

Types of crimes and length of prison terms vary; however, there has
been a significant increase in the number of inmates over the age of
55. From 1999 to 2016, this population increased by 280%, from 43,300
to 164,400 inmates (McKillop & Boucher, 2018). These amounts show
that there is an increase of inmates serving long prison terms, which
contributes highly to the cost of operating prisons. There needs to
be a change in how our society invests in people and communities;
especially in high-risk, low-income areas. The incarceration system
needs to be reformed so that Americans can invest more money toward
providing resources for people living in low-income communities,
improving equitable access to quality education, investing in the

healthy socio-emotional development of youth, and providing supportive services for those in need.

Generational Poverty

Generational poverty occurs when poverty transfers across two or more generations. It is a cycle of poor parents raising children with limited to no resources, minimal access to opportunities, and lack of child-rearing knowledge. Their lack of resources hampers their ability to transition out of poverty. Thus, they remain in poverty and raise children in poverty. In turn, their children also have limited access to resources. These limitations make it challenging to have a life that differs from their parents, so the cycle of poverty continues (Tough, 2008). For example, if you currently live in poverty with your children and your children raise their children in poverty, the cycle of poverty passes from one generation to the next. When families have high levels of capital, they often have access to many resources and opportunities, which provides them with privileges and life experiences that many low-income individuals struggle to obtain or may be unable to access. Lack of access and opportunities creates limitations for people in communities and for neighborhoods where people struggle and have low levels of human capital—qualities, abilities, skills, and resources that individuals possess.

There have been many debates on how to break the cycle of poverty. Before, policymakers believed that raising income levels of parents would create change. Others presented an approach that focused on providing poor children with the same resources that middle- and upper-class children have access too. Some economists believe that increasing human capital would help people transition out of poverty. Poverty is a lack of internal and external resources, so would providing individual access be enough to create change? What about the homes, families, and neighborhoods where poor children live? (Tough, 2008) There are numerous variables to consider when discussing how to break the cycle of poverty: Where do you begin? What is the best approach?

Lack of a Living Wage

Many Americans work 40 or more hours per week, and their income is not enough to provide family members with basic needs. According to a report by the U.S. Bureau of Labor Statistics (BLS) (n.d.a.), 79.9 million Americans age 16 and older were paid hourly wages in 2016, which is almost 60% of all wage and salary workers in America. Of those hourly wage earners, 701,000 earned the federal minimum wage of $7.25. About 1.5 million workers had wages that fell below the federal minimum (BLS, n.d.a.).

State minimum wage laws do vary by state. In 14 states, the minimum wage is $7.25. Five states do not have a minimum wage. Two states have minimum wages below the federal minimum. The remaining 29 states and District of Columbia have minimum wages greater than the federal minimum. See Figure 1.1 for the state minimum wages.

Applicable to Nonsupervisory NONFARM Private Sector Employment Under State and Federal Laws[1]			
Consolidated State Minimum Wage Update Table (Effective Date: 01/01/2019)			
Greater than federal MW	Equals federal MW of $7.25	Less than federal MW	No MW Required
AK $9.89	GA	CNMI $7.05	AL
AR $9.25	IA		LA
AZ $11.00	ID		MS
CA $11.00	IN		SC
CO $11.10	KS		TN
CT $10.10	KY		
DC $13.25	NC		
DE $8.75	ND		
FL $8.46	NH		
HI $10.10	OK		
IL $8.25	PA		
MA $12.00	TX		
MD $10.10	UT		

(Continued)

FIGURE 1.1 Consolidated Minimum Wage Table.

[1]Like the federal wage and hour law, State law often exempts particular occupations or industries from the minimum labor standard generally applied to covered employment. Some states also set subminimum rates for minors and/or students or exempt them from coverage, or have a training wage for new hires. Additionally, some local governments set minimum wage rates higher than their respective state minimum wage. Such differential provisions are not identified in this table. Users are encouraged to consult the laws of particular states in determining whether the state's minimum wage applies to a particular employment. This information often may be found at the websites maintained by state labor departments. Links to these websites are available at www.dol.gov/whd/contacts/state_of.htm.

Source: https://www.dol.gov/whd/minwage/mw-consolidated.htm.

Consolidated State Minimum Wage Update Table (Effective Date: 01/01/2019)			
Greater than federal MW	Equals federal MW of $7.25	Less than federal MW	No MW Required
ME $11.00	VA		
MI $9.25	WI		
MN $9.86	WY		
MO $8.60	PR		
MT $8.50			
NE $9.00			
NJ $8.85			
NM $7.50			
NV $8.25			
NY $11.10			
OH $8.55			
OR $10.75			
RI $10.50			
SD $9.10			
VT $10.78			
WA $12.00			
WV $8.75			
VI $10.50			
GU $8.25			
29 States + DC, GU, & VI	16 States + PR	CNMI	5 States

FIGURE 1.1 (Continued).

State minimum wages vary between $5.15 to $12.50, but none of the minimum wage amounts are "real" living wages. Even at $12.50, a worker will make $500 per week before taxes. In most places in the United States, a single person would barely be able to live off this income, so imagine a single-parent family with two children trying to live off the same income. Even a two-parent family, with both parents making $12.50 per hour, would barley be able to provide basic needs.

Imagine working 40 hours a week and barely being able to pay your bills and buy food. Each week and month, you live paycheck to paycheck. What happens if there is an emergency, if a family member becomes sick, or your spouse is laid off from work? One shift in the budget, a surprise bill, or mishap, could cause you to enter the negative on your budget. Then, what happens? People often turn to credit cards or quick high-interest loans to help them pay for their needs. A minimum-wage job, living paycheck to paycheck and accruing debt, can place people in a precarious situation.

A minimum wage, then, is very different from a living wage that allows you to provide basic needs, save for the future, and live a comfortable life. If you are working 40 plus hours a week, you should not have to worry about having enough money to live. Each individual's version of the American dream should be possible for all that put forth the hard work and effort to achieve it.

Single-Parent Families: Diverse Households and Military Families

The U.S. Census Bureau reported that 13,253,000 children were living in poverty in 2016; 59.5% lived in single-mother led homes; 8% lived in single-father families; and 32.5% lived in married-couple families. Of these 13.2 million children, 8.7 million lived in single-parent families, with the majority living in single-mother families (Children Defense Fund, 2017).

By definition, a single-parent family consists of one-parent with dependent children living in the same home. Some people start as single parents, while others become single parents as a result of divorce or becoming widowed. Regardless of the cause, many single-parent families struggle to provide basic needs for their families. Unlike in a dual-earner household, where there are two incomes, single-parent families only have one income to provide all resources for their family.

Single-parent families experience many stressors, including financial concerns, parenting and child care challenges, social isolation, role overload, and emotional and psychological issues. The support from extended family can help lessen some of the stress that single parents endure. Extended family may help with childcare or offer housing to the family. The presence of a strong support system helps single parents make strides toward getting their family out of poverty (Turner & Welch, 2012).

Military families sometimes function very similarly to single-parent families, where one parent is deployed and the other is home to manage the household and care for children. In these situations, as in other single-parent families, the family unit is supported by one income. If the parent is unable to access family or friends for support, he or she has to manage all household and child duties alone. Additionally, the family is subjected to deployment-specific stressors, such as separation from family and war-related trauma. Often, service families are not financially or emotionally prepared for these stressors (Turner & Welch, 2012).

For single-parent and military families, a lack of economic resources and support can create stress for the parent and negatively impact their relationships with their children. Stress can affect temperament, communication, and level of nurturing provided to children. Fortunately, for military families, there are financial counseling resources and programs to advise personnel and family members on how to improve their financial well-being. There are resources for single-parent families, too; however, unlike parents who are living on or near a military base, with access to military benefits, a civilian parent would have to identify resources, broker them, and then travel to receive services.

Limited Economic Opportunity

When I first moved to Stamford, Connecticut, my husband and I use to take day trips and explore surrounding areas. One day we decided to drive around Bridgeport to see more of the city. I knew very little about the area and decided to learn more about the city's history.

Bridgeport, like many American cities, was once a thriving city. Bridgeport was a hub of manufacturing for many industries. Items such as locomotive cars, sewing machines, ammunition, toy trains, and mechanical toys were all once produced in Bridgeport (Rabinowitz, 2017; Wasserman, 2016). Because manufacturing factory plants were the main employers in Bridgeport, the city fell quickly into economic decline during the period of deindustrialization. Deindustrialization, coupled with corrupt public officials, left the city in poor condition, which is reflected in many neighborhoods, the school system, and the increase in violence and crime throughout the city (Wasserman, 2016). I share Bridgeport's story because it is the story of many American cities. When the main employers leave and factory plants close, cities experience a drastic decline. The quality of everything in the city begins to decline because there is minimal to no economic growth and no stable tax base.

The effects of deindustrialization and corporate downsizing have long-lasting effects on people and communities. Unless they are able and willing to move, people live in declining conditions, send their children to schools that face massive budget cuts, and struggle to support their family with a low-wage job because there are limited economic opportunities in the community.

The American Dream

Many immigrants come to United States of America for economic opportunity, to flee political strife in their home countries, to access educational opportunities, and/or to obtain the "American dream." Others leave areas because there are limited to zero resources and opportunities, so they go to a new country to gain access to opportunities and start a new life. Many dream of a place where anything is possible and opportunity is accessible to all. The writer who introduced the phrase described the American dream as "that dream of a land in which life should be better and richer and fuller for everyone, with opportunity for each according to ability or achievement" (Adams, 1931, p. 214).

Unfortunately, America is not a land where everyone is treated equally with equal access to resources for all. After many immigrants arrive, they must face the reality that all people do not have equitable access to the American dream. These realties do not deter them from their goals, but they quickly learn that American society is organized according to a socially stratified system that creates an unequal distribution of income, wealth, access to resources, and power. Those at the top of the hierarchy possess greater social, economic, and political power than those who occupy the lower stratum of the system.

The U.S. Census Bureau refers to **immigrants** as **foreign-born individuals**. A foreign-born individual is someone who emigrates from another country and does not have U.S. citizenship at birth (U.S. Census Bureau, 2016). Since the founding of the nation, immigrants have faced many challenges when they first arrive in the United States, especially if they do not have economic resources, social supports such as family or friends to help them with their transition, or if they experience language barriers. Depending on how they enter the country, and their access to transitional resources, recent immigrants may find themselves quickly entering a state of poverty. In order to establish a life in the United States, they may have to work from the bottom up and live in poor conditions. Even immigrants who possess high levels of capital in their country of origin may experience challenges using their credentials to secure employment in the United States. If their credentials are deemed invalid, they too must work their way up the social hierarchy.

Imagine coming to a new country to live: You have limited understanding of English, your education and/or work credentials do not transfer over to the United States, you do not have a job or a permanent place to live, and you have limited savings—but you need to provide for yourself (and family). In some instances, parents come before children so that they can obtain work and a place to live. However, this option has challenges, too, because a family is separated for an extended period of time. In other situations, the entire family comes together and struggles through the transitional phase.

If immigrants are undocumented, often the only place they feel completely safe is their homes. If they are out, they are at risk of getting apprehended, detained, questioned, and possibly deported (Chavez, 1992). Living in a constant state of fear leads to added stress for all family members. Stress, coupled with living in poverty, places a lot of strain on each individual and family relationships. Imagine trying to be focused and productive at work or school with this heightened level of danger surrounding your family. You also are uncertain of where to go for legal assistance and who you can trust. There are many stories of immigrants who are taken advantage of by people who promise to help with securing citizenship, but they scam immigrants and take their money without providing them resources (Chavez, 1992). Risks are compounded for minors and young women, who have even fewer economic resources and are at greater risk of exploitation. Fortunately, there are some reputable organizations that work to help and protect immigrants when they first emigrate to the United States.

Other Causes of Poverty

Other causes of poverty are limited educational opportunities, chronic poverty, and devastating life events. Limited educational opportunities are correlated with all the causes that have been discussed. For example, if an individual or family suffers from generational poverty or social marginalization, then they will most likely experience limited educational opportunities too. Limited educational opportunities often lead to challenges with graduating high school, pursuing postsecondary schooling, and finding and sustaining employment. This will be discussed more in Chapter 2. People may struggle with chronic poverty, which is due to long-term physical disability or mental impairment. In other instances, people may experience a devastating life event such as accumulating medical debt from an illness, a death in the family, or a car accident. Due to the sudden life change and lack of economic resources, they may become poverty stricken for a short period of time or permanently.

Conclusion

According to the U.S. Census Bureau (2019), there were 38.1 million people living in poverty (Semega, Kollar, Creamer, & Mohanty, 2019). The 2018 poverty rate declined from the 39.7 million people that were reported in 2017. In 2016, there were 40.6 million people in poverty, so the poverty rate declined by 0.4% between 2016 and 2017. It has also declined since 2014; the number of Americans living in poverty decreased from 14.8% to 12% in 2017 (Fontenot, Semega, & Kollar, 2018).

Based on the data from the Census Bureau, poverty in the United States appears to be declining. Even though there has been a decline, there are still a significant number of people living in poverty. The poverty counts are unable to include every person living in poverty, so it is likely that the figures are slightly higher than what it is stated. Additionally, how accurate is the data on poverty when the poverty measurement system is outdated? Many people who live above the poverty line still live in poverty, but these people are not included in the poverty counts. It is important that Americans understand the data that is presented to them. Americans need to probe and ask questions so that citizens can become aware of the truth and understand the state of our society. Poverty and social class inequality are a threat to the stability of our society, and they are social issues that need to be taken very seriously

America has a history of creating greatness, but it also has a history of using marginalized populations to advance society without sharing the gains. Once areas are drained of natural or other resources, people are used for labor, and corporations have achieved their advancements, they often move on. What happens to communities and residents that are left behind?

In order to build support for efforts to alleviate poverty and social class inequality, it is important to understand how it negatively affects individuals, families, and society. The effects of poverty and social class inequality surpass the 38.1 million people who are identified as living in poverty, but the dominant group and data reporting institutions portray a different depiction of poverty and its effects. The truth is that our society compartmentalizes poverty; low-income and poor people are pushed to edges of cities, hidden in forgotten areas, and quietly ignored. Poverty and inequality are social issues that need our attention, and in the forthcoming chapters we will explore topics that explain the severity and urgency of recognizing poverty and social class inequality as issues that need immediate attention and action.

END-OF-CHAPTER ACTIVITIES

Discussion Questions

1. Is the current poverty measurement approach an accurate way to measure poverty? Explain.

2. Why are single-parent families prone to living in poverty? What are some of the challenges that they endure?

3. What cities or towns have recently experienced a shift in economic growth due to a factory plant closing or departure of a company from the area? How has the departure affected the area?

4. What are some of the challenges that immigrants may face when transitioning into a new country?

5. There are many reasons why poverty persists, and some are discussed in this chapter. Can you think of others that are not discussed in the chapter? What are they, and how do they contribute to the persistence of poverty?

Poverty Line Activity

You will work in small groups to complete the "Poverty Line" activity. Each group will become a family of four with two children, ages 3 and 6. You will need to create a basic needs budget for your family using the information listed. Choose one set of information to use; the information has been divided by cities.

- Los Angeles, California: The mother is a preschool teacher ($37,850), and the father is a security guard ($33,070)

- Austin, Texas: The mother is a nurse's assistant ($27,030), and the father is a dental assistant ($36,820)

- Miami, Florida: The mother is a cashier ($21,870), and the father is a physical therapist aide ($27,160)

- Manhattan, New York: The mother is a school social worker ($58,050), and the father is a cook ($32,800) (BLS, n.d.c.)

1. Refer to the federal poverty guidelines and find the income level needed for a family of four to be considered "above the poverty line."

2. Compare the annual earnings of your assigned *two-parent* household and the poverty line for a family of four. Are they above or below the poverty line?

3. Next, figure out the post-tax annual earnings for the two-parent household. To calculate the post-tax income (net income), you will need to take the total pre-tax income (gross income) and perform the following deductions:

4. Deduct 15% for income tax, 4.2% for Social Security tax, and 1.5% for Medicare. You will need to find your state tax; you can perform an Internet search to obtain this information.

5. Take the post-tax annual earnings from step 3 and calculate your family's monthly income. Next, explore whether that level of income can actually provide for all basic needs. Estimate the amount a family of four would spend in a month for the basic necessities listed. (If you are unable to pay for all basic needs, then go into the negative to demonstrate how much additional money you would need to cover basic necessities.)

In order to make this like real life, your group needs to perform research to complete the budget. To start, locate a map of your chosen city and choose a specific area within the city. Explore the area using the Google Maps street view feature. Remember that rent, day care, and car insurance costs will fluctuate based on the area that you choose. Additionally, make sure to research the gas costs in the area that you choose. Lastly, include a description of the neighborhood where the family lives.

Basic Needs:

> Food
>
> Meals away from home
>
> Rent/mortgage
>
> (If they are paying a mortgage, also include costs for insurance, property tax, and home maintenance costs.)
>
> Utilities
>
> Telephone
>
> Health care
>
> Toiletries (toothpaste, toilet paper, etc.)
>
> Transportation (gas, car maintenance, subway or bus pass)
>
> Car Insurance
>
> Day care
>
> (One child is in day care full time (age 3); the other child is school age (age 6).)

After your group completes their budget, answer the reflection questions.

ACTIVITY REFLECTION QUESTIONS

1. Did your group fulfill all basic needs? Did you have any money left over at the end of the month?

2. What additional expenses were not included in the budget? What would happen to your budget if you were to add those expenses?

3. People work full time and still are unable to afford basic needs for their family. Many Americans live paycheck to paycheck and struggle each month to provide for their families. What do you feel is a realistic living wage? Make sure to consider the variation in cost of living across the United States.

4. Based on your answer to the previous question, what should be the minimum wage in the United States? (Poverty USA, 2020)

Resources for Immigrant Families and Children

Research your community or the surrounding area to identify an organization that supports the healthy integration of immigrants into the community. Explore the organization's website, perform an Internet search to find recent news articles to review, and try to locate videos that discuss the organization and its programs. You should compile your research into a PowerPoint presentation that features the information listed. Presentations should include an introduction slide, photos, any pertinent tables or figures, and a slide with concluding points. Also, make sure to include a Works Cited slide.

- A summary that describes the history of the organization

- An overview on the programs and services that the organization offers

- Description of special or annual events that the organization hosts for their clients

- Discussion of volunteer and community service opportunities that the organization offers for individuals and groups

- A slide that lists your personal reflections: What do you think about the organization and the work that they are doing?

*This can also be a group activity. Students should divide tasks and work together to complete a PowerPoint. Students can work in groups and complete the assignment using Google Docs, which will allow students to collaborate and communicate throughout the assignment.

Service-Learning Activity: A Day of Service

This is a direct service activity.
Visit VolunteerMatch.com, Idealist.org, or a similar site to locate a local volunteer opportunity with an organization that provides resources to low-income individuals and families. After you complete the volunteer experience, write a one-page personal reflection that answers the following questions:

1. How does the organization work to alleviate the persistence of poverty?

2. How do the mission and goals of the organization connect to topics that were discussed in the chapter?

3. How do volunteers help to achieve the organization's goals?

4. What are your personal thoughts about the work that the organization does?

References

Adams, J. (1931). *The epic of America*. Little, Brown, and Company.

Associated Press. (2017, June 4). At $75,560, housing a prisoner in California now costs more than a year at Harvard. *LA Times*. https://www.latimes.com/local/lanow/la-me-prison-costs-20170604-htmlstory.html

Baldridge, S. (2017, March 12). *Pennsylvania secretary of corrections focuses on kids, early childhood education*. https://lancasteronline.com/news/pennsylva-nia-secretary-of-corrections-focuses-on-kids-early-childhood-education/article_589ad084-069b-11e7-835e-4372cff6869b.html

Bureau of Labor Statistics. (n.d.a.). *Occupational outlook handbook*. https://www.bls.gov/ooh/

Bureau of Labor Statistics. (n.d.b.). *Consumer Price Index*. https://www.bls.gov/cpi/home.htm.

Bureau of Labor Statistics. (n.d.c.). *May 2018 Occupational Employment and Wage Estimates*. https://www.bls.gov/oes/current/oessrcst.htm

Bureau of Prisons. (2018, April 30). *Annual determination of average cost of incarceration*. https://www.federalregister.gov/documents/2018/04/30/2018-09062/annual-determination-of-average-cost-of-incarceration.

Chavez, L. R. (1992). *Shadowed lives: Undocumented immigrants in American society*. Harcourt Brace.

Children Defense Fund. (2017). Child poverty in America 2016: National analysis. https://www.childrensdefense.org/wp-content/uploads/2017/11/child-poverty-in-america-2016-1.pdf

Cook, K. E. (2008). Marginalized populations. In L. Givens (Ed.), *The SAGE encyclopedia of qualitative research methods* (pp. 491–496). SAGE.

Dickerson, Caitlin https://www.nytimes.com/2018/04/20/us/immigrant-children-separation-ice.html

Fisher, G. M. (1992). Poverty guidelines for 1992. *Social Security Bulletin, 55*(4) (pp. 43–46).

Fisher, G. M. (2008). Remembering Mollie Orshansky—The developer of the poverty thresholds. *Social Security Bulletin, 68*(3). https://www.ssa.gov/policy/docs/ssb/v68n3/v68n3p79.html

Flaherty, A., & Owen, Q. (2018, November 29). *Can they do that? Trump administration fires tear gas, starts wait list for migrants seeking asylum.*

ABC News. https://abcnews.go.com/Politics/trump-administration-fires-tear-gas-starts-wait-list/story?id=59443487

Fontenot, K., Semega, J., & Kollar, M. (2018, September 12). *Income and poverty in the United States: 2017*. U.S. Census Bureau. (Report No. P60–263). https://www.census.gov/library/publications/2018/demo/p60-263.html

Fox, L. (2018). *The supplemental poverty measure: 2017*. https://www.census.gov/content/dam/Census/library/publications/2018/demo/p60–265.pdf

Glassman, B. (2019). *Multidimensional deprivation in the United States: 2017, American Community Survey Report*. U.S. Department of Commerce Economics and Statistics Administration U.S. Census Bureau.

Guggenheim, Davis. (2010). *Waiting for Superman*. USA: Paramount Vantage.

King, M. L., Jr. (1963). *I have a dream*. https://kinginstitute.stanford.edu/king-papers/documents/i-have-dream-address-delivered-march-washington-jobs-and-freedom

McKillop, M., & Boucher, A. (2018, February 20). *Aging prison population drive up costs*. Pew Charitable Trust. https://www.pewtrusts.org/en/research-and-analysis/articles/2018/02/20/aging-prison-populations-drive-up-costs

Miller, J. B. (2014). Domination and subordination. In P. Rothenberg (Ed.), *Race, class, and gender in the United States* (pp. 110–117). Worth Publishers.

Miller, J. B. (1986). *Toward a new psychology of women*. Beacon Press.

Oxford University. (n.d.). *Policy—A multidimensional approach*. https://ophi.org.uk/policy/multidimensional-poverty-index/

Poverty USA. (2020). *Hard living on the poverty line*. https://povertyusa.org/adult-education-activity-1

Rabinowitz, M. (2017). *The immigrant girl, radical woman: A memoir from the early twentieth century*. Cornell University Press.

Semega, J., Kollar, M., Creamer, J., & Mohanty, A. (2019, September 10). *Income and poverty in the United States: 2018*. U.S. Census Bureau. (Report No. P60–266). https://www.census.gov/library/publications/2019/demo/p60-266.html

Tough, P. (2008). *Whatever it takes: Geoffrey Canada's quest to change Harlem and America*. Houghton Mifflin.

Turner, P. H. & Welch, K. J. (2012). *Parenting in contemporary society*. Pearson.

United Nations Educational, Scientific and Cultural Organization (UNESCO). (n.d.). *Migration and inclusive societies*. http://www.unesco.org/new/en/social-and-human-sciences/themes/international-migration/glossary/poverty/

U.S. Census Bureau. (2016). Foreign born population. https://www.census.gov/topics/population/foreign-born/about.html#par_textimage

U.S. Census Bureau. (n.d.). *Poverty thresholds*. https://www.census.gov/data/tables/time-series/demo/income-poverty/historical-poverty-thresholds.html

U.S. Department of Agriculture. (2019). *SNAP eligibility.* https://www.fns.usda.gov/snap/eligibility

U.S. Department of Health and Human Services. (n.d.a.). *Prior HHS poverty guidelines and federal register references.* https://aspe.hhs.gov/prior-hhs-poverty-guidelines-and-federal-register-references

U.S. Department of Health and Human Services. (n.d.b.). *The development and history of the U.S. Poverty Thresholds—A brief overview.* https://aspe.hhs.gov/history-poverty-thresholds

U.S. Department of Health and Human Services. (1997, January 1). *History of poverty thresholds.* https://aspe.hhs.gov/history-poverty-thresholds.

Bureau of Labor Statistics. (n.d.). *Occupational employment statistics.* https://www.bls.gov/sae/

U.S. Department of Labor. (2019, July 1). *Consolidated minimum wage table.* https://www.dol.gov/whd/minwage/mw-consolidated.htm

Wasserman, J. (2016, April 18). Wasserman: The Bridgeport myth. *Yale Daily News.* https://yaledailynews.com/blog/2016/04/18/wasserman-the-bridgeport-myth/

Weber, L. (2010). Defining contested concepts. In *Understanding race, class, gender, and sexuality* (pp. 23–43). Oxford University Press.

2

Social Class Inequality

THOUGHT QUESTIONS

As you read the chapter, consider the following:

- How is modern capitalism different from Adam Smith's idea of capitalism?
- Why is the convertible property of capital important?
- According to Vygotsky's ideas, how does language impact cognitive development?
- How do the skills that middle-class children learn from concerted cultivation prepare them to navigate institutional settings?
- What do studies reveal about language use and achievement among children of different socioeconomic status?

Introduction

This chapter explores concepts related to social class inequality. Among many other constructs and lenses, American society may be described according to social status. Social status is based on an individual's possession of capital, ability to convert capital into other forms of capital, and access to resources. Individuals with high levels of capital often have economic and social advantages that provide them greater power and increase social standing in society. Further, individuals with high levels of capital are able to cultivate their children by exposing them to numerous social activities and provide them with resources, that can help them navigate and thrive in institutional settings. By contrast, low-income families often have low levels of capital; this lack of resources may hinder their ability to navigate institutional and social settings and rise from their low social status. Low levels of capital, coupled with limited access to resources, hamper the social mobility of many poor people. Similar to how wealthy people pass on wealth to their children, poor people may pass on low social standing and levels of capital to their children. Parents across social classes love their children and want the best for them, but the ability to provide access to more varies across social classes. This chapter explores the topics of capitalism, social class, forms of capital, child rearing techniques across social classes, and connections between social class and children's life experiences.

Capitalism

There is a difference between the original idea of **capitalism** and how it functions in the modern world. In 1776, theorist Adam Smith described capitalism as a group of small business owners who produced goods to sell to consumers. The entrepreneurs sold goods at competitive prices to ensure that consumers would be able to afford the items. This created competition among the producers, but the goal was to produce items that consumers needed at affordable prices. This initial entrepreneurial vision of capitalism has transformed over time and a new form of capitalism has emerged—monopoly capitalism (Johnson, 2018). Corporate entities that are owned by the wealthy elite dominate the business sector. A combination of money and power enables the elite to not only control the capitalist system but also to benefit from the political economy. Political resources are leveraged to shelter the elite and promote growth of the capitalist system, which then benefits a small collective of those who possess wealth and power (Johnson, 2018).

Modern capitalism has created a hierarchal system that has diminished democracy and spawned an oligarchic type of political governing that provides power and control to the top 10% of society. For example, presidential campaigns are very expensive to finance. In order to obtain funding, many candidates seek the support of wealthy individuals. Providing funding toward presidential campaigns give the wealthy elite a great deal of power as they become instrumental in providing resources to an individual who may potentially become the next president of the United States. This leads to elites possessing power to influence policy, laws, and the overall political economy. This capitalist system creates a government that works in the interest of the wealthy rather than cultivating a society that supports the social and economic prosperity of all American citizens. The main function of this system is for the elite to retain power and control and for those who have money to make more money (Johnson, 2018).

Capitalism and Social Class

Capitalism produces massive inequities in the distribution of wealth in our society and throughout the globe. As a result, the wealthiest 10% of Americans possess 75% of the wealth in the United States. This top 10% holds "seventy-five percent of cash, more than half of the land, more than ninety percent of business assets, and ninety-two percent of stocks" (Johnson, 2018, p. 39). The top 20% generates 59% of wage earnings in America, while 80% of Americans earn the remaining 41% of wages (Johnson, 2018).

These inequities foster a social class system that divides society into dominant and subordinate groups. The dominant group uses social class to organize people by economic and social status, which creates an oppressive system that perpetuates immense economic and social differences between social classes. Even though people across social classes subscribe to social class differences, the dominant group has the power to set societal norms and cultural beliefs. Since they possess this power, they are able to validate disparities that exist in society too. They are also able to engrain these beliefs into the principles that guide our society (Miller, 2014). Many people then adapt these beliefs, without questioning them, and accept them as truth. This distorted information contributes to the acceptance of inequality in our society.

Based on these socially constructed views, our society becomes organized into a categorical ranking system that is based on income, wealth, education, status, and power. When a society divides its population into groups based on socioeconomic status, this is known as **social stratification**. The dominant group creates a hierarchal system, which society supports, that results in an imbalanced distribution of access to resources. While capitalism does produce services and goods for consumers to acquire, it concurrently creates an environment of scarcity for those who exist on the bottom tier of society. Individuals who comprise the lower strata of the social system are pitted against each other, and the bulk of the American population is forced to divide the 41% of income that remains (Johnson, 2018). This unequal distribution of wealth creates a social class system that perpetuates profound differences in economic capital, social capital, and cultural capital, which leads to unequal access to resources, life opportunities, and power in society.

Forms of Capital

French sociologist Pierre Bourdieu (1986) provides a framework to examine different forms of capital. Capital is accumulated over time and has the capacity to produce profits and to reproduce itself in identical or expanded form. Bourdieu discusses three types of capital: **economic capital**, **cultural capital**, and **social capital**. Economic capital is the assets that you possess, cultural capital is the learned behavior from social relationships, interactions, and affiliations, and social capital is power that comes from mobilizing social connections.

High levels of capital provide individuals with power and access to resources. When individuals harvest their capital and convert it into other forms of capital, they experience social mobility and an increase in social status. This upward, vertical mobility provides the individual with access to higher levels of capital and resources, which has the potential to create wealth and an expansion of power (Miller-Smith & Cszimadia, 2014).

Economic Capital

Economic capital is a measure of the individual or family's income or wealth. These are assets that can be immediately and directly convertible into money (e.g., stock, mutual funds, real estate, etc.) (Bourdieu, 1986). Many people possess lots of things such as homes, cars, jewelry, furniture, clothes, electronic devices, and more; however, what do they really own? Possessing items and owning them are two different things. How many items are purchased with credit cards? Are the cars leased, or does the person pay a monthly car note? Is the home paid for, or how many years is left before the mortgage is paid in full? What is the individual or family's debt-to-income ratio? Anyone can appear to have wealth, as it is very easy to accumulate items and present a façade of being wealthy. However, the true measure of monetary wealth is what can be easily converted to cash and how much cash would be left after paying all debts.

People with high levels of economic capital have access to financial resources to aid them through challenging times. For example, many communities and homes were destroyed by Hurricanes Harvey, Irma, and Maria. Those who possess high levels of economic capital had financial resources to relocate to other places. While they experienced the trauma of displacement, they may also own another property, and they had resources to help them rebuild their damaged property. In contrast, people with little to no economic capital were displaced from their homes, and they had to process and handle all that happened to them without access to financial resources. Depending on the severity of damage, it may take months or over a year for individuals and families to acquire stable housing and return to their normal routine.

When properly managed, economic capital produces power; it provides individuals with access to resources and other forms of capital. It can provide resources to support academic achievement (Coleman, 1988), which can create access to greater levels of capital, resources such as better schools, extracurricular activities, tutors, and prep courses. Economic capital does not solve all problems; however, it does give the person economic power, and that power often produces additional resources, access, and opportunity.

Cultural Capital

Cultural capital is gained from socialization with family and peers. People become enculturated as they learn social practices in home and school settings. Over the lifespan, an individual may be able to accumulate cultural capital through social relationships, interactions, and affiliations. In contrast, people may have a lack of cultural capital due to not possessing economic capital, access to resources, or opportunities. Also, people who experience involuntary displacement due to unforeseen life events will often have low levels of cultural capital until they are able to re-stabilize their lives, as their focus is on providing basic needs and survival. There are three forms of cultural capital: embodied state, objectified state, and institutionalized state (Bourdieu, 1986).

EMBODIED STATE
Over the life span, people accumulate cultural capital through socialization with parents and peers (Bourdieu, 1986). When children are small, they are like sponges and absorb learned behaviors from their immediate environment. They learn through socialization and begin

to emulate those around them. With each interaction, children become cultivated and acquire social skills.

These learned practices become embodied and displayed in future social interactions.

PERSONAL REFLECTION

Think about your learned behaviors and social practices; where did you learn these behaviors? Really think back to times when your parents corrected your behavior or language. Also, try to recall your parent/caregiver(s) behavior. Do you believe that the behavior that your parent/caregivers(s) modeled, along with social interactions with them, helped to shape your social behavior?

OBJECTIFIED STATE

A moment ago, my daughter asked me to define the word *cultural*. When she and I were talking, she noticed the word "cultural" on the computer screen. I first explained the word *culture* as a group of people who share a common belief system, along with common social practices, cultural tools, and goods. I explained that she uses cultural tools every day. I asked her to name educational tools that she uses at school to help her learn. She named books, organizers, worksheets, and more. These cultural goods are also forms of cultural capital. Cultural goods are objects and media such as paintings, instruments, and other material objects that can be easily converted into other forms of capital. For example, a collection of paintings could be converted into economic capital. It is important to note that while the legal ownership of the paintings would be transferred (objectified state), the ability to understand or appreciate the art (embodied state) is not transmissible (Bourdieu, 1986). This is a perfect example of how capital functions in "real life."

INSTITUTIONALIZED STATE

The last form of cultural capital is the institutionalized state. This type of cultural capital comes from being affiliated with organizations (Bourdieu, 1986). Affiliations provide individuals varying levels of cultural capital. For example, all the students in my courses are members of the university. For most, this membership will lead to completing their degree. When graduates are looking for a job, they will list the university and degree on their resume. This affiliation and credential may help them to obtain interviews with different companies. The education gained from being a member of the university can potentially provide cultural capital, which may help in securing employment. Some graduates also have affiliations with fraternities and sororities. This affiliation is another great resource to mobilize when searching for job opportunities. People can often leverage affiliation connections to learn about job opportunities and gain direct access to job contacts.

Another example of the institutionalized state is being a member of country and recreational clubs. Being a member of a club provides you access to resources and opportunities to forge new social relationships. Affiliation and membership provide individuals with "power" that helps them navigate social institutions. This power also can be converted to other forms of capital and helps them to secure higher levels of capital, which has the potential to increase their level of "power" (Bourdieu, 1986).

Social Capital

A great percentage of Americans use social media. According to the Pew Research Center (2019), 7 in 10 Americans use social media. This means that 69% of Americans use some form of social media. When I discuss social capital in class, I often use social media to explain social capital. People use social media to connect with family, friends, and peers. Each time they add a new friend, their total number of friends increases. Some people have hundreds of friends, while others have thousands.

PERSONAL REFLECTION

Imagine that you were hosting a fundraiser, and you reached out to friends on social media for support. How many would support your efforts? How many would buy tickets to the fundraiser? How many of your Facebook friends could you access for resources?

The term *friend* as used on social media denotes something very different from the term applied to people we've met face to face or see each day. People can have hundreds or thousands of friends on social media, but social capital comes from having strong ties with friends and being able to mobilize relationships to access resources. It is also equally important that friends possess high levels of social capital because this increases their access and ability to mobilize resources.

High levels of social capital have the capacity to provide a great deal of power. Individuals with power occupy dominant roles in society; people in dominant groups can create social norms, set rules in society, and possess resources to create changes (Miller, 2014). A great example of social capital to create change can be seen in humanitarian efforts. After Hurricanes Harvey, Irma, and Maria, many companies, institutions nonprofit organizations, small business, and individuals used their social networks—both virtual and face to face—to leverage donations to help those affected by the hurricanes. Social connections, strength of ties, and ability to mobilize ties helped provide resources to those in need.

Human Capital

Human capital is knowledge and skills gained from education and experiences. Parents who possess high levels of human capital have the potential to create cognitive environments for their children that will encourage learning. Parents use their personal knowledge to aid their children's learning (Coleman, 1988). For example, imagine if your father taught you Spanish and Italian, or if your mother was a scientist who did experiments with you every week, or if your father was a lawyer who encouraged you to negotiate. Each parent is taking the time and asserting the effort to cultivate their child's intellect (Coleman, 1988). More importantly, the parent possesses the skill set to teach the foreign language, guide the experiments, and encourage the verbal negotiation.

Parents who have high levels of human capital will potentially impart knowledge to children, as seen with the examples. In contrast, parents who possess low levels of human capital may have limited ability to impart knowledge and skills to children. Many parents want to provide educational support to their children, but not all parents possess skills, knowledge, resources, or time to accomplish this task.

Conversions of Capital

Capital is accumulated over time, and it can be converted into other forms of capital (Bourdieu, 1986). As discussed earlier in the chapter,

TABLE 2.1 Conversions of Capital

Conversions of Capital
▪ Cultural capital into economic capital: If you decide to pursue a graduate degree to obtain a better paying job, then you are using cultural capital to create higher levels of economic capital.
▪ Economic capital into cultural capital: Parents with high levels of economic capital can afford to pay for educational resources and extracurricular activities, which increases the child's cultural capital.
▪ Social capital to cultural capital: If a friend provides a referral to an organization that you later join, your cultural capital increases because of your affiliation with the organization.
▪ Cultural capital to social capital: If you are a member of a country club and attend a social event, you may meet additional contacts. If you become good friends with the new contacts, your social capital has the potential to increase.
▪ Social capital into economic capital: Imagine that a friend gets you a job interview. You have a great interview and get the job. Since you were able to mobilize your social ties with your friend, who had strong social connections, you were able to secure a new job. Your new income will increase your economic capital.

capital can move, even across categories. For example, a parent can use knowledge to aid in educating their child. This is an example of how a parent uses human capital to provide their child with cultural capital. Additional examples of capital conversions are listed in Table 2.1.

Habitus, Capital, and Fields

Bourdieu's work can be used as a lens for exploring the relationship between socialization and social standing in society. His approach highlights the connection between systematic inequality, social conflict, and change. He discusses how people of different backgrounds undergo different socialization experiences. Bourdieu's model of structural inequality is centered on three core concepts: habitus, capital, and fields. Habitus are ways of being that individuals acquire from social interactions within their home. Children learn social and cultural skills that they adopt and use in external settings. Individuals across social classes gain varying levels of social dispositions based on their *habitus*. According to Bourdieu, these social dispositions later influence an individual's educational attainment, social relationships, and access to resources, which affects the individual's possession of *capital*. Bourdieu posits that social practices and capital impact how the individual navigates institutional settings and the social world, which are also known as *fields*. Thus, privilege often allows individuals to cultivate children so that they possess the social and cultural skills, along with access to resources, to thrive in the social world. Regardless of an individual's social class, they can eventually acquire social dispositions and increase their levels of capital so that they can successfully navigate institutional arrangements. However, when individuals are born into privilege, they begin life in an elite social position that provides them high levels of power in the social world (Lareau, 2011).

Sociocultural Theory

Theories provide a framework of understanding by using systematic principles, explanations, and observations. Developmental theories are ideas that explain the changes that people experience during each stage of development. Theories are based on the connections between scientific observations and facts. This collective information is used to establish common themes and patterns that help illuminate the various aspects of human growth (Berger, 2008).

Psychologist Lev Vygotsky was the pioneer of sociocultural theory. Vygotsky's theory embodies a constructivist perspective of learning. **Constructivism** emphasizes the learner's role in actively constructing meaning and contributing to the learning process. There are different views of constructivism, and Vygotsky's theory aligns with social and psychological constructivism. He believed that learning is developed through socialization, social activity, and cultural interactions, which reflects social constructivism. Sociocultural theory has psychological roots too, as it also discusses the internal development of individuals (Woolfolk, 2004). Vygotsky's theory creates a bridge between social and psychological constructivism. Social interactions, cultural practices, and cognitive development help to shape the developing person, and they are key pieces to sociocultural theory.

Sociocultural theory is centered on the idea that development occurs through social and cultural interactions. There are several key concepts within this theory: **guided participation**, **scaffolding**, and the **zone of proximal development**. Guided participation takes place when a skilled individual provides guided instruction to a new learner. The knowledgeable individual helps the novice learn a new skill by providing direction and sharing information. When the skilled individual provides the learner support to help them master a new skill, this process is known as scaffolding. According to Vygotsky, the learner is operating in the zone of proximal development (ZPD). The learner can perform the new skill with the assistance of a more experienced individual. With continual guidance and practice, the

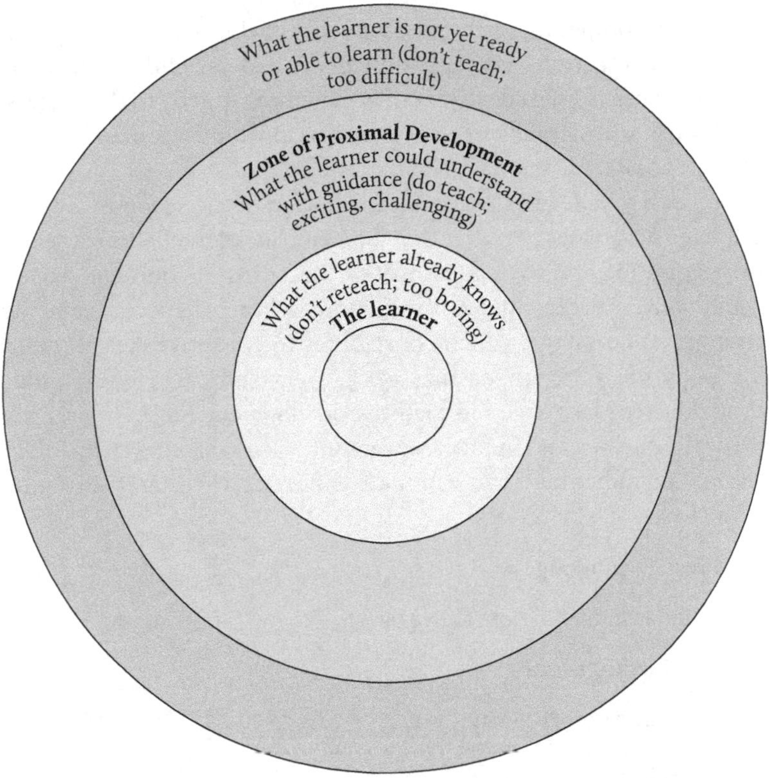

FIGURE 2.1 When the Learner Can Complete a Task with Guidance from a Teacher, They are Operating within the Zone of Proximal Development.

Source: Kathleen Berger, "Zone of Proximal Development," The Developing Person Through the Life Span, p. 47. Copyright © 2008 by Macmillan Publishing Company.

learner will eventually master the skill and complete it independently (Berger, 2008). The interaction between teacher and student produces learning and expands cognitive development. This experience leads to developing new cultural practices through social exchanges and problem solving (Woolfolk, 2004).

Vygotsky's sociocultural theory provides a framework for understanding language development. He believed that words were building blocks that developed cognition. The various components of language—listening, talking, writing, and reading—help advance the developing brain. Vygotsky identified two ways that language helps progress cognitive development. The first is through private speech. **Private speech** happens when the individual engages in personal discourse with themselves to generate new ideas (Vygotsky 1934/1987). Young children often demonstrate private speech when they talk out loud when completing a step-by-step process; they use private speech to guide their actions as they complete the task. As children mature, private speech is used silently, or they may speak quietly to themselves. Adults also use private speech as they develop and organize thoughts (Berger, 2008).

Vygotsky believed that social mediation is the second way that language progresses cognitive development. Social mediation develops language and cognitive skills through direct instruction and engaging in conversation. Guided instruction and verbal encouragements strengthen language, which contributes to cognitive development (Berger, 2008). Through socialization, parents (and/or caregivers) guide their children's language and cognitive development. Since children are naturally curious and inquisitive about the world around them, older and skilled individuals can stimulate children's learning by engaging in the following behaviors:

- Present challenges

- Offer assistance (not taking over)

- Provide instruction

- Encourage motivation (Berger, 2008)

Vygotsky used the term *apprentice* in thinking to describe the role of the child in the guided learning relationship. The child's learning is situated in a social environment and cognitive development is shaped through the guided direction by a mature and skilled individual. Guided instruction and verbal encouragements are integral actions for supporting children's cognitive development (Berger, 2008). When these behaviors are absent, a child's development can become compromised, which can negatively affect social, language, and cognitive development.

Unequal Childhoods

America is an unequal society that is divided into social classes. Before you can sit up, talk, or walk, you are ascribed a social standing within society that is based on the social class of your parents. If your parents are middle class, then you are middle class. If your parents are poor, then you are born into poverty. Children across social classes have very different life experiences. While the family's socioeconomic status can change drastically during a child's lifetime, each socioeconomic status experience will have an imprint on the developing individual.

Children from different socioeconomic backgrounds often experience differences in home environments, schooling, socialization practices, language use, and access to extracurricular and enrichment activities (Lareau, 2011). Parents with high levels of human capital are often able to provide their children with socialization experiences that help develop social, language, and cognitive skills. Due to low economic capital and limited access to resources, working-class and poor parents may struggle to provide similar experiences to their children. They may desire to provide their children with equitable experiences, but there may be institutional, environmental, and/or individual challenges that hinder their ability to achieve this goal.

In 1990, sociologist Annette Lareau began working on a study to analyze social class differences in family life. Lareau accessed the families through elementary schools in two areas in the Midwest; the first area was a community located near a small university, and the other area a large metropolitan neighborhood. Lareau studied African American and White families that were categorized into the following social classes: middle class, working class, and poor. Lareau studied a total of 88 families using an ethnographic approach. Researchers observed the families and children in their natural settings as they completed their daily routines. The sample size of the study is small, but small sample sizes often help with obtaining in-depth knowledge.

Lareau's research team observed parents' child rearing techniques and children's experience within their families (Lareau, 2011). The study revealed that there were vast differences in child rearing approaches across social classes. All parents displayed loved towards children, but they used different methods to raise their children. Middle-class parents engaged in **concerted cultivation**, while working-class and poor parents used the **accomplishment of natural growth** approach (Lareau, 2011). Lareau's study also includes a longitudinal component because she revisits 12 families (from the intensive study) 10 years later, and this provides information on the connections between social class, child rearing techniques, and development of the young adult.

Concerted Cultivation

In the study, middle-class parents took an active role in fostering the development of their children. This process was identified as concerted cultivation. Middle-class parents possessed the resources to invest in cultivating their children's language, skills, and talents. In many of the middle-class families, they organized their lives around a calendar that was filled with children's activities. During out-of-school time, parents chauffeured their children to different activities each day of the week. The children had activities such as soccer, ballet, jazz, gymnastics, choir, and Sunday school. Many of the activities had a similar structure to activities that children participated in at school because there were adults who provided direction, set schedules, and structured routines (Lareau, 2011).

Middle-class parents invested economic resources and time into their children's activities because they believed that the activities helped children with—correct language use, verbal negotiation, creativity, with organizing time, following rules, creating team-building skills, expanding knowledge, and developing fine and gross motor skills. Many of the social and cultural skills acquired from the numerous activities were skills that helped children navigate social arrangements. Additionally, middle-class parents were cultivating skills that would aid children as they matured into young adults and transitioned into adulthood. They were learning what was valued in institutional environments, appropriate social interactions, and how to navigate institutional settings (Lareau, 2011). Thus, middle-class parents were cultivating their children so that they could thrive in the social world.

Researchers observed that middle-class parents directed specific actions toward cultivating language through verbal negotiation. The parents actively stimulated their children's language by engaging in conversation, encouraging them to be inquisitive and guiding them to use their language to express their opinions. Some middle-class parents also demonstrated how to use effective language in institutional settings when they advocated for their children in school and in out-of-school settings. Parents mobilized their capital on behalf of their children to ensure that they received resources and to teach children how to use their skills to navigate institutional settings.

As their children acquired and practiced skills, some middle-class children developed an emerging sense of entitlement. They became outspoken and accustomed to speaking up for themselves and questioning adult authority. They felt entitled to share their opinions and use their language skills to assert their opinions (Lareau, 2011). Thus, a potential consequence of concerted cultivation is that children may develop a sense of entitlement.

Accomplishment of Natural Growth

In America's "Course on Poverty," offered for free by the Stanford Center on Poverty and Inequality, Annette Lareau (2011) shares her experiences conducting research for the book *Unequal Childhoods*. She discusses the relationship between socioeconomic status, education, and navigating institutional settings. In the study, the working class and poor parents did not have a college education, and many of the parents had not completed high school. Many of the parents had limited experience navigating educational institutions, making requests on behalf of children and communicating with school personnel. They were heavily dependent on the schools to provide them with direction, as they felt that the schools were responsible for educating the children. The parents relied on the schools to send home forms and provide them direction on the educational needs of their child.

Middle-class parents interacted differently with the schools. These parents acted as advocates for their children and sought out resources for their children. Unlike the working-class and poor parents, the middle-class parents were assertive and used their power to ensure that their children succeeded in school. They communicated regularly with the school and intervened when necessary (Stanford Center on Poverty and Equality, 2016). The differences in how parents interacted with the schools impacted the types of educational resources that children received, which influenced their overall development. Additionally, the children were able to observe the social interaction between their parents and educational institution (i.e., school personnel). This is an example of social learning; the parents were modeling behavior that the children observed and potentially would replicate in later social interactions.

Throughout the study, researchers observed that working-class and poor parents used a child rearing approach that reinforces the accomplishment of natural growth (Lareau, 2011). Working-class and poor parents were more focused on providing basic needs rather than creating a schedule of organized activities for their children. Unlike the middle-class children in the study, the working-class and poor children had less organized activities. Since they had fewer formal activities, they had more free time to engage in informal activities and play with neighbors and relatives who lived close by. During their free time, there was minimal to no adult supervision, so children learned how to structure their activities, utilize problem-solving skills, and resolve conflicts with their peers. Their informal activities encouraged the use of critical thinking and helped them develop a sense of independence. In comparison to the middle-class children in Lareau's research, they displayed more autonomy and were nicer to their siblings (Stanford Center on Poverty and Equality, 2016).

Working-class and poor parents also tended to establish distinct boundaries between adults and children. They did not encourage verbal negotiation; parents used directives when speaking to their children. They gave their children direction, and children were expected to follow directions without backtalk. While this type of compliance was beneficial in the home, it was a hindrance when children needed to navigate school and social environments. Children tended to develop a sense of constraint and distance in institutional and social settings (Stanford Center on Poverty and Equality, 2016). Working-class and poor children did not challenge authority. Instead, they exhibited constraint when receiving directives from adults, which resulted in a lack of verbal agility and negotiation when confronted with challenges in institutional environments. Table 2.2 lists the language use–related behaviors.

Researchers observed that the different child rearing approaches resulted in "the transmission of differential advantages to children" (Lareau, 2011, p. 5). Children from different social classes developed different social skills, which impacted their socialization with adults in authoritative positions in institutional settings and within in their household. Researchers reported less verbal communication in working-class and poor households. When adults cultivate language development, children develop bigger vocabularies, become comfortable engaging in conversations with peers and more mature individuals, and gain a better understanding of abstract concepts (Berger, 2008).

The cultivation of language through social interaction aligns greatly with Vygotsky's sociocultural theory. Vygotsky was an advocate

TABLE 2.2 Language Use in Families

	Middle-Class Parents	Working-Class and Poor Parents
	Child rearing approach	
	Concerted cultivation	*Accomplishment of natural growth*
Language Use	Children challenge parental authority using verbal negotiation Parents respond to children's demands	Clear directives to children Rare backtalk from children Children respectful of parental authority

Source: Stanford Center on Poverty and Equality, 2016

of social learning and believed that language and cognitive development occurred through social interaction. In *Mind in Society: The Development of Higher Sociological Processes*, Vygotsky (1935/1978) stated that "what children can do with the assistance of others might be in some sense even more indicative of their mental development than what they can do alone" (p. 5).

Revisiting Unequal Childhoods

Annette Lareau revisited 12 of the 88 families from her original study 10 years later. The 12 families were from Lareau's intensive study; she provided ethnographic case studies of each family in her book. At the time of the original study, the children were in third grade. Ten years had passed, and the children had become 19- and 20-year-old adults. Lareau (2011) wanted to find out if the child rearing differences that she identified in the original study remained constant over the 10-year period and how those differences affected the children's life experiences. She discovered as the children grew older that all parents continued to use the same approach to rear their children. Her findings revealed that social class, along with child rearing techniques, did create differences among their life experiences. There were differences in their high school experiences: Middle-class parents were able to provide resources, advocate for children, intervene if needed, and were active in the college application process. Working-class and poor parents were unable to provide as many resources, and their children relied more on school staff to guide them through the college application process. Working-class and poor parents did not possess as much knowledge on how to navigate the college application process, nor did they have the economic capital to support their children's college aspirations. Unfortunately, this deterred some of the working-class and poor children from pursuing higher education. For all families, social class and capital possession did influence accessible resources, parent interventions and advocacy in schools, and navigating institutions (Lareau, 2011).

Word Gap Among Children of Different Socioeconomic Classes

Language development can be influenced through social and cultural interactions with family members and peers. During childhood, children need their parents and caregivers to guide and support their language development. When children do not receive guidance and support, this area of development may be delayed and negatively impact other areas of development. There are many factors that impact language development, and one of these factors is social class. As discussed in the "Unequal Childhoods" section, there is a positive correlation between social class standing and language development. To further expand this discussion, this section highlights research studies that have explored these topics.

Hart and Risley

Researchers Betty Hart and Todd Risley (1995) conducted a research study to explore the differences in academic and linguistic achievement among children from all socioeconomic backgrounds. The landmark study revealed a 30 million "word gap" between high- and low-income children. Hart and Risley wanted to identify why low-income children lagged behind their economically advantaged peers in school, even after both populations attended preschool programs. For 2.5 years, researchers observed language use in the homes of 42 families. The families were categorized into four socioeconomic tiers: 13 were upper socioeconomic status, 10 families were middle socioeconomic status, 13 families were low socioeconomic status, and 6 families were on welfare.

Each month, researchers observed 7-month old children for 1 hour per week until the children reached the age of 3. Researchers recorded and analyzed three categories of language:

1. Language that was said to the children

2. Language that the children heard

3. Everything that the children said or did

Findings revealed that by the age of 3 the spoken language of the economically advantaged children was significantly larger than the low-income children (Hart & Risley, 1995). Table 2.3 provides an overview of the research findings.

The study revealed a correlation between socioeconomic status and children's later academic and linguistic development, which was directly connected to parents' language use and socialization practices with children. For example, in low-income families, parent-child language use tended to include parents providing directives to children,

TABLE 2.3 Word Gap Among Children of Different Socioeconomic Classes

	Number of Words Heard at Home Per Hour by 1- and 2-Year-Olds	Number of Words Heard by the Age of 4
Low-income child	620	13 million
Middle-income child	1,250	26 million
High-income child	2,150	45 million

Source: Hart & Risley, 1995

whereas in the economically advantaged families, language use between parent and child was more conversational (Hart & Risley, 1995).

This study is a landmark study because it was among the first to demonstrate that a child's vocabulary size could be linked to socioeconomic status and experience rather than an inherent language disorder. Additionally, the study revealed the need to view the child within the context of a language community. This is important because language development and exposure vary based on socioeconomic status and cultural ideologies regarding language use and communication with young children (Hart & Risley, 1995). While the Hart and Risley study is considered a landmark study, there are several limitations of the study.

- The 23-year-old study had a sample size of 42 families.

- One out of the thirteen upper social economic status families were African American, three out of the ten middle economic status families were African American, seven of the thirteen low socioeconomic status were African American, and all six of the welfare families were African American. Based on these numbers, some researchers believe that the racial composition across socioeconomic status was not balanced (Kamentez, 2018).

- Another limitation of the study is the way that the data was collected. According to Professor Paul Nation, a vocabulary expert at Victoria University of Wellington in New Zealand, low socioeconomic status families may have limited their language interaction with children due to their being an observer in the home. In comparison, the higher economic status parents may have become more engaged with children because they were being observed (Kamentez, 2018).

The last limitation aligns with the concepts discussed in the "Unequal Childhood" section of this chapter. In Lareau's study, lower-class parents and children often displayed a sense of constraint, while higher-status parents and children often enacted a sense of entitlement. Nation alludes to how the lower-status families could have exhibited constrained social interactions due to being observed, while the higher-class families increased their interaction because they were being watched by observers. Nation has also pointed out a discrepancy with how the researchers estimated vocabulary growth. He has questioned the ability to estimate growth from small bits of speech, especially when the samples have different quantities of words (Kamentez, 2018).

FERNALD, MARCHMAN, AND WEISLEDER

A study performed by Stanford psychologists (Fernald et al., 2013) revealed that there were significant differences in language processing and vocabulary among high- and low-income infants. The researchers observed 48 English-learning infants from 18 to 24 months. The researchers had two goals:

1. To monitor language and vocabulary processing efficiency across developmental stages.

2. To review the relationship between family socioeconomic status and language development and examine differences across social classes.

At 18 months, there were disparities in language and vocabulary processing between the populations. Researchers also identified a significant disparity at 24 months. Between the high and low socioeconomic groups, there was a 6-month difference in processing critical skills needed for language development (Fernald et al., 2013).

THE LENA STUDY

The LENA research foundation conducted a study in 2017 that was inspired by the 1995 Hart and Risley study. There was a sample size of 329 families, children ranging in age from 2 months to 4 years old, with 49,765 hours of recorded data. The researchers used a child-safe, small digital recorder that was in a vest worn by children to capture children speaking in their natural language settings (Kamenetz, 2018; Lena, 2018). The data was analyzed by the Language Environment

Analysis System (LENA). The software program estimated "(a) the number of adult words in the child's environment, (b) the amount of caregiver child interaction, and (c) the frequency of child vocal output" (Gilkerson et al., 2017, p. 248).

The study revealed that children of lower socioeconomic status had fewer adult words spoken to them daily, there were fewer caregiver-child interactions, and children expressed less vocalizations when compared to their upper socioeconomic status counterparts (Gilkerson et al., 2017). The data also showed that the word gap between low and upper socioeconomic children was closer to 4 million words rather than 30 million as Hart and Risley estimated (Kamenetz, 2018). Jill Gilkerson, senior director of research, stated that to get a figure close to 30 million words you would need to compare the most verbal 2% of children with the 2% of least verbal children.

SPERRY, SPERRY, AND MILLER

Douglas E. Sperry, Linda L. Sperry, and Peggy J. Miller examined language data from research studies in the late 1970s through the end of the 1990s. They analyzed data from families and children in five communities—two rural and three urban. The communities varied by social class: one was comprised of middle economic status families, two were working-class communities, and two were poor communities. Four of the five were European communities and one was an African American community. The research was gathered through ethnographic fieldwork and home observations. The researchers analyzed the following: (a) the quantity of words, in directed speech, that the primary caregiver spoke to children; (b) the quantity of words, in directed speech, that all caregivers spoke to children; and (c) the quantity of words that children overheard (not spoken directly to them) (Sperry et al., 2018a and 2018b).

Children from a low-income community in South Baltimore heard 1.7 times more words in comparison to the welfare group from the Hart and Risley study, and poor children in rural Alabama heard 3 times more words in comparison to the welfare group from the 1995 study (Kamenetz, 2018). Unlike the Hart and Risley study, this study did not have an upper socioeconomic status group, which did not allow for comparisons between low and high socioeconomic status children. However, this did not change that the low-income groups outperformed the low-income groups from the Hart and Risley study (Sperry et al., 2018b).

Review of Studies

During childhood, children are highly impressionable. They are learning from their environments and the people who are in their immediate surroundings. As children mature, they utilize their learned behaviors in social environments. Research has shown that parents (caregivers) from different socioeconomic backgrounds have different types of social and cultural interactions with their children, which results in developmental differences among children. These studies have described how social interactions between parents and children vary across social class, and how these interactions influence language development in children. In the studies that were discussed, higher exposure rates were observed in the higher-class families, and lower exposure rates were observed in the lower-class families.

So, how is this information related to social inequality? These studies demonstrate that there is a language gap between children of different socioeconomic backgrounds. Based on the information that has been reviewed in this chapter, it has shown that differences in language use can potentially lead to further differences in development among children, as language influences other areas of development (e.g. cognitive development). When inequality is rooted in childhood experiences, it creates an imbalance in how children across social classes develop. As children mature, there are often opportunities that may help working-class and poor children increase their cultural and social capital. However, some may still be exposed to environmental issues that negatively affect their development.

Conclusion

While America may be considered the place of great opportunity, it is also a land of great inequality. Different philosophies, child rearing approaches, and access to resources result in the *"transmission of differential advantages"* (Lareau, 2011, p. 5.) Parents (caregivers) use their knowledge, experiences, and resources to aid in developing their children, which in turn, can influence the life experiences and opportunities of the child. Working-class and poor families are often focused on providing immediate and basic needs—such as housing, water, electricity, and food—so conversations to develop language use and activities to foster children's development are not always a top priority. As a result, there are often differences in social, cognitive, and language development among youth of different socioeconomic backgrounds.

Economically advantaged parents often leverage their economic, cultural, and social capital to actively cultivate their children. Working-class and poor parents do their best to also provide resources to their children, but due to low levels of capital and environmental challenges, their resources are often limited and they do not have same the "institutional value" as the resources of their middle-class counterparts.

Parents' social class has profound impacts on children's life opportunities and experiences. Social class differences and child rearing techniques influence how children view themselves, their abilities, and role in the world. Children across social classes learn and acquire skills, but parents (caregivers) with high levels of capital have greater access to high-quality neighborhoods, schools, and valuable resources that can prepare youth to navigate institutional environments, effectively manage social arrangements, and thrive in future work environments. To create equitable developmental experiences for children, it is important for society to cultivate communities that can provide accessible, quality resources to support the healthy development of all families and children. This discussion on social class inequality will continue throughout the text, and the topics and concepts that were examined in this chapter will be discussed further in the chapters that follow.

END-OF-CHAPTER ACTIVITIES

Discussion Questions

1. What is the connection between capitalism, social class inequality, and poverty?

2. In what ways can cultural capital affect your life opportunities? Explain and provide examples.

3. Why are guided participation, scaffolding, and zone of proximal development important components of Vygotsky's sociocultural theory?

4. What are some consequences of rearing children using concerted cultivation?

5. How does the transmission of differential advantages create inequality among children, and how do these differences impact individuals when they transition into adulthood?

Capital and Conversions

This activity will help you to further understand the forms of capital. It can be completed independently or in small groups. You will need to provide examples of the different forms of capital (see list) and record them on a separate piece of paper. You will also provide a conversion example under each form of capital. See Table 2.1 for conversion examples. As you complete the activity, make sure to generate your own examples. Do not use examples that are listed in the book. Remember this is your opportunity to demonstrate your learning and understanding of concepts. Lastly, answer the discussion questions listed.

Economic Capital
Example 1:
Example 2:
Example 3:
Conversion example:

Cultural Capital
Example 1 (embodied state):
Example 2 (objectified state):
Example 3 (institutionalized state):
Conversion example:

Social Capital
Example 1:
Example 2:
Example 3:
Conversion example:

CAPITAL AND CONVERSIONS: DISCUSSION QUESTIONS

1. How can low-income and poor parents increase their human capital so that they can increase their families' capital? Consider all forms of capital.

2. When low-income and poor parents have low levels of capital, how can they increase their children's capital to help them thrive in academic and social settings? Explain and provide two to three examples.

3. What are some of the challenges, besides lack of economic capital, that low-income and poor parents may experience in increasing personal, family, and children's levels of capital? How can they overcome these challenges?

Learn More About a Poverty-Related Topic

Attend an event that promotes awareness on a poverty-related issue, for example, an event that is offered on your college campus. To find an event, check the college's calendar of events. Events may also be offered through local community organizations, libraries, or religious institutions.

1. Provide an overview of the event.

2. Discuss how the presented information connects to concepts from the textbook.

3. Explain what you thought of the event and the information that was presented.

Service-Learning Activity: Dress for Success

This is a direct service activity.
Dress for Success is a not-for-profit organization that provides resources to women that help them thrive in professional environments and in life. The organization provides empowering resources that help women in cultivating cultural capital, obtaining employment, and achieving economic security. There are over 150 affiliates in 29 countries, the organization collaborates with more than 5,000 organizations, and each year close to 13,000 people donate their time to help the organization fulfill their mission.

Visit the Dress for Success website (dressforsuccess.org/), and explore the site to learn more about the organization. Find a local affiliate in your area and find out what volunteer opportunities are available. Choose a volunteer opportunity that is of interest to you and sign up to volunteer. If there is not a local affiliate in your area, find an organization that is doing similar work in your community and identify a volunteer opportunity with this organization.

After you volunteer, complete a personal reflection that highlights your experiences. Write a summary of your volunteer experiences and discuss how the organization's mission and your volunteer experiences connect to information that you have read in the text.

References

Berger, K. (2008). *The developing person through the life span.* Worth Publishers.

Bourdieu, P. (1986). The forms of capital. In J. Richardson (Ed.), *Handbook of theory and research for the sociology of education* (pp. 241–258). Greenwood.

Coleman, J. (1988). Social capital in the creation of human capital. *American Journal of Sociology, 94*, S95-120.

Fernald, A., Marchman, V.A., & Weisleder, A. (2013). SES differences in language processing skill and vocabulary are evident at 18 months. *Developmental Science, 16*(2), 234–248.

Gestwicki, C. (2016). *Home, school, and community relations.* Cengage Learning.

Gilkerson, J., Richard, J. A., Warren, S. F., Montgomery, J. K., Greenwood, C. R., Oller, D. K., Hansen, J. H., & Paul, T. D. (2016). Mapping the early language environment using all-day recordings and automated analysis. *American Journal of Speech-Language Pathology, 26*(2), 248–265.

Hart, B., & Risley, T. R. (1995). *Meaningful differences in the everyday experience of young American children.* Paul H. Brookes.

Johnson, A. (2018). *Privilege, power, and difference.* McGraw-Hill Education.

Kamenetz, A. (2018). *Let's stop talking about the "30 million word gap."* NPR. https://www.npr.org/sections/ed/2018/06/01/615188051/lets-stop-talking-about-the-30-million-word-gap

Lareau, A. (2011). *Unequal childhoods: class, race, and family life.* University of California Press.

Lena. (2018). *What is Lena?* https://www.lena.org/about/

Miller, J. B. (2014). Domination and subordination. In P. Rothenberg (Ed.), *Race, class, and gender in the United States* (pp. 110–117). Worth Publishers.

Miller-Smith, M., & Csizmadia, A. (2014). Social mobility. In L. Ganong & M. Coleman (Eds.), *The social history of American family: An encyclopedia* (pp. 1244–1246. SAGE Publications, Inc.

Pew Research Center. (2019, June 12). *Social media fact sheet.* http://www.pewinternet.org/fact-sheet/social-media/

Sperry, D. E., Sperry, L. L., & Miller, P. J. (2018a). Reexamining the verbal environments of children from different socioeconomic backgrounds. *Child Development, 90*(4), 1303–1318.

Sperry, D. E., Sperry, L. L., & Miller, P. J. (2018b). *It's time to move beyond the word gap*. Brookings Institution. https://www.brookings.edu/blog/brown-center-chalkboard/2018/06/12/its-time-to-move-beyond-the-word-gap/amp/

Stanford Center on Poverty and Equality. (2016, April 23). *Unequal childhoods: Annette Lareau* [Video]. https://www.youtube.com/watch?v=6HN9ydNktAc

Woolfolk, A. (2004). *Educational psychology*. Allyn and Bacon.

Vygotsky, L. (1934/1987). *Thinking and speech*, Vol. 1 (R.W. Rieber & A. S. Carton, Eds., N. Minick, Trans.). Plenum Press.

Vygotsky, L. (1935/1978). *Mind in society: The development of higher sociological processes* (M. Cole, V. John-Steiner, S. Scriber & E. Souberman, Eds.). Harvard University Press.

3

Global Poverty

THOUGHT QUESTIONS

As you read the chapter, consider the following:

- What types of environmental, economic, and social consequences have communities experienced from climate change?
- What type of collective action are countries taking to combat issues like climate change, access to clean water, and poverty?
- In what ways does the rural-urban migration affect the poverty rate in a country?
- How does extreme poverty impact the development of children?
- Why were the millennium development goals revised to the sustainable development goals?

Introduction

Climate change is a social issue affecting people across the globe. Around the world, the hottest years on record have been: 2016 (highest temperatures), 2015 (second highest), 2017 (third highest), and 2018 (fourth highest) (National Oceanic and Atmospheric Administration (NOAA), 2018a, 2018b). Climate change is causing an increase in severe weather occurrences—flooding, storms, hurricanes, and droughts. These severe weather events negatively affect those who are directly impacted, but they also have significant, catastrophic effects on people who live in extreme poverty, as many may live in substandard housing, work in farming and agriculture sectors, and have limited access to recovery support. When people lose housing, employment, and lack resources, it can take them years to recover (World Bank, 2016).

Global Health Challenges

Ecosystems, such as rainforests, are an integral component of the water cycle. Access to fresh water depends on a thriving ecosystem. An **ecosystem** consists of animal, plant, and microorganism communities interacting with the nonliving environment (e.g., sun, climate, weather). Each element of the ecosystem occupies an important role; all organisms contribute to sustaining the productivity and health of the system. Terrestrial and aquatic ecosystems provide a water purification process that makes water useable for drinking, recreation, industry, and wildlife habitats. Each part of the ecosystem affects the global water cycle. Also, if a part of the ecosystem is affected, it can cause a disequilibrium to the system, which can lead to global water-related problems such as climate change, natural disasters, and water scarcity (UN Water, n.d.a.).

Addressing Climate Change

Some scientists attribute the increase and intensity of natural disasters to climate change. **Climate change** has profound effects on water availability. The United Nations Framework Convention on Climate Change defines the term as "a change of climate that is attributed directly or indirectly to human activity that alters the composition of the global atmosphere and that is in addition to natural climate variability observed over comparable time periods" (United Nations Framework Convention on Climate Change, 2011, p. 2). Increased temperatures and unpredictable weather patterns are predicted to affect distribution and availability of snowmelt, rainfall, groundwater and river flows, and to further threaten water quality. As humans have created advancements in our world, our environment has suffered. Our ecosystems are displaying the effects of increased greenhouse gases due to societal and landscape changes such as industrialization and deforestation. The ongoing increase in greenhouse gases has resulted in global warming and climate change. Two-thirds of greenhouse gases are carbon dioxide, and the burning of fossil fuels contributes greatly to the high levels in our atmosphere (United Nations, n.d.a.).

The World Meteorological Organization and United Nations Environment Programme established the Intergovernmental Panel on Climate Change (IPCC). The IPCC generated a special report on climate change that discussed the effects of global warming of 1.5 degrees

Celsius. The report details the environmental consequences of global warming (e.g., sea level rise and decline of coral reefs). To slow down the effects of global warming requires drastic changes across industries, energy production and consumption, transportation, the landscape and function of cities, along with numerous other changes. By enacting aggressive global changes, we can create a more sustainable world that will benefit people and preserve ecosystems (United Nations, n.d.a).

Climate Change and the Paris Agreement

World leaders gathered on December 5, 2015, in Paris, France, and committed to joining the Paris Agreement at the United Nations Climate Change Conference. One hundred and seventy-five countries publicly committed to signing the agreement, with 196 parties in attendance. All countries committed to creating global awareness on climate change and working collaboratively toward keeping global temperature rise below 2 degrees Celsius, or preferably 1.5 degrees Celsius. On April 22, 2016, the United Nations held the Paris Signing Agreement ceremony and representatives from the 175 countries signed the agreement. The agreement became fully active on November 4, 2016 (United Nations, n.d.d.). Since April 2016, all countries (197 parties) have signed the agreement, but not all countries have ratified the agreement. As of January 2019, 184 countries have ratified the agreement (United Nations, n.d.g.).

On June 1, 2017, President Trump announced his intention to withdraw the United States from the **Paris Agreement**, but the United States is unable to withdraw until 2020. The agreement states that once a country joins, they cannot depart the agreement for 3 years. The withdrawal date will fall on November 4, 2020, which is one day after the 2020 election. Depending on who is elected, the United States could easily re-join the Paris Agreement in January 2021. Until November 2020, the United States is still one of the 197 countries that is part of the Agreement (Mooney, 2018).

The Paris Agreement has created a unified partnership between countries so that they can collectively discuss how to address global climate change. Climate change is a social issue that affects all countries equally; it surpasses national borders, as emissions affect people everywhere. The Paris Agreement is motivating countries toward adopting alternative "green" methods and creating international climate change models that will help developed and developing countries shift toward a low-carbon existence and economy (United Nations, n.d.d.). Through communication, sharing best practices, and discussing challenges, countries can identify affordable, renewable, sustainable, and cleaner practices that people, communities, and countries can adopt.

Climate change is affecting countries across the globe, and it is causing catastrophic damage to people, communities, and national economies. Countries across the globe are beginning to experience the effects of climate change more than ever before. Sea levels are rising, weather patterns are changing, and more devastating weather events are continuing to occur—such as the hurricanes of summer 2017. It is necessary for people across the globe to change their lifestyles and become active in decreasing their carbon footprint, as human activities contribute greatly to greenhouse gas emissions. In order to lessen climate change, people must seek out planet-friendly alternatives for transportation, electricity, and personal lifestyle choices. If people do nothing, the planet's surface temperature will rise and likely increase over 3 degrees Celsius during the 21st century. The effects of this temperature rise will be felt across the globe, and those living in poverty will be affected the most (United Nations, n.d.d.).

Human Rights

In 2010, the Human Rights Council and United Nations General Assembly made an international resolution that all people must have access to safe drinking water and sanitation facilities. According to the resolution, water should be affordable and physically accessible. There should also be a sufficient supply of water for domestic and personal use. Additionally, everyone has the right to sanitation facilities that are near their home. The facilities should be safe, secure, and private. By ensuring that people have access to quality water and sanitation facilities, there could be a significant decrease in water-related disease outbreaks and illnesses.

Access to water and sanitation are fundamental necessities to sustaining a healthy life. However, this human right is not being upheld in many countries across the globe because some countries do not believe that access to water and sanitation is a human right (UN Water, n.d.b.). At the convention, the right to water resolution received 122 votes, and there were 41 countries that did not vote. The United States was one of these countries. The United States was committed to addressing the need for access to clean water, but the country did not support it as a human right (Goldberg, 2010). Four years later, the United States shifted its stance and supported the right to water resolution (Klasing, 2018).

In the United States, the Safe Drinking Water Act (SDWA) was signed into law in 1974 and later amended in 1986 and 1996. Under the SDWA, the United States Environmental Protection Agency (EPA) regulates and protects public drinking water. The EPA sets standards to protect water systems from contaminants. Water systems, states, and U.S. EPA work collaboratively to ensure that drinking water standards are properly enforced. Throughout the United States, there are over 170,000 water systems that provide public drinking water to everyone in America (U.S. Environmental Protection Agency, 2004). However, the United States has experienced challenges enforcing the human right to water resolution and effectively regulating healthy public drinking water standards. This is discussed more in Chapter 4 in the "Exposure to Pollutants" section.

Access to Clean Water

There is currently not a global water shortage, but countries across the globe need to monitor and address the current water problems across the world. With ecosystems being dramatically affected by climate change and natural disasters, water scarcity is a potential problem that needs to be taken very seriously. According to the United Nations (n.d.b.), 40% of the globe experiences water scarcity, and this figure is projected to increase. Additionally, almost 1.7 billion people live in the area of a river basin where water usage exceeds river recharge. If our environment continues to struggle to replenish global water supplies, everyone will suffer, but those who live in poverty will be the ones who suffer the most.

By the year 2050, nearly one in four people will live in an area that experiences chronic shortages of *clean* water (United Nations, n.d.b.). Having access to clean water is an essential part of one's existence. Although most of the planet is covered by water, much of it is salt-water, and the portions that are fresh are not equally accessible to all people in all regions, or may be locked in glaciers, contaminated, or overused for irrigation. So, while there may currently be enough water in the world for everyone, in some countries there are challenges in providing access to people.

Water scarcity is increasing in certain areas, causing droughts and thus negatively affecting people's health. There are countries that suffer from poor economic infrastructure, which leads to millions of disease-related fatalities, mostly children, due to deficient water supply, substandard sanitation facilities, and inadequate hygiene practices. Water scarcity and contaminated water heighten the risk of illness, such as diarrhea. Diarrhea kills 2.2 million people each year (UN Water, n.d.b.).

Droughts can also create water shortages in poor countries, leading to high rates of hunger and malnutrition, which can lead to an increase in mortality rates. Higher temperatures and less rainfall are projected to decrease crop production in many tropical countries, where access to food is already a problem. Limited access to water also affects a country's food security and sustainability, and how can a country grow food without a continuous water supply?

In other places, water and sanitation systems are at risk of being destroyed from flooding, which can contaminate water supply. Developing countries and low-income populations, who have challenges with access to water and poor water quality, are most likely to experience the worse effects from climate change (UN Water, n.d.b.). Poor access to water can also negatively impact educational opportunities, as people, mostly girls and women, in developing countries tend to spend a good portion of the day collecting water for their families (United Nations, n.d.b.).

Ending Open Defecation

Another global health challenge that affects millions of people is lack of sanitation facilities. Four and a half million people lack safe access to a toilet, and 892 million people defecate in open spaces that are not meant for sanitation purposes (United Nations, n.d.e.). When people practice open defecation, human waste is not being contained or treated. A lack of containment leads to waste exposure, which can cause environmental problems, disease outbreaks, and epidemics; create poor working and living conditions, nutritional concerns, and educational challenges; and affect economic growth. Lack of sanitation facilities also means that there is no place for hand washing, which also can spread disease. To bring attention to this issue, the United Nations made November 17 World Toilet Day (United Nations, n.d.e.).

To address the issues described, India is undergoing a toilet revolution. The government of India is working with UNICEF to end open defecation in the country. Currently, 100 million people in the country do not have a toilet. People practice open defecation in urban and rural spaces. For those who live in rural locations, they risk encountering snakes and scorpions when using the bathroom in field and forest areas. Women and girls often suffer the greatest. Many women use the bathroom when the sun is not out to avoid shame. Also, it is unsafe for girls and women to use the bathroom when the sun is not out. Using the bathroom before sunrise or after sunset places women and girls in danger of being attacked (Gale & Pridham, 2018).

Open defecation is also an economical burden in India. Poor sanitation costs India $116 billion each year. People are constantly suffering from open defecation–related health issues, such as gastrointestinal infections. Sick employees are unable to work, do not consume as much, and have shorter lifespans. Constant illness prevents individuals from saving money, and they are unable to pay for university schooling for their children (Gale & Pridham, 2018).

In 2014, the prime minister launched a $20 billion initiative, "Clean India," to end open defecation in India by installing a 110 million toilets in the country by the end of 2019. The campaign resulted in bathrooms for girls and boys at public schools, and UNICEF is conducting a study on how newly built school toilets are affecting female students' attendance and dropout rates. Clean India met the goal of having all toilets installed by October 2, 2019, Mahatma Gandhi's birthdate, which was the 150th anniversary of his birth. Gandhi recognized the importance of sanitation; he once stated that "sanitation is more important than political independence" (Gale & Pradhan, 2018, p. 52.).

Anticipating Urbanization

Over 50% of the world's population lives in urban areas, and by the year 2050, it is predicted that this figure will increase to two-thirds of the population. This is the only time in history that so many people have lived in towns and cities. Growth is occurring at a higher rate in urban sections of developing countries, and the population is predicted to increase from 3.9 billion to 6.3 billion by 2050. This population growth is attributed to an increase in the world's population and other causes. Climate change, natural disasters, and conflict also cause migratory shifts in countries. For example, if farmers are unable to produce crops due to limited rain or drought, then they are unable to make money. When farmers and agriculture workers begin to have economic struggles, they are forced to look for new jobs (UN Water, n.d.c.).

This often causes a "**rural-to-urban migration**," where people living in the outlying areas of cities migrate into urban communities. Communities that are currently densely populated will absorb the newcomers, which will cause areas to become overpopulated. This leads to an increase in overpopulated slums, which worsens access to water and sanitation facilities. Since many of these communities already lack proper water access and piping systems, wastewater goes into the nearest water drain or drainage channel, often without or with minimal treatment. Hospitals, car garages, and other businesses also lack the proper resources to properly dispose of medical waste and toxic chemicals. Even in areas where the water is treated, the effectiveness varies by the treatment system that is used (UN Water, n.d.c.).

Densely overpopulated slums that lack appropriate sanitation facilities can also lead to open defecation, which has massive health and environmental implications. Urban areas become breeding grounds for widespread health issues and make communities vulnerable to disease and epidemic outbreaks (UN Water, n.d.c.). Further, the lack of water and sanitation facilities, wastewater, open defecation, and increased risk of disease affect ecosystems within the surrounding area. For example, the water sources can become contaminated, which can potentially cause widespread illness. In Chapter 7, I continue the discussion on the health consequences of people having poor access to clean water and sanitation facilities in the United States. To read more about these topics, see the "Homeless Encampments" section.

Summary

Nearly 2 billion people around the globe access drinking water that has been contaminated with fecal matter, and 4.2 billion do not have access to adequate sanitation facilities (UN Water, n.d.d.). The reality is that these numbers are much higher, as millions of poor people living in informal conditions go uncounted. Limited access to water and sanitation are connected to poverty. Poor people suffer from low status in society and inadequate access to resources. When you combine low levels of capital and inequality, along with environmental and social challenges, people living in poverty are facing a major human rights crisis that needs to be addressed (United Nations Human Rights et al., 2010).

The rural-to urban-migration will increase over the next 35 to 40 years in areas around the globe, and poor areas will be impacted the most by overpopulation with limited access to water-related resources. To avoid pandemics, protect the ecosystem, and decrease potential negative effects to the economy, it is important that urban areas in poor communities and developing countries become more sustainable. To achieve this, these areas need strong governmental infrastructure, leadership, and resources. While individuals can take steps to protect their own drinking water supplies, a community-wide response requires organized planning.

Extreme Poverty

When people live off less than $1.90 per day, they live below the international poverty line and are considered to live in **extreme poverty**. There are over 700 million people living in extreme poverty, and they struggle to satisfy basic needs such as access to water and sanitation, education, and health (United Nations, n.d.h.). Some causes of global poverty are similar to those discussed in Chapter 1, but, unlike poor people in the United States, people who suffer from extreme poverty in developing countries often experience greater deprivations.

Those who live in developing countries with poor infrastructure often face numerous challenges due to geographical limitations. Countries may struggle with access to electricity, quality health care, clean water, schooling opportunities, and other services (World Bank, 2019). Other global poverty causes include conflict-affected areas, human trafficking, and remote locations. Seventy percent of people living in extreme poverty live in sub-Saharan Africa and Southern Asia. Specifically, close to 50% of extremely poor people live in Nigeria, India, Indonesia, and China (United Nations, n.d.h.)

Children and Extreme Poverty

Children, by far, are the greatest victims of poverty. They are affected by so many factors that are out of their control because they are only children. Children are born into their parent(s) social class, and their parent(s) level of capital (economic, cultural, and social) will affect all aspects of their development. All children should have an opportunity to live a successful and prosperous life. Unfortunately, for children who are born into poverty, they are often exposed to the disadvantages of intergenerational poverty (UNICEF, 2016).

Millions of children are born into the ongoing cycle of poverty, which threatens their health, education, and overall future. It also greatly affects the future of their communities, as the poverty cycle is continuously perpetuated with each generation and their surroundings reflect their poor class standing. Children are often denied basic rights and lack basic needs because of their families' socioeconomic status and limited resources in their communities. Children who grow up in extreme poverty are at heightened risk to experience hunger, illiteracy, and disease. They also often face obstacles in completing school such as having to enter the workforce at an early age to help their family maintain basic needs (UNICEF, 2016).

TABLE 3.1 The Effects of Global Poverty on Children by 2030

If the World Does Not Address Inequity, It is Predicted That by 2030
60 million primary school aged children will not attend school;
69 million children below age 5 will die between 2016 and 2030;
167 million children will be in extreme poverty; and
750 million women will have been child brides.

Source: UNICEF, 2016a, 2016b

Ending Poverty

Ending poverty in all its forms everywhere is the first sustainable development goal that has been adopted by the United Nations and its member states. The sustainable development goals (SDGs) are 17 goals that address health and education disparities, social class inequality, climate change, and other global issues. The due date for fulfilling the SDGs or making considerable progress toward achieving the goals is 2030. The goals were established in 2015, and each year there are annual progress reports released for each goal. For the ending poverty goal, there was a decrease in poverty from 10% in 2015 to 8.6% in 2018. However, the rate of decline has slowed. It is projected that by 2030, 6% of the population will still be living in extreme poverty (United Nations, n.d.f.).

People who experience extreme poverty are deprived of basic needs; there are limited resources through social protection programs, and there may be no programs to access. In 2016, 4 billion people did not receive cash subsidies from a social protection program. Most (87%) lived in sub-Saharan Africa in comparison to 14% in Northern America and Europe. People's experience of multiple deprivations is confounded by conflicts within their country and by environmental challenges such as droughts, flooding, and other natural disasters. Natural disasters can destroy an area, fracture the economy, and often produce more poverty. Over a 9-year period (1998 to 2017), there was a $3 trillion economic loss due to natural disasters, and 77% was allocated toward climate change–related disasters. Countries are taking strides to identify and implement risk-reduction strategies but the environmental, social, and economic factors are profound and have long-lasting effects on countries, communities, and people (United Nations, n.d.f.). These topics and the sustainable development goals will be discussed more later in the chapter.

Conflict

Political conflict is prominent in countries with limited to no economic development. There are three economic factors that make a country have a greater likelihood for **conflict**:

- Dependence on primary commodities
- Low per capita income
- Overall economic decline

A major determinant of conflict is a lack of economic growth. Countries with low **gross national income** per capita that are reliant on export revenue from primary commodities are vulnerable to volatile community pricing. Items categorized as fuel, minerals and metals, and food are identified as a **primary commodity**. If a country is highly dependent on commodity export earnings, the people who work in those industries, which are typically people living in poverty (e.g., farmers and those working in agriculture) become greatly affected by fluctuations in commodity pricing (United Nations Development Program (UNDP), n.d.).

When countries are marginalized from global markets, they lack economic development and have minimal access to resources. Limited resources and economic opportunities contribute to an increase in poverty. Financial distress combined with scarce resources can potentially create a competitive environment, as most people would go to great lengths to provide basic resources for their families. When there becomes a large economic divide between rich and poor, the social climate of a country can change. The unequalled distribution of resources can cause tension within a country. In some countries, tense social relationships between groups and social classes cause armed movements (Bailey, 2006).

Social Effects of Conflict

Conflict causes a heightened state of tension among people and is highly counterproductive. Countries plagued by conflict experience social, health, and economic burdens. The social costs of war are vast. There typically is a breakdown of the country's infrastructure as resources are diverted to support war, and some countries experience an increase in disease from lack of health resources (which can lead to an increase in mortality rates), presence of landmines, and psychosocial damage from exposure to traumatic events and stress (Bailey, 2006).

Population rates often decline during and after a conflict. The population decrease is due to the high number of conflict-related fatalities and population displacement. During times of war, many lives are taken, and communities are damaged and broken. **Population displacement** occurs when people flee conflict-affected areas and seek refuge in other countries. There are also many health-related effects of conflict. When there is a mass migration of refugees to other

FIGURE 3.1 Building Ruins from War Conflict.

Source: Copyright © 2018 Depositphotos/photo_zaur.mail.ru.

countries, it increases risk of infectious diseases and decreases access to clean water and food in new communities. Additionally, there are limited funds to provide preventative and continual care to refugees.

Conflict also tends to cause separation between community members and negatively affect social ties. This fracture in the community weakens social relationships and makes the community at risk to crime and deviant behavior. Civil war creates regions that become safe havens for terrorists to seek refuge. When resources are directed toward war, the infrastructure is weakened and countries are often easily infiltrated by outsiders and susceptible to disorder. Countries may also experience an increase in criminal activities, such as drug distribution and trafficking (Bailey, 2006).

Economic Effects of Conflict

Conflict can cause great economic effects to countries engaged in conflict and to bordering countries. Economic effects include military costs, transport costs, and an influx of refugees to borders, and the investment potential countries suffer due to the negative reputation that is associated with being involved in civil war. Many countries become economically depressed after war. War drains countries of economic resources that could have supported productivity and community improvements. Also, war creates major destruction over vast geographic areas; the cost of repairing war-damaged areas is another economic burden caused by conflict. The money used to pay for destruction could have been used for life-sustaining development or productivity. Postwar, many conflict-affected countries have severely damaged economic, social, and physical infrastructures. If countries remain economically stagnant for long time periods, they tend to have a greater likelihood of relapsing back into conflict. As mentioned in the beginning of this section, lack of economic development is a key cause of conflict. In many countries, the cycle of poverty and conflict are ongoing social problems that create turbulent social conditions over long periods of time (Bailey, 2006).

Immigration Policy in the United States

Under the Trump administration, there has been a drastic shift in immigration policy. From October 2017 to June 2018, there was a "zero tolerance" immigration policy being enforced at the southern United States' border with Mexico. After traveling through dangerous conditions for weeks, and sometimes months, with children, migrants who were seeking asylum, often from political and gang violence, were arrested and separated from their children once they reached the border. The Office of Refugee Resettlement, which operates under the Department of Health and Human Services, reported that 700 immigrant children were separated from their parents between October 2017 and April 2018; 100 of these children were less than 4 years old (Dickerson, 2018). According to the U.S. Department of Homeland Security (DHS), when an immigrant attempts to enter the U.S. illegally, it is legal to arrest the person. By law, an illegal entry arrest can result in a 6-month maximum conviction for first-time illegal entry and 2 years for those who are repeat offenders. When adults attempted to enter with children, the parents were arrested and the children were turned over to the Department of Health and Human Services (CBS News, 2018). DHS stated that there were other reasons why they separated children from adult caregivers. When they were unable to verify a familial relationship between adult and child, they separated "the family," as there were fraudulent cases when adults used children to gain entry into the United States. While this was a valid concern, the Center of Immigration Studies stated that family separation should be implemented as a "last resort" (Dickerson, 2018). Jessica Vaughn, director of policy studies at the center, agreed that if a child is being used to gain unlawful entry into the United States, then the adult caregiver should be convicted. However, every immigrant case at the border should not be flagged as a fraud attempt to enter the United States (Dickerson, 2018).

In June 2018, DHS reported that an additional 2,000 children were separated from their families between April 17 and May 31, 2018. After public outrage against family separation at the border, President Trump signed an executive order to keep detained families together at the U.S.-Mexico border. DHS reported that another 2,342 children were taken from 2,206 adult caregivers from May 5 to June 9, 2018 (Hegarty, 2018). After the signing of the executive order, the immigration controversy continued. There were reports that families were still being separated, there were migrants who continue to make the dangerous trek from Central America and Mexico hoping to seek asylum and entrance into the United States, and there were images of border police using tear gas on adults and children to deter them from getting close to the border, which according to U.S. law is legal. However, one main takeaway from the immigration debate is that enforcing laws does not always produce humane results. While the United States has the right to protects its border against illegal entry, how can laws be upheld and still protect people's human rights? Legally, according to international and U.S. law, people are allowed to seek asylum "if they fear persecution in their home country on the grounds of race, religion, nationality, membership in a particular social group or political opinion" (Flaherty & Owen, 2018.) The Migration Policy Institute reports that asylum claims have increased since 2010. In 2010, there were 9,000 credible asylum claims and 79,000 in 2017. Additionally, in the past, 1 in 10 adults traveled with a child when crossing the border. Now, 1 in 3 people travel with a child. Based on information from the Migration Policy Institute, the increase of adults traveling with children to the southern border is attributed to the violence that families are enduring in Central America (Flaherty & Owen, 2018).

The quest for safety, opportunity, education, and a new life is what motivates many migrants to make the journey through Central America and Mexico. Many travel with little to no belongings, other than the clothes that they are wearing. By the time adults and children arrive at the border, many are malnourished, suffer from medical conditions, and are in dire need of basic necessities. They exist in a state that exceeds extreme poverty because they have nothing but a desire for a better life.

Summary

In some countries, people flee to escape the conflict. However, if there is a mass movement to flee, other countries begin to feel the effects of accepting refugees. Eventually, the efforts to aid refugees will need to give way to longer-term, stable economic arrangements, allowing the refugees either to thrive in place or to return home. This is only one of many long-term effects of warfare that affect the social, economic, and physical structure of conflict-affected countries and neighboring countries.

The cost of war, damage to country, trauma experienced by people, mass migration of people to other countries, and fatalities are only some of the effects of conflict. By the year 2030, it is predicted that the population of poor people living in conflicted areas will reach 46% (World Bank, 2019). Heightened tension and complicated disagreements between conflict-affected countries can mean that the desire for power and control (or the battle between who is wrong and who is right) overshadows thinking about postwar damage and fatalities.

Human Trafficking

Human trafficking is an issue that affects people across race, gender, and class. Human trafficking is a form of modern slavery, and victims are exploited and forced into some form of servitude, typically as a laborer or sex worker (U.S. Department of State, 2017). The 2018 "Trafficking Persons" report addresses seven categories of trafficking: sex trafficking, child sex trafficking, forced labor, bonded labor or debt bondage, domestic servitude, forced child labor, and unlawful recruitment and use of child soldiers. According to the global estimates of modern slavery, of forced labor and forced marriage, there were a total of 40 million people living in modern slavery in 2016. Fifteen million victims were reported living in forced marriages, and there were 25 million forced labor victims. Additionally, 71% of these victims were female. Worldwide in 2016 there were 5.4 victims per 1,000 people, 4.4 child victims per 1,000 people, and 5.9 adult victims per 1,000 people (International Labour Organization and Walk Free Foundation, 2017).

Sex trafficking occurs when a person (above or under the age of 18) is forced, coerced, or tricked into participating in commercial sex acts. If an adult consents to participate in prostitution, then is later held against their will and coerced into committing acts using physical violence and psychological manipulation, they are considered a victim of sex trafficking. Child sex trafficking occurs when children under the age of 18 are obtained, recruited, or harbored using coercion or fraud and then forced to participate in commercial sex acts. Using children in prostitution is against the law in the United States and prohibited under statutes in a lot of countries throughout the world (U.S. Department of State, 2017). However, it is still a social issue that is worldwide, including in the United States. In the United States and other countries, technology has allowed traffickers to use websites, social media, and apps to identify, recruit, and communicate with potential victims and buyers (Sadwick, 2016).

Forced labor is another type of human trafficking. When a person is forced to work against their will, they are victims of labor trafficking. Migrants often fall victim to this type of trafficking, as they are vulnerable and in desperate need of work. One type of coercion that sex and labor traffickers use is bonded labor. Some workers inherit their family's debts, so they are forced to work off their relatives' debts. In South Asia, there are millions of people held under debt bondage. Women and girls who experience bonded and forced labor are also typically exploited and sexually abused, especially those who are forced into domestic servitude (U.S. Department of State, 2017).

Domestic workers who are underpaid, abused, and not free to leave their employment are victims of involuntary domestic servitude. These workers tend to provide domestic services to private homes, so, at times, they live at the residence. The employer controls the worker's life and limits free time and days off. Due to this isolation, domestic workers are highly vulnerable to abusive treatment (U.S. Department of State, 2017).

Children can be forced into working in slave-like conditions too. In some cultures and locations, particularly those with an agricultural economy, it's considered acceptable for children to perform certain work, such as child care, farming, or tending livestock. However, when children are enslaved and forced to perform work that provides financial gains for someone else, it can be considered forced child labor. Child soldiering is another type of child trafficking. Children who are forced into military labor by armed forces become child soldiers. Child soldiers, male and female, are often exploited and sexually abused. These children experience many of the same physical and psychological effects that child victims of sex trafficking experience (U.S. Department of State, 2017).

The "Trafficking Persons" report (2018) organizes countries into three trafficking tiers. Countries in tier 1 have complied with the minimum standards of the Trafficking Victims Protection Act (Div. A of Pub. L. No. 106–386, § 108):

1. The government of the country should prohibit severe forms of trafficking in persons and punish acts of such trafficking.

2. For the knowing commission of any act of sex trafficking involving force, fraud, coercion, or in which the victim of sex trafficking is a child incapable of giving meaningful consent, or of trafficking which includes rape or kidnapping or which causes a death, the government of the country should prescribe punishment commensurate with that for grave crimes, such as forcible sexual assault.

3. For the knowing commission of any act of a severe form of trafficking in persons, the government of the country should prescribe punishment that is sufficiently stringent to deter and that adequately reflects the heinous nature of the offense.

4. The government of the country should make serious and sustained efforts to eliminate severe forms of trafficking in persons.

Countries in tier 2 are not in compliance with the minimum standards. However, they are making efforts toward becoming compliant with standards. There is also a tier 2 watch list; these countries are not in compliance but are slowly making strides toward achieving compliance. In these countries:

1. The percentage of trafficking victims is significantly high or increasing.

2. The country has failed to produce records that demonstrate an increased effort to combat human trafficking. If there is no progress from the previous year, the country is not making strides towards compliance.

3. The country will be identified as making strides if there is a commitment and plan presented that highlights steps to be followed over the next 12-month period.

Tier 3 countries have not met standards, and they are not making concerted efforts to meet standards (U.S. Department of State, 2018).

2018 TRAFFICKING IN PERSONS REPORT TIER PLACEMENTS				
TIER 1				
ARGENTINA	COLOMBIA	GERMANY	NEW ZEALAND	SWITZERLAND
ARUBA	CYPRUS	GUYANA	NORWAY	TAIWAN
AUSTRALIA	CZECH REPUB-	ISRAEL	PHILIPPINES	UNITED KING-
AUSTRIA	LIC	ITALY	POLAND	DOM
THE BAHAMAS	DENMARK	JAPAN	PORTUGAL	UNITED
BAHRAIN	ESTONIA	KOREA, SOUTH	SLOVAKIA	STATES OF
BELGIUM	FINLAND	LITHUANIA	SLOVENIA	AMERICA
CANADA	FRANCE	LUXEMBOURG	SPAIN	
CHILE	GEORGIA	NETHERLANDS	SWEDEN	

(continued)

FIGURE 3.2 Tier Placement by Country.

Source: https://www.state.gov/wp-content/uploads/2019/01/282798.pdf.

2018 TRAFFICKING IN PERSONS REPORT TIER PLACEMENTS				
TIER 2				
AFGHANISTAN	CROATIA	KAZAKHSTAN	NEPAL	SRI LANKA
ALBANIA	CURAÇAO	KENYA	OMAN	TANZANIA
ANTIGUA &	DJIBOUTI	KOSOVO	PAKISTAN	THAILAND
BARBUDA	DOMINICAN	LATVIA	PALAU	TIMOR-LESTE
ARMENIA	REPUBLIC	LEBANON	PANAMA	TONGA
AZERBAIJAN	ECUADOR	LESOTHO	PARAGUAY	TRINIDAD &
BARBADOS	EGYPT	MACEDONIA	PERU	TOBAGO
BENIN	EL SALVADOR	MALAWI	QATAR	TUNISIA
BOTSWANA	ETHIOPIA	MALTA	ROMANIA	TURKEY
BRAZIL	GHANA	MARSHALL	RWANDA	UGANDA
BRUNEI	GREECE	ISLANDS	ST. LUCIA	UKRAINE
BULGARIA	HONDURAS	MAURITIUS	ST. VINCENT &	UNITED ARAB
BURKINA FASO	ICELAND	MEXICO	THE GRENA-	EMIRATES
CABO VERDE	INDIA	MICRONESIA	DINES	URUGUAY
CAMBODIA	INDONESIA	MOLDOVA	SERBIA	VIETNAM
CAMEROON	IRELAND	MOROCCO	SINGAPORE	ZAMBIA
COSTA RICA	JAMAICA	MOZAMBIQUE	SOLOMON	
COTE D'IVOIRE	JORDAN	NAMIBIA	ISLANDS	
TIER 2 WATCH LIST				
ALGERIA	CUBA	HUNGARY	MALI	SOUTH AFRICA
ANGOLA	ESWATINI	IRAQ	MONGOLIA	SUDAN
BANGLADESH	FIJI	KUWAIT	MONTENEGRO	SURINAME
BHUTAN	THE GAMBIA	KYRGYZ RE-	NICARAGUA	TAJIKISTAN
BOSNIA & HER-	GUATEMALA	PUBLIC	NIGER	TOGO
ZEGOVINA	GUINEA	LIBERIA	NIGERIA	UZBEKISTAN
CENTRAL	GUINEA-	MACAU	SAUDI ARABIA	ZIMBABWE
AFRICAN	BISSAU	MADAGASCAR	SENEGAL	
REPUBLIC	HAITI	MALAYSIA	SEYCHELLES	
CHAD	HONG KONG	MALDIVES	SIERRA LEONE	
TIER 3				
BELARUS	COMOROS	EQUATORIAL	LAOS	SYRIA
BELIZE	CONGO,	GUINEA	MAURITANIA	TURKMENI-
BOLIVIA	DEMOCRATIC	ERITREA	PAPUA NEW	STAN
BURMA	REP. OF	GABON	GUINEA	VENEZUELA
BURUNDI	CONGO,	IRAN	RUSSIA	
CHINA (PRC)	REPUBLIC OF	KOREA, NORTH	SOUTH SUDAN	
SPECIAL CASE				
LIBYA	ST. MAARTEN	SOMALIA	YEMEN	

FIGURE 3.2 (Continued).

Mariposa DR Foundation

Fortunately, there are organizations that are educating and empowering youth so that they can promote change within their families and communities. The Dominican Republic (DR) is a tier 2 country, and prostitution is very visible in many areas. In Cabarette, Dominican Republic, Mariposa is an organization that provides educational and social resources to girls ages 8 to 18. The organization invests in empowering girls so that they can begin to break the cycle of poverty that persists in their communities. The organization provides academic support, art classes, health resources, service learning, sports, field trips, and environmental education (Mariposa DR Foundation, n.d.).

The organization is in a building that once was home to a small hotel. Mariposa has transformed the old building into a beautiful space with classrooms, a music room, a library, a sewing/merchandise production room, a kitchen, an edible garden, a pool, and art throughout. One collection of artwork features images of influential women from around the world. The images are displayed on the pillars of the outside courtyard and on the walls of the buildings, and there are placards with each woman's story of empowerment. Each day, the Mariposa girls are surrounded by these beautiful images and reminded of the women's empowering stories. Organizations like Mariposa plant seeds of change in communities by providing resources and opportunities to youth. By investing in youth, organizations are empowering them to become leaders and agents of change in their communities. This is one way that social issues, like poverty and human trafficking, can be addressed and communities can become strengthened.

United Nations Millennium Development Goals

World leaders gathered in September 2000 at the United Nations headquarters in New York to discuss how countries across the globe could mobilize resources to alleviate eight global issues. The leaders committed to a global partnership and established the United Nations Millennium Declaration and developed a set of global goals known as the **millennium development goals** (MDGs). The declaration set a time-bound goal for the series of MDGs; all goals were to be achieved by 2015 (United Nations Development Programme, n.d.).

TABLE 3.2 Millennium Development Goals

The Eight Millennium Development Goals
1. Eradicate extreme poverty and hunger
2. Achieve universal primary education
3. Promote gender equality and empower women
4. Reduce child mortality
5. Improve maternal health
6. Combat HIV/AIDS, malaria, and other diseases
7. Ensure environmental sustainability
8. Be a global partnership for development

Source: United Nations Development Programme, n.d.

Over the 15-year time period, the United Nations worked with national governments, organizations, the private sector, civil society, and other partners to meet the goals that were declared in September 2000. The millennium development goals guided a highly successful anti-poverty movement that produced poverty declines across the globe. The millennium development goal report of 2015 discussed the progress that was achieved over the 15-year time period. The following are highlights from the report:

- Goal 1: Eradicate extreme poverty and hunger: The number of people in extreme poverty declined from 1.9 billion in 1990 to 836 million in 2015.

- Goal 2: Achieve universal primary education: The number of primary school-aged, out-of-school children declined from a 100 million in 2000 to 57 million in 2015.

- Goal 3: Promote gender equality and empower women: Developing countries made progress toward gender equality in education. There were more girls attending schools in developing regions in 2015 in comparison to the year 2000.

- Goal 4: Reduce child mortality and improve maternal health: The global mortality rate of children under five declined from 12.7 million in 1990 to close to 6 million in 2015.

- Goal 5: Improve maternal health: From 1990 to 2015, the maternal mortality rate decreased by 45% across the globe.

- Goal 6: Combat HIV/AIDS, malaria, and other diseases: From 2000 to 2015, more than 6.2 million malaria deaths were averted.

- Goal 7: Ensure environmental sustainability: 1.9 billion people gained access to piped drinking water. The numbers have increased from 2.3 billion people (1990) to 4.2 billion in 2015.

- Goal 8: Be a global partnership for development: From 2000 to 2014, development assistance from developing countries increased by 66%, reaching $135.2 billion. (United Nations, 2015)

The millennium development goals proved that goal setting and the global mobilization of resources can create profound change in the world. The 8-goal framework resulted in the greatest anti-poverty movement in history and in global progress toward alleviating poverty, improving well-being and health, creating equitable access to education, and providing resources for expanded life opportunities. However, by the end of 2015, the goals were not completely accomplished. Yes, much progress was made from 2000–2015, but inequities across the globe persist. The world's poverty rates are highly concentrated in specific regions of the world, gender disparities in education and employment are prevalent in many nations, low-income and disadvantaged populations have limited access to resources and economic opportunities, and vast social and economic conditions exist between urban and rural communities (United Nations, 2015).

Sustainable Development Goals

Sustainable development efforts focus on creating a sustainable, resilient, and inclusive future for people and the environment. It is development that fulfills the current needs of people while considering the needs and state of the planet for future generations. There are three core elements of sustainable development: social inclusion, economic growth, and environmental protection. These elements are interconnected and guide the framework of sustainable development. To achieve effective, sustainable success for individuals and societies, it is crucial for each element to be addressed and for sustainable solutions to be explored. This approach is beneficial for the well-being of present and future generations and the planet (United Nations, n.d.c.). The 17 **sustainable development goals** are listed in Table 3.3.

TABLE 3.3 The 17 Sustainable Development Goals

1. No poverty
2. Zero hunger
3. Good health and well-being
4. Quality education
5. Gender equality
6. Clean water and sanitation
7. Affordable and clean energy
8. Decent work and economic growth
9. Industry, innovation, and infrastructure
10. Reduced inequalities
11. Sustainable cities and communities
12. Responsible consumption and production
13. Climate action
14. Life below water
15. Life on land
16. Peace, justice, and strong communities
17. Partnerships for the goals

Source: United Nations, n.d.c.

In September 2015, world leaders gathered at a United Nations summit to discuss poverty, inequality, and climate change. The leaders worked collaboratively to develop a new set of global goals similar to the millennium development goals. Instead of eight goals, they developed 17 sustainable development goals to be achieved by 2030. Like the MDGs, the sustainable development goals are a set of goals that rely on collaborative efforts by countries of all economic levels, poor, middle income, and rich, to mobilize resources that will end poverty and promote prosperity. The SDGs are unique because they also include goals that focus on environmental protection and climate change. While countries are not legally required to adopt the sustainable development goals, it is encouraged that governments develop national frameworks to aid them in accomplishing the goals. The goals are a tool to support countries in developing strategies that will decrease poverty rates, increase economic growth, and address social needs such as health, education, job opportunities, and safety, while also encouraging practices that will protect the planet (United Nations, n.d.c.).

The evidence and experiences from efforts to fulfill the millennium development goals demonstrate that collective, global mobilization of resources and adopting a goal-setting framework are highly effective methods for decreasing poverty and other social issues across the globe. Moving forward, it is important that world leaders explore root causes of issues, expand on achievements, and develop sustainable solutions. By building on successes and reflecting on experiences, countries can work collaboratively toward creating a more equitable and sustainable world (United Nations, 2015).

Conclusion

Everyone should have access to basic needs, resources, and opportunities, but due to social, economic, and environmental factors this is not possible for all people. Even though people have their personal struggles living in poverty, many poor people share common experiences, challenges, and desires. Everyone deserves basic human rights and the opportunity to achieve their goals. Social inequality and unequal distribution of power create an imbalanced distribution of capital and access to resources, which produces a world where a great portion of the population lives in poverty and extreme poverty and a small percentage of the population controls most of the wealth and power in our society.

To address global social, economic, and environmental inequities, the United Nations, along with member states, have established the sustainable development goals. The SDGs help to collectively mobilize all countries toward eradicating global issues that plague our world. When 2030 arrives, the hope is that we will have collectively worked together to make progress that benefits all people and generations to come. As each country makes strides toward achieving each of the 17 SDGs, hopefully there will be a shift toward empowering people, communities, and countries with innovative tools and supportive resources to stimulate growth and promote sustainability.

END-OF-CHAPTER ACTIVITIES

Discussion Questions

1. Why is climate change being discussed more on a global level than in the past?

2. How does water scarcity and access to clean water affect people living in poverty?

3. What are some of the economic, social, and global effects of conflict?

4. What types of health challenges do victims of human trafficking experience?

5. "End poverty in all its forms everywhere" is the first sustainable development goal. What type of progress is being made to achieve this goal? Consider what is happening on a local, regional, national, and global level.

Human Trafficking in the United States

As discussed in the chapter, human trafficking is a worldwide issue. The United States is only considered a tier 1 country, but daily there are people who are victims of human trafficking in each state. Conduct research on the Internet to complete the following assignment.

Which 10 states have the highest human trafficking rates? List the states and total number of human trafficking cases reported. Choose three of the ten states and research what the states are doing to address human trafficking. Write a summary of your findings. Also, discuss if the states are involved in similar initiatives or taking different approaches to address the issue.

Creating a Sustainable School Community

You will work in small groups to complete this activity. You are a group of teachers at a K–5 school who are working together to create awareness on the sustainable development goals. Review the 17 sustainable development goals that are listed in the chapter. Visit the following website to learn more about the goals: www.un.org/sustainabledevelopment/sustainable-development-goals/.

You will be using *Frieda: The Universal Message of the Sustainable Development Goals* with each grade to help explain the purpose of the goals. Visit the following website to learn more about the storybook and to download a copy of the book: www.un.org/sustainabledevelopment/blog/2018/12/frieda-the-universal-message-of-the-sustainable-development-goals/.

Your group has the task of choosing six of the goals and creating projects for each grade to complete. For example, grade 5 could work on goal 14: life below water. The students could create videos that explain why it is important to avoid using plastic bags to keep the ocean plastic free. The videos could be shared at a school assembly or posted on the school's website or on one of the school's social media pages. The entire grade could also perform a beach clean-up. As you design the projects, make sure that they are grade appropriate.

Service-Learning Activity: Creating a Sustainable School Community

This is a direct service activity.
The "Creating Sustainable Communities" activity can also be completed as a service-learning project. Write a proposal for your program and find a school, after-school program, or community organization to become your group's community partner. Throughout the project, make sure to document each step of the process by taking photos and recording video clips. Also, make sure to have students write personal reflections. Depending on the grade, it may be easier for students to write and draw reflective comments. Your group members should also complete one-page personal reflections after each session and a summative personal reflection after the program is complete. In your

personal reflections, provide an overview of your experiences and discuss connections to information from the textbook.

At the end of the project, you can host an event to share the project with the school community, families, and community members. This is a great opportunity for all students to share their personal experiences and reflective thoughts with the community.

References

Bailey, L. E. (2006). *The impact of conflict on poverty.* World Bank, Operational Policy and Country Services (OPCS). http://siteresources.worldbank.org/PSGLP/Resources/TheImpactofConflictonPoverty.pdf

CBS News. (2018, May 8). Sessions: *"Zero-tolerance" policy may cause families to be split at border.* https://www.cbsnews.com/news/sessions-zero-tolerance-policy-may-cause-families-to-be-split-at-border/

Dickerson, C. (2018, April 20). *Hundreds of immigrant children have been taken from parents at U.S. border.* https://www.nytimes.com/2018/04/20/us/immigrant-children-separation-ice.html

Flaherty, A. & Owen, Q. (2018, November 29). Can they do that? Trump administration fires tear gas, starts wait list for migrants seeking asylum. https://abcnews.go.com/Politics/trump-administration-fires-tear-gas-starts-wait-list/story?id=59443487

Gale, J., & Pradham, B. (2018, November 5). India's toilet revolution. *Bloomberg Businessweek*, 45–53.

Goldberg, M. L. (2010, July 28). Why the United States did not support "water is a human right" resolution. *UN Dispatch.* https://www.undispatch.com/why-the-united-states-did-not-support-water-as-a-human-right-resolution/

Hegarty, A. (2018, July 25). *Timeline: Immigrant children separated from families at the border.* https://www.usatoday.com/story/news/2018/06/27/immigrant-children-family-separation-border-timeline/734014002/

International Labor Organization & Walk Free Foundation. (2017). *Global estimates of modern slavery: Forced labour and forced marriage.* Author.

Klasing, A. (2018, July 11). *Water is a human right—in Flint, in Michigan, and the US.* Human Rights Watch. https://www.hrw.org/news/2018/07/11/water-human-right-flint-michigan-and-us

Mariposa DR Foundation. *Creating a model for the world.* https://mariposa-drfoundation.org/

Mooney, C. (2018, December 12). Trump can't actually exit the Paris deal until the day after the 2020 election. That's a big deal. *Washington Post.*

https://www.washingtonpost.com/energy-environment/2018/12/12/heres-what-election-means-us-withdrawal-paris-climate-deal/?noredirect=on&utm_term=.cb1a6c06feae

National Oceanic and Atmospheric Administration. (2018a, January 28). *NOAA: 2017 was 3rd warmest year on record for the globe.* https://www.noaa.gov/news/noaa-2017-was-3rd-warmest-year-on-record-for-globe

National Oceanic and Atmospheric Administration. (2018b, October 17). *September 2018 and year to date were 4th hottest on record for the globe.* https://www.noaa.gov/news/september-2018-and-year-to-date-were-4th-hottest-on-record-for-globe

Sadwick, R. (2016). 7 ways technology is fighting human trafficking. *Forbes.* https://www.forbes.com/sites/rebeccasadwick/2016/01/11/tech-fighting-human-trafficking/#a0d9c1c6cac9

World Bank. (2016, November 14). *Breaking the link between extreme weather and extreme poverty.* http://www.worldbank.org/en/news/feature/2016/11/14/breaking-the-link-between-extreme-weather-and-extreme-poverty

World Bank. (2019). *Fragility, conflict, and violence.* http://www.worldbank.org/en/topic/fragilityconflictviolence/overview

UNICEF. (2016a). *The state of the world's children 2016, a fair chance.* https://www.unicef.org/sowc2016/

UNICEF. (2016b). *A call to action.* https://www.unicef.org/sowc2016/index_91478.html

UNICEF India. (n.d.). *Eliminate open defecation.* http://unicef.in/Whatwedo/11/Eliminate-Open-DefecationUnited Nations

United Nations. (2015). *The Millennium Development Goals report 2015.* United Nations. https://www.un.org/millenniumgoals/2015_MDG_Report/pdf/MDG%202015%20rev%20(July%201).pdfUnited Nations. (n.d.a.). *Climate change.* http://www.un.org/en/sections/issues-depth/climate-change/

United Nations. (n.d.b.). *Clean water and sanitation.* https://www.un.org/sustainabledevelopment/water-and-sanitation/

United Nations. (n.d.c.) *Sustainable development agenda.* https://www.un.org/sustainabledevelopment/development-agenda/

United Nations. (n.d.d.). *Climate action.* https://www.un.org/sustainabledevelopment/climate-action/#ParisAgreement

United Nations. (n.d.e.). *World Toilet Day, 19 November.* http://www.un.org/en/events/toiletday/

United Nations. (n.d.f.) *Sustainable Development Goals. Goal 1: End poverty in all its forms everywhere.* https://www.un.org/sustainabledevelopment/poverty/

United Nations. (n.d.g.). *Paris Agreement—Status of ratification.* https://unfccc.int/process/the-paris-agreement/status-of-ratification

United Nations. (n.d.h.). *No poverty: Why it matters.* https://www.un.org/
sustainabledevelopment/wp-content/uploads/2018/09/Goal-1.pdf

United Nations Development Programme. (n.d.). *Millennium development goals.*
http://www.undp.org/content/undp/en/home/sdgoverview/mdg_goals.
html

United Nations Framework Convention on Climate Change. (2011, February). *Fact sheet: Climate change science—the status of climate change science
today. https://unfccc.int/files/press/backgrounders/application/pdf/press_factsh_
science.pdf*

United Nations Human Rights, UN Habitat, & World Health Organization.
(2010). *The right to water: Fact sheet No. 35.* Author.

UN Water. (n.d.a.). *Water and ecosystems.* https://www.unwater.org/water-facts/
ecosystems/

UN Water. (n.d.b.). *Human rights to water and sanitation.* http://www.unwater.
org/water-facts/human-rights/

UN Water. (n.d.c.). *Water and urbanization.* https://www.unwater.org/
water-facts/urbanization/

UN Water. (n.d.d.). *Water, sanitation, and hygiene.* https://www.unwater.org/
water-facts/water-sanitation-and-hygiene/

U.S. Department of State. (2017). *Trafficking in persons report June 2017.* U.S.
Department of State Publication Office of the Under Secretary for Civilian
Security, Democracy, and Human Rights.

U.S. Department of State. (2018). *Trafficking in persons report June 2018.* U.S.
Department of State Publication Office of the Under Secretary for Civilian
Security, Democracy, and Human Rights.

U.S. Environmental Protection Agency. (2004). *Understanding the Safe Drinking
Water Act.* US EPA Office of Ground Water and Drinking Water.

PART II

HEALTH DISPARITIES

4

Poverty and Health Disparities

THOUGHT QUESTIONS

As you read the chapter, consider the following:

- How does exposure to chronic, toxic stress affect the developing person across the life span?
- Why are many low-income communities classified as food deserts?
- What forms of capital do low-income individuals need to improve oral health care?
- What are the health impacts of human trafficking and child marriage?
- Why do some seniors become poverty-stricken during retirement?

Introduction

Poverty affects all domains of human development—biological, cognitive, and psychosocial. These domains of development are each greatly affected by social class differences. When people live in poverty, these areas of development can be negatively affected by possessing low levels of capital, lack of resources, and the inability to provide and sustain basic needs. **Biological development** encompasses all the changes that occur in a person's body across the life span. People experience physical and biological changes throughout their lives, from holding a bottle, taking their first steps, learning to swim, experiencing puberty, and driving a car. **Cognitive development** includes the mental capacity to think, learn, and decide. It encompasses the processes that people use to acquire knowledge and how people perceive the world. Cognition-related mental processes include language, memory, perception, imagination, and judgement. Cognition is influenced by family, peer relationships, and education. People acquire knowledge in non-formal (e.g., immediate surroundings) and formal settings (e.g., school). **Psychosocial development** is the third domain of development. This domain includes development in the following areas: temperament, emotions, and social skills. Psychosocial development comes from social relationships and interactions with family and friends. This domain is also influenced by culture, community, school, and the larger society (Berger, 2016).

Individuals and children who live in poverty often experience many health challenges, such as chronic stress, hunger, nutritional deficiency, poor dental health, obesity, high blood pressure, heart disease, and depression. Exposure to these challenges can lead to short- and long-term declines in health. People who live in poor communities are often exposed to high rates of crime and violence too. Unsafe areas prevent children from going outside to play, which can affect gross motor skill development and contribute to childhood obesity. Poor communities are often situated near highways, industrial areas, and densely populated locations within a city. Location of communities can play a key role in exposure to pollutants and can place people at higher risk for illness and disease. People may also live in communities that are known as food deserts, which are neighborhoods that have limited access to healthy foods. Those who live in food deserts have greater access to unhealthy foods, which can cause an array of health issues in children and adults. This chapter will review the factors that contribute to health disparities among poor families and children in the United States, including intergenerational influences, chronic stress, hunger, environmental injustices, lack of access to healthcare, and fragile support systems among elders.

Early Influences

Poverty has harsh, long-term effects on children, and these negative effects begin before children are born, through lack of access to prenatal care or poor health of one or both parents. They may live in toxic home environments with high levels of stress. Lack of nutrition and poor access to health care are contributing factors to a long history of potential health issues. There is also a high incidence of low-income babies with low birth weight, which heightens the risk of health and educational challenges. According to Dr. James Duffee, a community pediatrician who works with low-income families and children in Ohio, stress, coupled with poverty, affects the brain and the likelihood of cardiac disease and diabetes (Esposito, 2016).

Brain Development

In order to understand how poverty affects the brain, it is important to understand the anatomy of the brain and the specific functions of areas that are affected. The **prefrontal cortex** is located at the very front of the brain. It controls executive functions, such as organizing thoughts, attentiveness, and planning. This area is also labeled as "executive" because the other sections within the cortex are controlled by prefrontal processes. As children mature, the prefrontal cortex develops more (Berger, 2016).

The **limbic system** consists of the **amygdala**, **hippocampus**, and **hypothalamus**, and these areas of the brain influence emotional regulation and expression. The amygdala is a set of almond-shaped structures that are at the lower part of hippocampus. They are located deep in the temporal lobe. The amygdala registers positive and negative emotion, especially anxiety and fear. If a child experienced high levels of fear and/or anxiety, it would excite the amygdala and could result in the child having nightmares or terrors. Too much activity in this region could also negatively affect the executive functions of the prefrontal cortex (Berger, 2016).

The hippocampus processes memory; it is primarily a central processor of location-related memory. The hypothalamus is also part of the limbic system. It works closely with the amygdala and hippocampus. It reacts to signals that come from both areas. The amygdala sends arousing signals while the hippocampus sends suppressing signals that result in the moderate production of hormones. These hormones then stimulate different areas within the brain and throughout the body. If this area of the brain is imbalanced and experiences heightened activity, there becomes an increase in hormone production. When the brain receives too much stress hormones, areas of the hippocampus can suffer from permanent damage, which can result in permanent declines in memory and learning. For these reasons long-term exposure to poverty-related stress for developing children can be detrimental. It

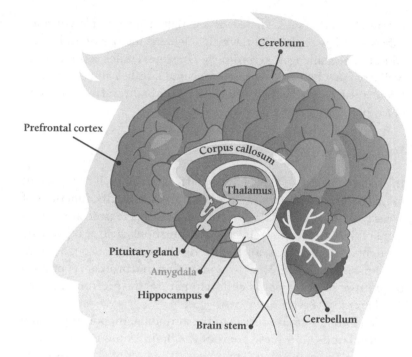

FIGURE 4.1 Diagram of the Brain.

Source: Copyright © 2018 Depositphotos/VectorMine.

can result in long-term and permanent damage to cognitive and emotional functions, leading to mental and physical impairments and lack of emotional regulation, along with numerous other developmental challenges (Berger, 2016).

Chronic Stress

Poor children and their families tend to endure high levels of stress over long periods of time. Low socioeconomic (SES) families are affected by numerous factors that contribute to increased levels of stress. They worry about providing basic needs: Will they have enough money for rent, the electric bill, and groceries? In some situations, food is sacrificed to afford the other needs, so families suffer from hunger. They often worry about financial problems and job insecurity too. Low SES communities are often plagued with violence and crime, which creates a sense of fear, heightened tension, and stress.

When people are constantly struggling to provide for themselves and families, they live under stressful conditions. This type of ongoing stress can negatively affect the brain's ability to function at an optimal level. When your body is under a lot of stress it produces high levels of cortisol, high levels of the hormone make the body enter a high alert state (Conway, 2016). For example, if you were camping and saw a bear, your body would produce cortisol. Your blood pressure would increase, other functions would temporarily shut down, like reproduction and digestion, and your body would use glucose to provide energy for the escape. It is normal for a person's body to react this way in a stressful situation, but it is not beneficial for the body to constantly remain in this heightened state. People who continue to experience heightened levels of stress may develop an **allostatic load**—health declines due to stress.

These people have a high cortisol level that never decreases. Their heightened state causes a change in their endocrine system, which causes overproduction of cortisol. This shift in their body places them at risk of cardiovascular disease. In contrast, other people who experience chronic stress sometimes suffer from a "hypo-response," which causes the body to not produce cortisol. A lack of cortisol production places people at risk for autoimmune diseases, such as arthritis (Conway, 2016). Poverty is a disease with long-lasting negative effects that can last throughout adulthood. Even after life circumstances change, the effects of poverty linger. In some instances, it influences maternal health and can affect children before they are born.

Parental stress levels affect parent' childrearing practices and influence how parents across social classes raise their children. When parents are under high levels of stress, it affects their parenting practices, how they communicate with their children, and the level of care provided to their children. Stress contributes to behavioral and emotional issues, which also affects parenting. Additionally, parental stress and depression have been connected to poor emotional regulation and behavioral issues in children. Research shows that stress affects children's developing brains, which directly affects their cognitive abilities. Research also states that nurturing relationships with parents can lessen the effects of chronic stress (Center for Youth and Wellness, n.d.). When children are made to feel safe, this buffers and reduces the negative effects of the stress. Chronic stress often comes from adverse childhood experiences. When children have continual exposure to chronic, toxic stress (e.g., witnessing domestic violence, being exposed to substance abuse, and experiencing homelessness), their overall human development is negatively affected. Long-term exposure to stress can led to poor mental and health outcomes during adulthood. People may suffer from emotional, social, and cognitive declines. Toxic stress can also harm neurodevelopment. As people age, stress can lead people to adopt unhealthy behaviors such as smoking, developing disabilities or diseases, experiencing social problems, and having an early death (Center for Youth and Wellness, n.d.). Poverty, stress, and development will be discussed more in Chapter 5.

Access to Healthy Food

Economic inequality often leads to unequal access to opportunities and resources. There are massive differences between access to healthy foods in affluent and low-income communities. In affluent neighborhoods, there is greater access to quality grocery stores and farmer's markets that offer fresh fruits and vegetables, while in lower-income communities, there is often greater access to corner stores and fast-food restaurants. Community residents in low-income communities often need to advocate for access to affordable, healthy foods, which should be a right that all Americans possess (Elmes, 2018). Moreover, this right is denied to people with lower levels of economic capital. Without access to healthy foods, low-income communities become food deserts with high levels of food insecurity, hunger, obesity, and community members that suffer from diabetes, cardiovascular issues, and other health issues.

Food Deserts

Throughout the United States, there are communities in low-income areas that lack access to healthy foods; the U.S. Department of Agriculture refers to these areas as **food deserts** (Ploeg, M.V., Nulph, D., &

Williams, R., 2011). According to the U.S. Department of Agriculture's Economic Research Service (ERS) department (2019), there were 39.4 million people who lived in low income and low access census tracts in 2015. Low-income and low-access census tracts are defined as:

> Low-income census tract (LI): Tract has a poverty rate (income at or below the federal poverty thresholds by family size) of at least 20% or the median family income is below 80% of the median income for the metropolitan area or state (U.S. Department of Agriculture, ERS, 2019).

> Low-access census tract (LA): At least 500 people or at least 33% of the tract's population live more than 1 mile from the nearest food store (supermarket, supercenter, or large grocery store) if residing in an urban area or more than 10 miles away from such a store if residing in a rural area (U.S. Department of Agriculture, ERS, 2019).

Typically, there is a lack of grocery stores and healthy food options in these areas. Instead, people in impoverished communities have greater access to convenience stores and fast-food eateries. In low-income communities, people can afford to buy food that is cheap. When they eat out, they choose places that are affordable and accessible. These locations offer unhealthy food options with processed foods that are high in sugar and fat, which contributes to the rising obesity epidemic that plagues many youth and adults across our country. These are foods like potato chips, soda, candy, French fries, fried chicken, hamburgers, and chicken nuggets. While these foods are okay to eat occasionally, it is not healthy to consume these foods on a regular basis each week.

There are food activists who are advocating for healthier food options in low-income communities. In South Central Los Angeles, Ron Finley has been working toward creating access to fresh foods for a decade. Ron Finley grew up in the inner city and had limited access to fresh foods. South Central Los Angeles is classified as a food desert, and Finley's family had to travel 45 minutes to gain access to fresh foods. Having grown up with no access to fresh foods motivated Finley to create change in his community (Ron Finley Project, n.d.a.). In 2010 Finley took his first step toward starting a food revolution: He planted an edible garden on the curbside, which is space that is owned by the city of Los Angeles. Even though the space is owned by the city, the property owner is expected to maintain it. The space is referred to as a parkway, and Finley received a citation from the city for gardening in the space. After receiving the citation, Finley shared his story and refused to remove the garden. A reporter from the *Los Angeles Times* wrote an article on Finley, and one of his fellow food activists circulated a petition that would allow people to garden and produce food in their community. The petition had over 900 signatures, and the city felt the pressure from the organized collective. One of the city council people contacted Finley to let him know that the city would endorse his gardening project. The collective activism, from the community, resulted in the city allowing people to garden freely on parkways in their communities (Ron Finley Project, n.d.a.).

Finley wants to spread this movement to other communities so that everyone can have equitable access to fresh foods. Over time, he envisions that food deserts will transform to food forests. He hopes that more communities will embrace this gardening movement and that children will become avid gardeners. Finley's next project, HQ, is a community edible garden that will be a communal gathering location. HQ will provide jobs to the community, and the communal space will provide resources to the community members such as fresh foods, food education, and cooking instruction (Ron Finley Project, n.d.b.).

Food Insecurity

Food insecurity occurs when people lack access to food. Food insecurity can lead to several health issues: chronic morbidity, nutritional deficiency, obesity, and higher levels of stress (Nguyen et al., 2015). It is ironic that there are people in our society who suffer from food insecurity because 30% to 40% of food produced is wasted and ends up in the trash (Hall et al., 2009). In September 2015, the U.S. Department of Agriculture released 2014 data that reported 48.1 million people, or 17.4 million households, experienced food insecurity. Further, 6.9 million people suffered from very low food insecurity, and there were higher rates of food insecurity in rural areas than in metropolitan communities. Additionally, African American and Hispanic households had above national averages of food insecurity; the food insecurity rate of African American households was 26.1% and 22.4% for Hispanic households (Coleman-Jensen et al., 2015).

Food insecurity is a social issue that many college students endure too. Many students do not have the economic resources to pay for college and afford money for food. In some instances, students may also struggle to pay for housing. Researchers from the Wisconsin HOPE lab and Temple University conducted a study to explore the hunger and homelessness rates among college students (Romo, 2018). They found that one-third of college students lack stable housing and struggle to buy food. The findings also revealed that food insecurity affected 36% of students attending college, an additional 36% were unable to maintain stable housing, and 9% were homeless. Among community college students, 42% experienced difficulties providing food for themselves. Nine percent of students reported that they would go 24 hours without eating due to not having money for food. Another 46% had challenges paying for housing and household-related bills (Romo, 2018).

In response to this issue, many colleges are opening food pantries for students to access. For students who are poor, a food pantry is a great resource. Without enough food, students are unable to focus in class and test grades may decline, which affects their ability to pass courses and eventually graduate (Romo, 2018). Food pantries on campuses are more common than in 2008 when there were only four colleges with a food pantry. There are currently over 300 colleges with food pantries. College such as Georgetown University, Michigan State University, and Cornell University all have food pantries on campus (George Washington University, 2016). Colleges have reported high student usage and that students are grateful that there is a food pantry on campus (NPR Staff, 2016). Many students would continue to not eat meals if the food pantries were not on campuses.

Isabella Community Soup Kitchen (ICSK) in Mount Pleasant, Michigan, provides free meals to single parents, children, teens, college students, seniors, and community members. The soup kitchen was started by a college student, Gary Taylor, who attended Central Michigan University. In 1990, Taylor witnessed another student eating a sandwich that only had ketchup on it. The student was from another country, and his sponsorship money only covered tuition, books, and room and board (ICSK, 2019). When Taylor searched for food resources, there were none available in the area. For a class project, Taylor decided to start a small soup kitchen to feed people in Isabella County. Within 3 years, the kitchen outgrew its space and relocated to the basement of Trinity Methodist Church. The basement housed a large kitchen, which allowed for them to serve a greater amount of people. The soup kitchen operated out of this space for 10 years. Once again, the kitchen outgrew its space and it moved to a new building. The Isabella Community Soup Kitchen has been serving the community since 1990. This kitchen has been a great resource to the community by providing food to those who experience food insecurity (ICSK, 2019).

Obesity

When people have limited access to healthy foods, they tend to gravitate toward the foods that are readily available in their community. These foods tend to be highly processed and contain high levels of salt, refined sugar, and saturated fat. Snack and fast foods are cheaper than healthy alternatives and are packed with empty calories. The non-nutritious foods are often highly addictive due to the salt, sugar, and fat. Individuals who sustain unhealthy diets may experience excessive weight gain, suffer from obesity, and develop numerous other health issues. Research has shown that people experiencing food insecurity have high caloric diets that lack appropriate nutrients, but the poor diet helps to satisfy hunger. These same individuals often skip meals and others may have limited food toward the end of the month due to their food assistance running out (Elmes, 2018).

Food insecurity and obesity contribute to economic inequality, as these social issues result in large numbers of poor children and adults who suffer from declines in health. These declines affect productivity in school and work and lead to food-related diseases that often require additional medical visits, which can cause excessive medical debt. Additionally, in order to avoid hunger, individuals may find themselves having to access other food resources, such as food banks, grocery outlets, and soup kitchens, to provide for their families. In these cases, food options may be limited and processed foods may be more available at food banks rather than fresh foods.

Dental Health

Poor social status, limited economic resources, and lack of dental insurance lead to poor oral health among low-income children. Minority and low-income children are at great risk for tooth decay. Dental caries (tooth decay) is the greatest chronic early childhood disease. When children have dental issues that go untreated, the problems typically worsen and affect speaking, eating, sleeping, and learning (Huff, 2015).

Food insecurity and quality can greatly impact the presence of dental caries. When children have inadequate access to nutritious foods, they are not absorbing the proper nutrients to produce healthy, strong teeth. Low-income individuals are more prone to buying fast food and cheaper groceries that have high fat and calories with limited nutritional benefits, such as foods that are high in simple carbohydrates and sugar (Huff, 2015). They gravitate toward these foods because they are accessible, cheap, and quickly curb hunger.

Lack of access to dental providers is another reason many low-income individuals and children have poor dental health. Many low-income individuals use Medicaid benefits for dental coverage (Fielding, 2016). Some children who rely on Medicaid receive adequate dental coverage, but most states have poor quality dental programs for children and adults. Many states designate barely 2% of their Medicaid budget toward dental services. The credentialing process to accept Medicaid payments deters many dentists from becoming a Medicaid provider because it is an arduous, lengthy process. Also, once approved, there is ongoing paperwork that is added to the dentist's workload. Additionally, Medicaid reimbursement payments are low in comparison to the cost of running a dental office. For many providers, seeing Medicaid patients is not profitable and becomes a financial loss (Feinberg, 2015). Massive amounts of administrative work, coupled with funding issues, result in a small number of dental providers that accept Medicaid. This makes it challenging for many low-income individuals to find a dental office that will accept Medicaid (Fielding, 2016). Thus, having Medicaid eligibility does not guarantee access to dentists or medical treatment. If people are unable to locate Medicaid dental providers, they will often go without dental care, as they are unable to pay out-of-pocket dental expenses.

It is recommended that people with low risk of gum disease and cavities visit the dentist once a year. If people forgo visiting the dentist for regular cleanings and X-rays, consider the number of dental problems the person may experience (Huff, 2015). It is important that people are educated on the importance of maintaining good oral health so that they can limit their probability of developing oral diseases.

According to the Centers of Disease Control and Prevention (CDC), there are many health disparities in oral health care. Disparities are especially based on the following categories: gender, race/ethnic background, age, geographic location of residence, and socioeconomic status. The following disparities are experienced: poor overall oral health, tooth decay among children and adults, oral health education, oral cancer, and periodontal diseases (CDC, 2016). Children between the ages of 5 and 19 who are low income are two more times likely to experience tooth decay in comparison to children who are part of families with higher incomes (CDC, 2019). Additionally, adults who attended some college are three times less likely to have untreated tooth decay when compared to adults who have lower than a high school education (CDC, 2016).

Untreated dental issues can result in children missing school and performing poorly academically (Fielding, 2016). Imagine trying to focus at school or work while trying to ignore the taste of a rotting tooth (teeth) in your mouth. Or, imagine if you had two or three dental problems while trying to focus. Trying to learn or work while having ongoing dental pain is an experience that many poor people endure. For some families, it is difficult to afford oral products: toothbrush, toothpaste, or dental floss (Huff, 2015). With economic constraints and, sometimes, lack of dental knowledge, poor people may sacrifice medical and dental needs. Unfortunately, the sacrifice results in long-term negative consequences that are often irreversible.

According to Pew Charitable Trusts, decaying teeth that are left untreated can be painful and lead to a dental infection and other health issues (Fielding, 2016). Further, people who have high levels of tooth decay as children tend to also have tooth decay in adulthood and continue to experience other health issues. The American Dental Association reports that adults may exacerbate other medical issues due

TOOTH DECAY

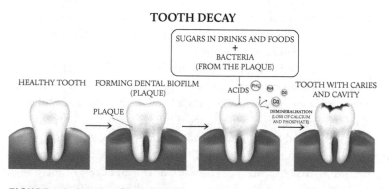

FIGURE 4.2 Stages of Tooth Decay.

to poor oral health, or poor health may also be a contributing factor to oral health issues (American Dental Association, 2013).

Healthy People 2020

The Office of Disease Prevention and Health Promotion, which is an office that is under the U.S. Department of Health and Human Services, oversees the Healthy People initiative. Healthy People 2020 builds on the work of the 2010 health initiative that was aimed at improving the health of Americans. Healthy People has four key goals:

1. Help people live longer without suffering from physical or health challenges.

2. Provide equitable access to health care and resources.

3. Establish and sustain healthy physical and social habitats that promote healthy living.

4. Support healthy development across all stages of the lifespan. (CDC, 2013)

The initiative has 42 topic areas, 600 objectives, and 1,200 detailed measures. There are 17 objectives that focus on oral health. The goals of the objectives are to ensure that all people have access to oral health care, regardless of their socioeconomic status, and promote oral health education to prevent oral craniofacial conditions, injuries, and diseases (CDC, 2013). With the extension of the 2010 nation's health initiative, hopefully over the next decade there will be improvements in health access, care, and resources for people across the nation.

Exposure to Pollutants

Children who live in poverty are often exposed to a greater number of health risks in their immediate physical surroundings, such as lead exposure. They tend to live in older housing structures that may contain lead paint. Before 1950, over 50% of the homes were painted with lead-based paint (Schnur & John, 2014). If the paint has not been removed, then people can potentially be exposed to lead. Even small traces of lead in water can result in increased blood lead levels and eventual cognitive declines. Lead exposure can have negative effects on children's neurodevelopmental functions and level of intelligence (Schnur & John, 2014). In previous decades, lead-contaminated water was a major health hazard, and in some communities it was not discussed as much as other health issues. As of the year 2014, lead-contaminated water became a topic that was being openly discussed due to the Flint, Michigan, water crisis.

Starting in April 2014, residents of Flint, Michigan, experienced lead contamination in their water. While a new pipeline was being constructed to source water from Lake Huron to Flint, the city shifted to using the Flint River as a water source. After the switch, residents noticed a drastic change in the color, taste, and smell of the water. When the water was tested by the Environmental Protection Agency in 2015, there were dangerous levels of lead discovered in the water. From 2014 to 2015, there were ongoing issues with the water such as fecal coliform bacterium, high levels of chlorine, and disinfectants being detected in the water. In 2015, the city finally switched back to accessing Detroit's water, but only after much damage had been done to the people and community. People were exposed to detrimental water conditions for over a year and a half. Being exposed to lead-contaminated water can affect nerves, heart, and kidneys. Specifically, children can experience delayed puberty, hearing problems, behavioral disorders, and impaired cognition (CNN Editorial Research, 2019).

From 2014 to 2017, there were numerous lawsuits filed against the city, city officials, and the state. Unfortunately, money is unable to reverse the damage that was done to the people of Flint, Michigan. Flint residents will be dealing with the effects of the water crisis for many years to come. The Community Foundation of Greater Flint established the Flint Child Health and Development Fund to provide resources to affected children. Some children have displayed apparent negative developmental effects such as low weight, memory loss, and poor eye-hand coordination. Others may not experience effects for 10 to 20 years; sometimes it takes many years for the effects of lead exposure to become apparent (Gulledge, 2017).

Human Trafficking

In Chapter 3, the topic of human trafficking was discussed. Human trafficking victims suffer from physical, psychological, sexual, and emotional trauma from the physical and mental abuse that they endure. Due to unsafe and unsanitary work environments, they often have limited access to health care, poor nutrition, substandard living conditions, and high exposure to communicable and sexually transmitted diseases. In forced labor situations, victims often work long hours and in dangerous working environments. Working without the correct protective gear, near-lethal chemicals, and in fear of being abused or sexually assaulted can lead to injury or illness. Sex trafficking victims also experience great health risks. They are at risk for sexually transmitted infections, pelvic inflammatory disease, and HIV/AIDS. If victims become pregnant, traffickers force women (and girls) to have abortions in unsafe locations (U.S. Department of State, 2017).

The level of physical and emotional harm that trafficking victims experience can cause panic attacks, anxiety, depression, and other health disorders. Victims of human trafficking are often prevented from seeking medical care or lack medical insurance (or money) to seek preventative services such as annual health and dental screenings. Often, if victims do have medical conditions, they will go untreated. When issues are not diagnosed and treated, the health of the individual begins to decline and the issue gets aggressively worse. Untreated medical issues, especially contagious conditions, can greatly affect the health of the individual and cause widespread health epidemics across communities (U.S. Department of State, 2017).

Child Marriage and Maternity

In many countries, child marriage is still a widespread practice, partially because of gender inequality and poverty. In the United States, there are 25 states that have no legal minimum marriage age and other states that allow children to marry at the age of 13, 14, 15, 16, and 17. Some states do require judicial and parental approval, but there are others that do not. Between the years 2000 and 2015, there were close to 207,500 child marriages in the United States (Tsui et al., 2017). This number reflects the amount of legal marriages, but it does not include the number of children who are part of common law marriages, in arranged unrecorded marriages, and forced relationships where girls are held against their will.

In developing regions, one in every nine girls is married before they reach age 15. One in five girls gets married before the age of 18 in developing countries; this equates to tens of thousands of girls each day. Child marriage in all countries has many negative effects on girls' health and lives. When girls are child brides, they often become pregnant. Young girls tend to have increased risks and complications during their pregnancy. In developing countries, pregnancy complications are the main cause of maternal death among older teen girls, ages 15 to 19 (United Nations Population Fund (UNPF), n.d.).

Child marriage also causes other social and health issues. In the United States, studies have revealed that child marriage is correlated with dropping out of school, divorce, spousal abuse, and physical and mental health issues (Hamilton, 2012; Strat et al., 2011). After girls get married, they are often forced to drop out of school. Instead of furthering their education, they are forced to perform domestic duties (UNPF, n.d.). They are expected to shift from being girls to women rather quickly, but psychologically and physically they have many years before they will become women. Developmental psychologists estimate that adults do not achieve full brain development until approximately age 25 (Simpson, 2008). One study has shown that women who were child brides, in the United States, were at an increased risk for developing psychiatric disorders in comparison to women who were married during adulthood years (Strat et al., 2011).

Although some religious and societal groups continue to practice child marriage, it is considered by many scholars to be supported by gender inequality and poverty. In developed and developing nations, child marriages are more prevalent in rural areas (Syrett, 2016; UNPF, n.d.). Often, poor parents believe that their daughters will have a better life if they are passed on to another person (or family) (UNPF, n.d.). In other cases, it is part of familial tradition that is passed on from generation to generation.

Retirement, Poverty, and Health

Heath care is a costly expense that many people in poverty sacrifice when trying to afford immediate basic needs. So, what happens when poor people with declining health begin to age? According to Fidelity, when you calculate expenses for a couple seeking to retire at the age of 65, they will spend $275,000 on medical costs over a 21-year time period. These are out-of-pocket expenses that are not covered by Medicare, such as Medicare premiums and additional medical expenses. A large expense post-retirement is long-term care. In 2017, the annual cost of assisted living was $45,000, a private room at a nursing home was $97,500, and a daily home health aid was $64,000 (Ambrose & Lankford, 2018).

For seniors who live in poverty, they will be stuck in a cycle of never ending low-wage work in order to provide for themselves. Since poor people struggle to survive, they are unable to save money for retirement. When many poor seniors become retirement age, they are heavily dependent on Social Security income. However, if they have barely worked or worked primarily low-income wage jobs, their monthly benefit amount may only cover their monthly rent. To subsidize costs, poor seniors may acquire credit card debt to help pay bills and out-of-pocket medical costs. Seniors may also access local food banks to offset the costs of groceries (Semuels, 2018).

As people approach retirement age, many are discovering that they are not prepared financially. Nearly half of retirees (ages 55 and above) do not have retirement savings, nor do they have non-retirement savings (U.S. Government Accountability Office (GAO), 2015). According to the National Institute on Retirement Security (a nonprofit organization),

FINANCIAL PLANS FOR ALL
ASPECTS OF LIFE

☑ Goal Projections

☑ Retirement Projections

☑ Tax Planning

☑ Investment Analysis

☑ Education Planning

☑ Eldercare Planning

☑ Estate Planning

☑ Risk Analysis

FIGURE 4.3 Checklist for Financial Planning.

the average 401k savings for ages 55 to 65 is only $15,000 (Semuels, 2018). A government accountability study (2015) reported that 48% of households 55 and older had some retirement savings. The median savings for 55 to 64 is $104,000 and $148,000 for ages 65 to 74. The study also found that Social Security was the main source of income for households that were 65 and older (U.S. GAO, 2015).

To be prepared for retirement, people should start saving 15% of their income starting at the age of 25 years old. However, nearly half of the population will face economic hardships during retirement or have to return to work because they are unable to sustain themselves financially. If full-time workers are not properly prepared for retirement, part-time workers are facing greater challenges as they approach retirement age.

For many part-time workers, retirement plans are not offered through their employer, so lack of savings forces people to spend less and work into elder age. In some situations, people who were never poor are experiencing a downward mobility shift. These people are entering poverty for the first time when they transition into elder age. For those people who were already poor, they are sliding further into poverty (Semuels, 2018).

The United States retirement savings system has three components: individual savings, employer-sponsored retirement plans, and Social Security. With a decrease in pensions and an increase in less stable employment opportunities, a great portion of elder Americans are depending solely on Social Security income to survive. Sadly, many older Americans do not have savings or pensions to support them during their retirement years. According to the United States Census Bureau, two-thirds of people who live in the United States do not save money in a retirement or 401(k) account (USAgov, 2020).

Conclusion

Poverty takes a debilitating toll on people, families, communities, and cities. Poverty affects all aspects of development and has profound long-term effects on health. According to Tom Boyce, chief of developmental medicine at the University California San Francisco's Department of Pediatrics, socioeconomic status is the main predictor of injury, disease, disorder, and mortality. Income provides insights on life expectancy; people living in poverty live 7 to 8 years less than people who have income levels that are four times higher than the federal poverty line (Conway, 2016).

Poverty and health collide every day for many low-wage earners in America. For those who live in poverty, maintaining personal and family health is a daily struggle (Conway, 2016). When people barely have enough money to provide basic needs, how can they afford to pay for health-related costs? Even if they visit clinics and doctors for emergency care, the lack of preventative care may cause untreated problems to become bigger issues.

Food activist Ron Finley said that in order "to change the community, you have to change the composition of the soil. We are the soil" (Finley, 2013). The reality is that if you do not make changes, things will not improve. Poor adults with ailing health problems will become poor seniors with severe health issues and lack of resources.

Poverty and health disparities cause long-term health, social, and economic burdens within communities; however, people, communities, and institutions can make small and big steps toward addressing these social issues. If starting a small garden on a parkway can start a revolution, imagine what could happen if we all planted gardens on parkways through the nation. To address issues and create change, sometimes doing something small can make a lasting, profound impact.

END-OF-CHAPTER ACTIVITIES

Discussion Questions

1. What types of community resources would help adults, children, and families buffer the effects of chronic, toxic stress?

2. How can communities that are classified as food deserts increase fresh food options for community members?

3. What is the connection between lack of healthy foods and poor dental health? What are some of the health consequences of having poor dental health?

4. Why are low-income communities more susceptible to being exposed to environmental pollutants?

5. Why are people not prepared financially for retirement?

Dental Health Clinics

Many universities have dental health clinics that offer low or no-cost dental care in a teaching and learning environment. University clinics offer people access to quality dental care for a discounted price. Some universities have mobile dental clinics that provide services to people who live in remote areas. They may also offer study-abroad programs to volunteer dental services in another country.

Choose a university that offers a low-cost/no-cost dental health clinic and provide a summary about the clinic and services it offers. Also, if they have a mobile dental clinic or study abroad program, make sure to provide a summary on these programs too. Try to find patient reviews from the clinic and discuss positive and negative reviews.

Everytable

In the chapter, you read about the Ron Finley project in South Central Los Angeles. Another organization that is creating change in South Los Angeles is Everytable, whose mission is to provide equal access to healthy and fresh foods. Everytable has developed a model of offering healthy, sliding-scale meals at an affordable cost. In affluent areas, the grab-and-go menu is slightly higher than in low-income areas. The goal is to provide low-income communities with healthy eating options without the excessive costs. Everytable currently has seven locations throughout the Los Angeles area; two of the locations are in affluent areas, and five are in underserved communities. The price of items at the affluent locations are priced $7 to $8 dollars, while items in the underserved communities are priced at $5 dollars (Everytable, 2019). Visit the Everytable website to learn more about the company and their business model: www.everytable.com.

After you review the website, answer the following questions:

1. What do you think about the Everytable business model?

2. Review the menu options and pricing of items. If there was an Everytable location in your community, would you eat at the location? Explain.

3. How might Everytable alter the prevalence of health disparities among adults and children living in South Los Angeles?

4. Why do you think that there are not more companies like Everytable operating in communities throughout the United States?

Service-Learning Activity: Alternative Break

This is a direct service activity.

Many college campuses have Community Outreach departments that offer alternative break trips offered throughout the year. Often, the trips will range from a few days to several weeks. These trips allow students to immerse themselves in a community service experience that supports their learning, promotes civic engagement, and fulfills a community need.

Visit the Community Outreach department website for your college and research alternative break trips. There will most likely be local, regional, and abroad offerings. The trips will have different focuses, such as food insecurity, environmental conservation, healthcare access, and community development. Choose an experience that is related to one or more of the topics that are being discussed in the book. Prices of trips will vary by location, type of experience, and length of time. If you need assistance with funding the experience, you should inquire about scholarships.

After participating in the alternative break, complete the following reflection assignment:

- Write an overview of your experience.

- Discuss how the service experience connects to the topics that have been discussed in the book.

- Explain how the experience has impacted you personally. Provide specific details and examples.

References

Ambrose, E., & Lankford, K. (2018, March 4). Health care costs can swamp retirees. *Chicago Tribune*. http://digitaledition.chicagotribune.com/tribune/article_popover.aspx?guid=cabaece4-59ca-4a84-89a8-5527f44e0448

American Dental Association. (2013). *Action for dental health: Bringing disease prevention into communities*. Author. https://www.ada.org/~/media/ADA/Public%20Programs/Files/bringing-disease-prevention-to-communities_adh.ashx

Berger, K. (2016). *Invitation to the lifespan*. Worth Publishers.

Centers for Disease Control and Prevention. (2013, July 10). *Healthy people 2020: Oral health objectives*. https://www.cdc.gov/oralhealth/about/healthy-people.html

Centers for Disease Control and Prevention. (2016, May 17). *Disparities in oral health.* https://www.cdc.gov/oralhealth/oral_health_disparities/index.htm

Center for Disease Control and Prevention. (2019, May 14). *Children's oral health.* https://www.cdc.gov/oralhealth/basics/childrens-oral-health/index.html

Center for Youth Wellness. (n.d.). *An unhealthy dose of stress: The impact of adverse childhood experiences and toxic stress on childhood health and development.* https://centerforyouthwellness.org/translating-aces-science/

CNN Editorial Research. (2019, December 13). *Flint water crisis facts.* CNN. https://www.cnn.com/2016/03/04/us/flint-water-crisis-fast-facts/index.html

Coleman-Jensen, A., Rabbitt, M. P., Gregory, C., & Singh, A. (2015). *Household food security in the United States in 2014* (Economic Research Report: No. 194). U.S. Department of Agriculture. http://www.ers.usda.gov/publications/pub-details/?pubid=45428

Conway, C. (2016). *Poor health: When poverty becomes disease.* University of California San Francisco. https://www.ucsf.edu/news/2016/01/401251/poor-health-when-poverty-becomes-disease

Elmes, M. B. (2018). Economic inequality, food insecurity, and erosion of equality of capabilities in the United States. *Business & Society, 57*(6), 1045–1074.

Esposito, L. (2016). *The countless ways poverty affects people's health: Many gaps persist, from lower birth weights to shorter life spans.* U.S. News & World Report. https://health.usnews.com/health-news/patient-advice/articles/2016-04-20/the-countless-ways-poverty-affects-peoples-health

Everytable. (2020). *Mission.* https://www.everytable.com/mission/

Fielding, J. (2016, November 9). *Take care of children's teeth: Tooth decay disproportionately affects low-income kids with limited access to dental care.* U.S. News & World Report. https://www.usnews.com/opinion/policy-dose/articles/2016-11-09/low-income-children-deserve-better-access-to-dental-care

Finley, R. (2013). *A guerilla gardener in South Central LA.* TED. https://www.ted.com/talks/ron_finley_a_guerilla_gardener_in_south_central_la?language=en#t-341640

George Washington University. (2016). The store's—GW's food pantry. https://students.gwu.edu/sites/g/files/zaxdzs1186/f/downloads/The-Store.pdf

Gulledge, J. (2017, January 31). *Flint water crisis leaves long-term impact on children's health.* CNN. https://www.cnn.com/2017/01/31/health/iyw-flint-water-crisis-two-years-later/index.html

Hall, K. D., Guo, J., Dore, M., & Chow, C. C. (2009). The progressive increase in food waste in the U.S. and its environmental impact. *PLOS ONE, 4*(11). http://www.ncbi.nlm.nih.gov/pmc/articles/PMC2775916/

Hamilton, V. E. (2012). The age of marital capacity: Reconsidering civil recognition of adolescent marriage. *Faculty Publications*, Paper 1430. Author.

Huff, Q. A. (2015, July 8). *A perfect smile comes at a cost: How poverty and food insecurity cement disparities in oral health.* Campaign for Dental Health. https://ilikemyteeth.org/a-perfect-smile-comes-at-a-cost-how-poverty-and-food-insecurity-cement-disparities-in-oral-health/

Isabella Community Soup Kitchen (ICSK). (2019). About us. http://www.isabellacommunitysoupkitchen.org/aboutUs.html

Nguyen, B. T., Shuval, K., Bertmann, F., & Yaroch, A. L. (2015). The supplemental nutrition assistance program, food insecurity, dietary quality, and obesity among U.S. adults. *American Journal of Public Health, 105*(7), 1453–1459.

NPR Staff. (2016, October 14). *More colleges open food pantries to address campus hunger.* https://www.npr.org/sections/thesalt/2016/10/14/497948224/more-colleges-open-food-pantries-to-address-campus-hunger

Ploeg, M. V., Nulph, D., & Williams, R. (2011, December 1). *Mapping food deserts in the United States.* USDA. https://www.ers.usda.gov/amber-waves/2011/december/data-feature-mapping-food-deserts-in-the-us/

Romo, V. (2018, April 3). *Hunger and homelessness are widespread among college students, study finds.* NPR. https://www.npr.org/sections/thetwo-way/2018/04/03/599197919/hunger-and-homelessness-are-widespread-among-college-students-study-finds

Ron Finley Project. (n.d.a.). *The gangsta gardener.* http://ronfinley.com/meet-ron-finley/

Ron Finley Project. (n.d.b.). *The Ron Finley project.* http://ronfinley.com/the-ron-finley-project/

Semuels, A. (2018). This is what life without retirement savings looks like. *The Atlantic.* https://www.theatlantic.com/business/archive/2018/02/pensions-safety-net-california/553970/

Schnur, J. & John, R. M. (2014). Childhood lead poisoning and the new Centers for Disease Control and Prevention guidelines for lead exposure. *Journal of the American Association of Nurse Practitioners, 26*(5), 238–247.

Simpson, A. R. (2008). *Brain changes.* Cambridge, MA: Massachusetts Institute of Technology. http://hrweb.mit.edu/worklife/youngadult/brain.html

Strat, Y. L., Dubertret, C., & Foll, B. L. (2011). Child marriage in the United States and its association with mental health in women. *Pediatrics, 128*(3), 524–530.

Syrett, N. L. (2016). *American child bride: A history of minors and marriage in the United States.* University of North Carolina Press.

Tsui, A., Nolan, D., & Amico, C. (2017). *Child marriage in America by the numbers.* Frontline. http://apps.frontline.org/child-marriage-by-the-numbers/

United Nations Population Fund. (n.d.). *Child marriage*. https://www.unfpa.org/child-marriage.

USAgov. (2020). *Retirement*. https://www.usa.gov/retirement

U.S. Department of Agriculture, Economic Research Service. (2019). *Food access research atlas: state-level estimates of low income and low access populations*. https://www.ers.usda.gov/data-products/food-access-research-atlas/state-level-estimates-of-low-income-and-low-access-populations/

U.S. Government Accountability Office. (2015, May 12). *Retirement security: Most households approaching retirement have low savings*. https://www.gao.gov/products/GAO-15-419

5

Adverse Childhood Experiences

As you read the chapter, consider the following:

- What are the categories and types of adverse childhood experiences (ACEs) that have been studied?
- When people are exposed to one ACE, what is the likelihood of exposure to additional ACEs?
- How does exposure to ACEs affect health during adulthood?
- Why was the original ACEs pyramid revised?
- How does chronic stress affect children's brain development?
- How can resiliency and positive communication help families cope with the effects of ACEs?

Introduction

Nearly 50% of the United States population has experienced adverse childhood experiences. **Adverse childhood experiences** (ACEs) are traumatic events that occur during childhood, such as abuse, neglect, household dysfunction, witnessing or experiencing domestic violence, exposure to neighborhood violence, and economic hardships. Continual exposure to ACEs can negatively affect an individual throughout their life. ACEs can cause physical, mental, social, psychological, emotional, and cognitive challenges, along with other declines in health.

People across social classes are exposed to one or more ACEs; however, people of lower income experience ACEs at greater rates than people of higher income levels. Exposure to ACEs does not always lead to poor health outcomes, and positive experiences can protect children from developing poor health and life outcomes. However, negative experiences can make children more susceptible to developing poor health and life outcomes.

Adverse Childhood Experiences

In 1995, a collective group of physicians and scholars led a collaborative study with the **Centers for Disease Control and Prevention** (CDC) and Kaiser Permanente to examine the relationship between adverse childhood experiences and health outcomes in adulthood. The study was based at Kaiser's San Diego Health Appraisal Clinic (Felitti et al., 1998). In 1995 and 1996, 13,494 members who completed physical evaluations were eligible to enter the study. After the medical examinations, participants were mailed a questionnaire with questions that asked about their exposure to household dysfunction, abuse, and neglect during their childhood. The sample number decreased due to participants not completing the questionnaire or failing to answer all questions that were listed. There were 8,056 respondents who fully completed the questionnaire (which was 59.7% of the initial sample), and they were used in the statistical analysis. The final sample was 79.4% White, the mean age was 56.1 years, 52.1% identified as women, 43% were college graduates, and 6% had not received a high school diploma (Felitti et al., 1998).

Researchers adapted questions from previous studies to design the ACE study questionnaire: Conflicts Tactic Scale, 1998 National Health

TABLE 5.1 Participant Demographics, CDC-Kaiser Study (n = 8,056)

Characteristic	Sample Size (N)
Age group (years)	
19–34	807
35–49	2,063
50–64	2,577
> or equal to 65	2,610
Gender	
Women	4,197
Men	3,859
Race	
White	6,432
Black	385

(continued)

TABLE 5.1 (Continued).

Characteristic	Sample Size (N)
Hispanic	431
Asian	508
Other	300
Education	
No HS diploma	480
HS graduate	1,536
Any college	2,541
College graduate	3,499
All participants	**8,056**

Source: Felitti et al., 1998

Interview, Behavioral Risk Factors Surveys, Third National Health and Nutrition Examination Survey, the National Institute of Mental Health's Diagnostic Interview Schedule, the Kaiser Health Appraisal Clinic questionnaire, and several questions from Wyatt's Sexual Abuse of Afro-American and White-American women in childhood study (Felitti et al., 1998). The ACE study questionnaire listed questions that asked about exposure to abuse and household dysfunction. Specifically, the questions asked about the following categories: psychological, physical, and sexual abuse; and household dysfunction with substance abuse; mental illness; mother treated violently; and criminal behavior in household.

There were two sets of questionnaires administered, and both had male and female versions of the questionnaires. One questionnaire collected a family health history, and the other was a personal health appraisal questionnaire. The female and male versions of the questionnaires are in the Appendices; see Appendix A and B for the family health history questionnaires and Appendix C and D for the health appraisal questionnaires.

Sample questions from the family health history questionnaire are as follows:

Sometimes physical blows occur between parents. While you were growing up in your first 18 years of life, how often did your father (or stepfather) or mother's boyfriend do any to these things to your mother (or stepmother)?

- Push, grab, slap or throw something at her
- Kick, bite, hit her with a fist, or hit her with something hard

TABLE 5.2 Relationship Between Categories of Adverse Childhood Experiences

Percent Exposed to Another Category										
First Category of Childhood Exposure	Sample Size*	Psychological Abuse	Physical Abuse	Sexual Abuse	Substance Abuse	Mental Illness	Treated Violently	Imprisoned Member	Any One Additional Category	Any Two Additional Categories
Childhood abuse:										
Psychological	898	–	52*	47	51	50	39	9	93	74
Physical	874	54	–	44	45	38	35	9	86	64
Sexual	1770	24	22	–	39	31	23	6	65	41
Household dysfunction:										
Substance abuse	2064	22	19	34	–	34	29	8	69	40
Mental illness	1512	30	22	37	46	–	26	7	74	47
Mother treated violently	1010	34	31	41	59	38	–	10	86	62
Member imprisoned	271	29	29	40	62	42	37	–	86	64
median	29.5	25.4	40.5	48.5	38	32	8.5	80	54.5	
range	(22–54)	(19–52)	(34–47)	(39–62)	(31–50)	(23–39)	(6–10)	(65–93)	(40–74)	

*Number of exposed to first category, for example, among persons who were psychologically abused, 52% were also physically abused. More persons were a second category than would be expected by chance (P < .001; chi-square).

Source: Felitti et al., 1998

- Repeatedly hit her over at least a few minutes
- Threaten her with a knife or gun, or use a knife or gun to hurt her

Sample questions from the health appraisal questionnaire are as follows:

- Do you sometimes drink more than is good for you?

- Do you use street drugs?

- Have you ever been raped or sexually molested as a child? (CDC, 2019a)

The data from the study shows that there is a relationship between categories of ACEs (see Table 5.2). Researchers found that 52% of the participants experienced one or more ACEs, and 6.2% of the participants reported four or more ACEs (1998). The category that was reported the most was substance abuse within the home (25.6%), and the category with the lowest prevalence (3.4%) was "evidence of criminal behavior in the home" (Felitti et al., 1998).

The study also showed that there was a relationship between adverse childhood experiences and poor health outcomes (see Table 5.3). The findings showed that there was an increase in prevalence and health risks associated with childhood exposures to abuse, neglect, and household dysfunction. The findings also showed that adults were at risk for developing cancer, heart disease, chronic lung disease, and liver disease. Additionally, the researchers discovered a positive correlation

TABLE 5.3 The Relationship Between the Number of Adverse Childhood Experience Exposures and Number of Risk Factors for the Leading Causes of Death

Number of Categories of Childhood Exposure	Sample Size	% with Number of Risk Factors				
		0	1	2	3	4
0	3,861	56	29	10	4	1
1	2,009	42	33	16	6	2
2	1,051	31	33	20	10	4
3	590	24	33	20	13	7
> Or = 4	545	14	26	18	17	7
Total	8,056	44	31	15	7	3

Source: Felitti et al., 1998

between an increase in the number of childhood exposures and an increase in risk and prevalence for suicide attempts, depression, obesity, physical inactivity, and smoking among respondents. A great number of respondents who experienced one ACE had also been exposed to one or more additional categories of ACEs. For participants who reported exposure to one category, the probability that they had experienced another ACE ranged from 65–93% (median = 80%); exposure to two or more ACEs ranged from 40–74% (median = 54.5%) (Felitti et al., 1998).

A question that the researchers generated from their observations was, "Exactly how are adverse childhood experiences linked to health risks behaviors and adult diseases?" (Felitti et al., 1998). Researchers reported that long-term exposure to ACEs could potentially cause children to develop anxiety and depression and display high levels of anger. Based on observations, researchers stated that poor health risk behaviors may be used as coping mechanisms (Felitti et al., 1998). For example, participants may engage in behaviors such as substance abuse, smoking, drug use, overeating, and risky sexual behaviors to cope with the childhood experiences and stressors associated with abuse and dysfunction. By chronically engaging in these behaviors, there is potential negative, long-term health consequences. Repeated use may cause long-term damage to mental and physical health, which ultimately places people with adverse childhood experiences at great risk of engaging in negative health practices and developing health diseases that are reported to be leading causes of death among adults (Felitti et al., 1998).

Limitations

As with any study, there are potential limitations that should be discussed. First, the sample was not diverse; nearly 80% of the respondents were White and almost 45% were college graduates. Additionally, the data was collected from self-reported answers. There are instances when respondents may have over- or under-reported adverse childhood experiences and disease conditions (Felitti et al., 1998). Inaccurate reporting of both items can hamper the potential to demonstrate causality. Additionally, there may be other risk factors respondents experience that were not identified in the study. For instance, ACEs may affect how people view health care and personal health maintenance, or they may cause cognitive impairments and declines. To further understand the relationship between ACEs and health outcomes, it is important to review other ACE-related studies that examine the relationship between adverse childhood experiences and mental and physical health during adulthood (Felitti et al., 1998).

Behavioral Risk Factor Surveillance System ACE Data

An adverse childhood experience module was developed by the Centers for Disease Control and Prevention in 2008 to be used for collecting data in the Behavioral Risk Factor Surveillance System (BRFSS). The BRFSS is a state-based, random telephone survey that collects health-related information from non-institutionalized adults in the United States. The survey is administered annually and collects information on health care access, health risk behaviors, and health conditions. The BRFSS ACE module was designed using information from the CDC-Kaiser Permanente Study and collects information on household challenges and childhood abuse (CDC, 2019b). From 2009–2018, the District of Columbia and 42 states have added ACE questions on their state's survey. Each state that has participated has included questions for a minimum of 1 year. Some states use their own resources to design and collect ACE data. It is optional for them to share data and findings with the CDC.

TABLE 5.4 States Collecting BRSSS ACE Data by Year, 2009–2018

Year	States
2009	AR, CA, LA, NM, TN, WA
2010	DC, FL, HI, ME, NE, NV, OH, PA, UT, VT, WA, WI
2011	CA, ME, MN, MT, NE, NV, OR, VT, WA, WI
2012	CT, IA, NC, OK, TN, WI
2013	AK, CA, IL, IA, MI, OR, UT, WI
2014	AK, AZ, CO, FL, IA, KS, LA, MD, NV, NC, OK, OR, SC, TN, WI
2015	AK, CA, IA, KS, KY, LA, MD, NV, NH, OH, OR, SC, TN, TX, WI
2016	AZ, AR, GA, IA, LA, MI, NH, NV, NY, OK, OR, PA, SC, TN, UT, VA, WI
2017	CT, CA, IL, IA, NV, OR, SC, SD, TN, VA, WI
2018	AZ, AR, GA, ID, IN, IA, KY, NV, NJ, OK, OR, SC, SD, UT, VA, WV, WI

Source: CDC, 2019b

From 2011 to 2014, 23 states added the module. During that time frame, data was collected on 214,157 participants. Similar to the CDC-Kaiser sample, this sample also lacks racial diversity. This sample was 68.15% White, and the CDC-Kaiser sample was 79.4% White. See Table 5.5 to review participant demographics.

TABLE 5.5 Participant Demographics, 2011–2014 BRFSS ACE Module (n = 214,157)

Demographic Information	Percent (N = 214,157)
Gender	
Female	51.5%
Male	48.5%
Race/Ethnicity	
White	68.1%
Black	8.4%
Other	6.3%
Multiracial	1.6%
Hispanic	15.6%
Age (years)	
18–24	12.3%
25–34	17.3%
35–44	16.5%
45–54	18.3%
55–64	16.2%
65+	19.4%
Educational attainment	
Less than high school	13.8%
High school diploma/GED	28.1%
Some college	32.6%
College degree	25.5%

Source: Merrick et al., 2018

The BRFSS ACE module questions refer to experiences that may have occurred from birth through age 18 (see Table 5.6). The questions collect information on the following categories and subcategories: psychological, physical, and sexual abuse; and household dysfunction with substance abuse; mental illness; mother treated violently; and criminal behavior in household (CDC, 2019b). See Appendix E for BRFSS ACE survey.

TABLE 5.6 Prevalence of ACEs by Category for Participants Completing the ACE Module on the 2011–2014 BRFSS

ACE Category	Women	Men	Total Percent
Abuse			
Emotional	33.9%	34.9%	34.4%
Physical	17.5%	18.4%	17.9%
Sexual	16.3%	6.7%	11.6%
Household Challenges			
Intimate partner violence	18.2%	16.8%	17.5%
Substance abuse	28.7%	26.3%	27.6%
Mental illness	19.2%	13.7%	16.5%
Parental separation or divorce	27.8%	27.5%	27.6%
Incarcerated household member	7.3%	8.6%	7.9%

Source: Merrick et al., 2018

TABLE 5.7 ACE Score Prevalence for Participants Completing the ACE Module on the 2011–2014 BRFSS

Number of Adverse Childhood Experiences (Ace Score)	Women	Men	Total Percent
0	37.6%	39.3%	38.5%
1	22.7%	24.5%	23.5%
2	12.9%	13.9%	13.4%
3	9.0%	8.6%	8.8%
4 or more	17.8%	13.7%	15.8%

Source: Merrick et al., 2018

Two-thirds of the participants who completed the BRFSS ACE questionnaire reported at least a single exposure to an adverse childhood experience (see table 5.7). The findings also showed that one in five participants had experienced three or more exposures to ACEs. Both findings are similar to the findings from the CDC-Kaiser Study. Also like the CDC-Kaiser study, the BRFSS ACE data showed a dose-response relationship between adverse childhood experiences and poor health outcomes (CDC, 2019b). This means that the data from both studies showed that exposure to many ACEs can potentially result in people being at a greater risk of having poor health.

Limitations

From 2009–2018, 42 states and the District of Columbia have collected ACE data. However, the BRFSS ACE data that has been discussed is from 23 states during 2011–2014. Since only a fraction of the data has been analyzed, there is a great deal of ACE information from the other states that needs to be reviewed. This study, like the original ACE study, used self-reporting, which can result in participants who under- or overreport when completing a questionnaire. Additionally, the sample, similar to the CDC-Kaiser sample, was primarily White. To learn more about ACEs and its effects on people, it is important that researchers actively ensure that studies include a diverse sample of participants. People have different adverse experiences based on their home environment, condition of their community, socialization experiences, socioeconomic status, and numerous other factors.

Philadelphia Urban ACE Survey

In 2012, the Institute for Safe Families created a task force to study the prevalence and effects of ACEs in Philadelphia. The ACE task force distributed a follow-up survey to the Public Health Management Corporation's Southeastern Pennsylvania Household Health Survey (SEPA HHS). The Philadelphia Urban Ace Survey benefitted from being a follow-up survey, as responses could be aligned to the health and demographic information that was collected by SEPA HHS. SEPA HHS gathered data from over 13,000 residents using a random telephone-based survey that digitally dialed landlines and cellphones. The HHS survey collected information on health care access, health status, health screenings, health behaviors, and chronic health conditions (Public Health Management Corporation (PHMC) et al., 2013).

Nearly 1,800 Philadelphia residents that were age 18 and older participated in the study from November 2012 through January 2013. Interviewers contacted interviewees by landline and cellphone, and the average interview was around 12 minutes long. Interviews took place in both English and Spanish. Interviewers and interviewees were matched based on gender, so men interviewed male respondents and women interviewed female respondents. The gender matching was done because researchers hoped that it would help increase the respondent cooperation rates (PHMC et al., 2013).

In comparison to the CDC-Kaiser study and BRFSS Survey, the Philadelphia survey had a more diverse sample of participants. See the participant demographics in Table 5.8.

TABLE 5.8 Demographics Characteristics of Philadelphia Urban Ace Survey Respondents

Race	
White	44.1% (n = 786)
Black	42.5% (n = 758)
Latino	3.5% (n = 63)
Asian	3.6% (n = 63)
Biracial	3.8% (n = 68)
Other	2.4% (n = 43)
Education	
Less than high school	10.3% (n = 184)
HS graduate	31.4% (n = 558)
Some college	22.7% (n = 402)
College graduate	35.7% (n = 634)
Gender	
Male	41.7% (n = 744)
Female	58.3% (n = 1,040)
Age (years)	
18–34	29.7% (n = 529)
35–64	52.2% (n = 931)
65+	18.1% (n = 323)
Total	1,784

Source: Public Health Management Corporation et al., 2013

The Philadelphia Urban ACE Survey was designed collaboratively by PHMC and the ACE Task Force. Researchers included questions from the CDC-Kaiser and BRFSS survey. Respondents were asked about the exposure to ACEs during childhood, from birth to age 18. The survey included questions about the following ACEs-related categories and subcategories: (a) abuse and neglect: physical abuse, emotional abuse, sexual abuse, emotional neglect, and physical neglect; (b) household dysfunction: household member with substance use disorder, household member who is mentally ill, and domestic violence; and (c) household member in jail (PHMC et al., 2013).

Researchers also wanted to examine exposure to adverse childhood experiences that were related to living in an urban community. The survey included questions that measured exposure to living in an unsafe environment, observing violent acts, and experiencing racial discrimination. PHMC and the task force collectively developed questions that were adapted from several surveys/questionnaires: the CDC Family Health History and Health Appraisal questionnaires, the Adverse Childhood Experiences International Questionnaire, the National Survey on Children's Exposure to Violence, and the California Health Interview Survey Adult Questionnaire. Specifically, the questionnaire included questions that accessed the following: neighborhood safety and trust, bullying, violence witness, racism, and foster care. There were also additional questions that inquired about health conditions and health behaviors (PHMC et al., 2013).

The Philadelphia Urban ACE Survey found that 69.9% of the respondents reported exposure to a least one or more ACEs. This was based on the indicators from the CDC-Kaiser study. Also, many of the ACEs rates are higher in the Urban ACE Survey in comparison to those reported in the Kaiser study (PHMC et al., 2013). Tables 5.9 and 5.10 show the abuse, neglect, and household dysfunction findings from both studies.

Findings from the Urban ACE survey also revealed that respondents had exposure to community-related ACEs, such as not feeling safe in their community or seeing a violent act take place. Specifically, 27.3% lived in a community where they did not feel safe, 40.5% witnessed or heard violence, and 34.5% experienced discrimination. The ACE score for 63% of the respondents increased when adding the Urban ACE indicators. When scores from the Urban ACE survey indicators were added to the ACE indicators scores, respondents who had exposure to at least one ACE increased from 69.6% to 83.2%. The survey also revealed that there was a relationship between economic hardship

TABLE 5.9 Abuse and Neglect Indicators Among Philadelphia Urban ACE Survey and Kaiser ACE Study

	Philadelphia ACE Survey (n = 1,784)	Kaiser ACE Study (n = 17,337)
Emotional abuse	33.2% (n = 1,784)	10.6% (n = 1,838)
Physical abuse	35.0% (n = 624)	28.3% (n = 4,906)
Sexual abuse	16.2% (n = 289)	20.7% (n = 3,589)
Physical neglect	19.1% (n = 340)	14.8% (n = 2,566)
Emotional neglect	7.7% (n = 136)	9.9% (n = 1,716)

Source: Public Health Management Corporation et al., 2013; Felitti et al., 1998

TABLE 5.10 Indicators of Household Dysfunction Among Philadelphia Urban ACE Survey and Kaiser ACE Study

	Philadelphia ACE Survey (n = 1,784)	Kaiser ACE Study (n = 17,337)
Substance abusing household member	34.8% (n = 620)	29.6% (n = 4,664)
Mentally ill household member	24.1% (n = 429)	19.4% (n = 3,363)
Domestic violence witness	17.9% (n = 319)	12.7% (n = 2,202)
Household member in jail	12.9% (229)	4.7% (n = 815)

Source: Public Health Management Corporation et al., 2013; Felitti et al., 1998;

and prevalence of ACEs. Respondents who lived below a 150% of the federal poverty level displayed a greater likelihood of being exposed to four or more ACES (50%) when compared to those who had an income that was equivalent to a 150% of the poverty level or higher (PHMC et al., 2013).

Health behaviors and physical health outcome were also measured. The findings showed that there was a relationship between income and smoking behavior. Respondents who lived below a 150% of the poverty level and experienced four or more ACEs smoked at a greater rate and had higher rates of mental health diagnosis and depression than respondents with one to three ACEs or no ACEs (PHMC et al., 2013).

Limitations

The sample size of the Urban ACE survey was small, and this does pose challenges when proving a definitive relationship between ACEs and health outcomes. To support and expand the findings from this survey, there needs to be additional ACE studies performed in Philadelphia and in other communities with similar community and population demographics.

The small sample size may be connected to how the data was collected. Respondents were interviewed over the phone by an interviewer, which may have caused some people to not participate. Individuals may have felt uncomfortable discussing personal information with a stranger. For example, there was a difference between respondents' reported exposure to sexual abuse on the Urban ACE survey and CDC-Kaiser study. With the Kaiser study, respondents completed questionnaires that were received in the mail rather than answering questions administered by an interviewer. This difference in data collection methods may have resulted in respondents who underreported exposure to ACEs in the Urban ACE study.

2011/12 National Survey of Children's Health

The Health Resources and Services Administration's (HRSA) Maternal and Child Health Bureau developed the National Survey of Children's Health (NSCH). The NSCH "is the only nationally representative survey that considers children's health and well-being within the contexts of the family and community" (Health Resources, and Services Administration, 2014). It was administered by the National Center for Health Statistics of the Centers for Disease Control and Prevention in 2003, 2007, and 2011/2012. The 2011/2012 data was examined to identify the prevalence of exposure to adverse childhood experiences among youth (birth to age 17) (HRSA, 2014). About 2,000 parents per state were interviewed, which resulted in a sample of 95,677 children. More than half of the sample were boys (51.2%) and

48.8% were girls. The racial composition of the sample was 57.5% were White, non-Hispanic; 23.7% were Hispanic; 13.5% were Black, non-Hispanic; and 10.3% were other races. The children were categorized by three age groups: 0–5 years (32.7%), 6–11 years (33.2%), and 12–17 years (34.1%) (HRSA, 2014).

Parents or guardians of the 95,677 children were interviewed by telephone. Interviewers spoke with a knowledgeable adult in each household. If respondents did not answer all questions, the interviews were not included in the analysis (HRSA, 2014). There were nine questions included to measure the children's exposure to adverse childhood experiences. They measured whether the child had experienced the following:

1. Economic hardships

2. Parental separation/divorce

3. A parent who was incarcerated

4. Witnessed domestic violence

5. Death of a parent

6. Neighborhood violence

7. Lived with someone who was mentally ill or suicidal

8. Lived with an adult who had an alcohol or drug addiction

9. Unfair treatment due to their race or ethnicity (HRSA, 2014)

When the survey data was analyzed, the findings revealed that almost 50% of children in the United States had been exposed to at least one adverse childhood experience. Specifically, 25.3% had been exposed to one adverse childhood experience, and 22.5% of the sample had been exposed to two or more ACEs. Additionally, there was a common theme identified in the findings; the most reported ACE was economic hardship. Across the United States, one out of every four children were exposed to economic hardship. The second most prevalent ACE was parental divorce or separation. In most states, the third highest reported ACE was living in a household with an adult who suffers from a substance use disorder (i.e., alcohol or drug use). Other ACEs that were frequently reported, in many states, included experiencing violence in the neighborhood and exposure to mental illness in the household (HRSA, 2014).

Additionally, children who lived at 100% of the federal poverty level (FPL = $22,350 for a family of four in 2011) were more likely to have been exposed to adverse childhood experiences when compared to children who lived in households that were above the federal poverty level (FPL); 66.5% percent of children who lived below the FPL had been exposed to one or more ACEs, 59% of children who lived in households with incomes between 100 to 199% of the FPL had been exposed to one or more ACEs, 45.1% of children who lived in households with incomes between 200 to 299% of the FPL had been exposed to one or more ACEs, and 27.2% of children who lived in households with incomes of 400% or greater than the FPL had been exposed to one or more ACEs. These findings show that children who live in lower income households are more susceptible to ACEs (HRSA, 2014).

2016 National Survey of Children's Health

The NSCH was revised and administered in paper form through the mail and electronically as a Web-based survey. The U.S. Census Bureau conducted the NSCH in 2016, 2017, and 2018. In 2016, the NSCH combined information from the previous NSCH and the National Survey of Children with Special Health Care Needs (Data Resource Center for Child and Adolescent Health, n.d.). Parents reported information on 50,212 children (ages 0–17 years), and the findings from the 2016 NSCH are similar to those from the 2011/12 NSCH. Nationally, 46.3% of children had been exposed to one or more ACE, and 21.7% of children were exposed to two or more ACEs. Similar to the 2011/12 NSCH, economic hardship was the most reported ACE (25.5%), followed by parent/guardian divorce or separation (25%), and the third highest reported ACE was living in a household with a person who had an alcohol or drug problem (9%) (Bethell et al., 2017).

The findings from this study showed that children of lower income had a greater prevalence of ACEs in comparison to children of higher social classes; 61.9% of children who lived in a household with an income less than 200% of the FPL were exposed to one or more ACEs and 31.9% had been exposed to two or more ACEs. Additionally, 43.2% of children from households with an income between 200% and 399% of the FPL were exposed to one or more ACEs and 19% had been exposed

TABLE 5.11 National and Across-State Prevalence of ACEs Among Children and Youth

Adverse Childhood Experiences (ACEs)	National Prevalence by Age of Child				Range Across States
	All Children	Age 0–5	Age 6–11	Age 12–17	
Child had more than or equal to one ACE	46.3%	35.0%	47.6%	55.7%	38.1% (MN) – 55.9 (AR)
Child had more than or equal to two ACEs	21.7%	12.1%	22.6%	29.9%	15.0% (NY) – 30.6% (AZ)
Nine assessed on the 2016 NSCH					**% with more than one additional ACEs**
Somewhat often/very often hard to get by on income	25.5%	24.1%	25.7%	26.5%	54.4%
Parent/guardian divorced or separated	25.0%	12.8%	27.5%	34.2%	68.0%
Parent/guardian died	3.3%	1.2%	2.9%	5.9%	74.7%
Parent/guardian served time in jail	8.2%	4.5%	9.2%	10.6%	90.6%
Saw or heard violence in the home	5.7%	3.0%	6.1%	8.0%	95.4%
Victim of violence or witnessed neighborhood violence	3.9%	1.2%	3.7%	6.5%	92.1%
Lived with anyone mentally ill, suicidal, or depressed	7.8%	4.4%	8.6%	10.3%	82.4%
Lived with anyone with alcohol or drug problem	9.0%	5.0%	9.3%	12.7%	90.7%
Often treated or judged unfairly due to race/ethnicity	3.7%	1.2%	4.1%	5.7%	75.3%

Source: Bethell et al., 2017

to two or more ACEs; 26.4% of children who resided in homes with an income equal to or greater than 400% of the FPL had been exposed to one or more ACEs and 9.2% had been exposed to two or more (Bethell et al., 2017). ACEs were prevalent across social classes, but there was a greater prevalence of ACEs among children who lived in a household with an income less than 200% of the FPL. This data is consistent with data from the 2011/2012 NSCH.

Limitations

Like the other studies, the parents responded to the surveys. Parents may report accurately, underreport, or overreport. Parents may be hesitant to disclose their personal information, or they may not accurately remember information that is being asked in the questions. In either situation, parents may report inaccurately, which affects the accuracy of the data.

The data collections methods changed from the 2011/2012 NSCH to the 2016 NSCH; the 2016 NSCH was administered through mail and Web-based survey, so people were able to answer questions privately. However, since respondents completed the surveys independently, they could have been confused by a question or distracted while completing the survey. It is possible for the collection method to influence the reported data.

Summary

Based on findings, we know that almost half of the U.S. population has been exposed to adverse childhood experiences. We also know that people of lower income are exposed to ACEs at higher rates than people of higher income. Exposure to ACEs can potentially lead to a number of poor mental and physical health outcomes during adulthood. The effects of ACEs can be buffered and individuals can recover from exposure. The next section provides more information on these topics and discusses the importance of implementing ACEs screenings in pediatric care.

Center for Youth Wellness

Nearly 35 million children from all socioeconomic backgrounds have been affected by ACEs; however, poor children have higher levels of exposure to toxic stress. To alleviate the effects of ACEs, it helps when pediatric clinicians use early detection measures to identify ACEs. Early intervention leads to treatment and supportive services, which can decrease and prevent damage to the developing child (Center for Youth Wellness, 2017a).

The **Center for Youth and Wellness**, founded by Dr. Nadine Burke in February 2014, is part of a collective national movement to transform how society identifies and treats children who have been exposed to high levels of toxic stress and ACEs. The center has partnered with Bayview Child Health Center in San Francisco and uses a community-based health model approach that combines ACEs science, research, health care, and family-centered medical services to support the healthy development of families and children (Center for Youth Wellness, 2017b).

The pediatric patients are seen at the primary care clinic, and every patient receives an ACE screening. Through coordinated clinical care, children and families have access to effective treatments that address toxic stress. With treatment and supportive services, the center can help families and children begin to heal from the exposure to stress. The pediatric treatment, which focuses on "addressing the neuro-endocrine-immune dysregulation of toxic stress," results in a decline of ACEs-related damage to the developing child's nervous, cardiovascular, immune, and endocrine systems (Center for Youth Wellness, 2017c).

The Center for Youth and Wellness (2017d) shares research and practices to:

1. educate parent/caregivers about the effects of ACEs,

2. establish a national collective of pediatric clinicians that screen for ACEs, and

3. advocate for early interventions screenings, trauma-related care, and promote change in policy.

Dr. Nadine Burke and the Center for Youth and Wellness are making extraordinary progress in the areas of treating toxic stress and ACEs. The center's community-based health model is being recognized and studied on a national level. As momentum builds behind the national ACEs movement, families across socioeconomic backgrounds will benefit from the awareness that the organization is creating, research that is being conducted, and health practices that are replicated by pediatric clinicians serving patients with high levels of toxic stress and ACEs.

As discussed in Chapter 4, poverty-related stress has profound negative effects on brain development. Adverse childhood experiences

(ACEs) affect children of all SES backgrounds, but children living in poverty tend to have higher rates of exposure. There are a total of 10 ACEs, and they are divided into three categories: abuse, neglect, and household dysfunction (see Table 5.12). Research is being conducted to identify other ACE-related life events, such as homelessness, neighborhood violence, being in the foster care system, and experiencing bullying in school (Center for Youth Wellness, 2017e).

TABLE 5.12 Three Types of Adverse Childhood Experiences

Adverse Childhood Experiences
Abuse: Physical, emotional, and sexual
Neglect: Physical, emotional
Household dysfunction: Mental illness, mother treated violently, divorce, substance abuse, incarcerated relative

Source: Center for Youth Wellness, 2017e

Repeated exposure to ACEs may alter the developing brain, hormone production, and the immune system. These changes can often lead to learning challenges, behavioral changes, the restructuring of DNA, immunity problems, and developing chronic health issues like asthma. In some cases, ACEs may have long-lasting effects that are prevalent throughout the life span (Center for Youth and Wellness, 2017e). Figure 5.1 shows the original and revised ACEs pyramids. The original version shows the initial hypothesis that was formulated from the CDC-Kaiser study findings. The revised version was developed 15 years later to reflect how ACEs affects cognitive and physical development during early childhood.

One way to buffer the effects of ACEs is for children to have safe, nurturing, and healthy home environments. Even if they are exposed to stress, the supporting and nurturing relationship with the caregiver will help to counter the effects of toxic stress. By providing basic resources such as food, play time, and sleep, the parent (caregiver) is helping to shape the development of the child. It is also equally important for parents to take appropriate care of themselves so that they can effectively provide care to children in a healthy, supportive environment (Center for Youth Wellness, 2017e).

Variations of Stress

There are different types of stress, and the body responds to each one differently. Positive stress is a brief, mild stress response. For example,

Original ACEs pyramid

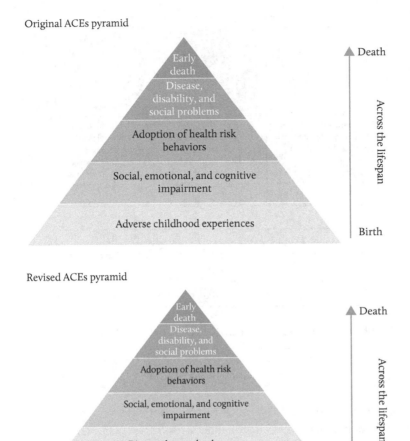

Revised ACEs pyramid

FIGURE 5.1 Ways That ACESs Affect Development Throughout the Life Span (Center for Youth Wellness, 2017E).

Source: https://www.cdc.gov/violenceprevention/childabuseandneglect/acestudy/about.html.

when a student experiences stress when studying for a midterm exam, the body's reaction has a moderate response; there is a slight increase in heart rate and a release of stress hormones. It is normal to experience **positive stress**, and it prepares people to handle stressful life events. When stress levels are more heightened but remain brief, a person experiences **tolerable stress**. Since the exposure to stress is infrequent, tolerable stress only has short-term, negative effects on a child's development. If a relative dies and a child receives supportive care from an adult, this buffers against the effects of the stress and

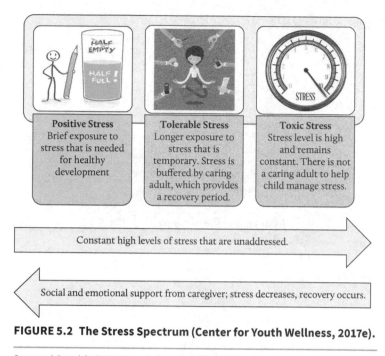

FIGURE 5.2 The Stress Spectrum (Center for Youth Wellness, 2017e).

Sources: a) Copyright © 2014 Depositphotos/trueffelpix b) Copyright © 2015 Depositphotos/
VectorStory. c) Copyright © 2014 Depositphotos/BigAlBaloo.

makes it more tolerable. When children do not have a caring adult to
help them manage stress, the tolerable stress can transition into **toxic
stress** (Center for Youth Wellness, 2017d).

Toxic stress comes from constant exposure to traumatic stressful
life events. When the body is exposed to chronic stress, the body's stress
response system activates to respond to the stress and stays activated until
the stress decreases. Unlike tolerable stress, the child's stress level does
not decrease; rather, it remains constant or increases. The body reacts by
producing stress hormones, adrenaline, and **cortisol**. If the body produces
too little or too much cortisol, it can cause issues to the body. The body
should be in a state of balance; however, when a child is always anticipating
and experiencing stress, the brain triggers the stress response. Instead of
the body reacting to a stressful situation, the body remains in a reactive
state, known as "fight or flight," and produces cortisol to manage the
threat of stress. This heightened, constant level of stress causes damage
to the developing child. It can have negative effects on different areas of
development: biological, social, emotional, and cognitive. High levels of
cortisol can suppress the immune system, which can make the individual
prone to disease and infection (Center for Youth Wellness, 2017e).

Toxic stress can also be very damaging to the brain because of the changes that the brain experiences during the childhood years. From birth to the age of 5, there are significant changes happening within the brain. During early childhood, the brain is being molded by daily experiences; this process is called **neuroplasticity**. For children who are under the age of 5, there are two kinds of neuroplasticity that are taking place—synaptic and cellular plasticity. Synaptic plasticity refers to the strength of connections that exist among the brain cells. Cellular plasticity is the amount of connections that are among all the brain cells. Synaptic plasticity is an ongoing process across the life span, while cellular plasticity occurs primarily from birth to age 5. Due to the brain's plasticity during this stage, positive and traumatic events can have profound impacts on the brain. Positive life experiences can promote optimal brain development while traumatic events can lead to developmental challenges (Center for Youth Wellness, 2017e).

Conclusion

It is not uncommon for children to experience an emotional or social challenge at some point during their childhood. However, children who have experienced trauma from ACEs are at a higher risk for developing poor mental and physical health outcomes. ACEs can create significant challenges for individuals and families, but there are ways to combat the effects of ACEs. It is important that families establish stable and safe home environments for their children. Positive, nurturing relationships between a caring adult and child also help to buffer the effects of ACEs.

The CDC has created a comprehensive list of ways that individuals, families, and communities can help people recover from the effects of ACEs:

1. Strengthen economic supports to families
   - Strengthening household financial security
   - Family-friendly work policies
2. Change social norms to support parents and positive parenting
   - Public engagement and enhancement campaigns
   - Legislative approaches to reduce corporal punishment

3. Provide quality care and education early in life

- Preschool enrichment with family engagement
- Improved quality of child care through licensing and accreditation

4. Enhance parenting skills to promote healthy child development

- Early childhood home visitation
- Parenting skill and family relationship approaches

5. Intervene to lessen harms and prevent future risk

- Enhanced primary care
- Behavioral parent training programs
- Treatment to lessen harms of abuse and neglect exposure
- Treatment to prevent problem behavior and later involvement in violence (CDC, 2019c)

Resiliency can also help hamper the effects of ACEs. When individuals and families learn coping skills, they can begin to heal from ACEs. Undergoing the process of healing helps families become healthier and more resilient. Resiliency skills coupled with a supportive community environment can be instrumental in helping individuals and families recover from ACE-related, traumatic stress (Bethell et al., 2017).

Positive communication is another way that individuals and families can combat the effects of ACEs. Establishing positive communication habits within a family helps foster an environment that supports open communication. This creates a safe space where family members can speak freely and work through challenges, which also contributes to families becoming more resilient (Bethell et al., 2017).

It is also beneficial when people engage in positive communication with health care providers. Positive communication helps people feel more comfortable discussing sensitive topics with a health care practitioner. Parents (and caregivers) who have positive communication with their child's health care provider tend to practice daily, healthy family routines such as eating together, less television time, and reading to children on a regular basis. Continual positive communication with children's health care providers also strengthens family resilience and builds a healthy patient-healthcare provider relationship (Bethell et al., 2017).

It is pivotal that individuals and families remain resilient when faced with adversity. Resiliency skills help to buffer the effects of ACEs and strengthen families who are recovering from the effects of ACEs. It is imperative that communities support the development of healthy children and families. Families, community leaders, policymakers, and health care providers can all be active participants in creating safe, supportive community environments that nurture children and families (Bethell et al., 2017).

END-OF-CHAPTER ACTIVITIES

Discussion Questions

1. What are some of the poor health outcomes that adults may develop from exposure to adverse childhood experiences?

2. Why is it important to examine the effects of ACEs on children and adults? Why is it important to examine the effects of urban community-related and low-income related ACEs?

3. What are the different types of stress and how are they different?

4. What happens to developing children when their body remains in a constant "fight-or-flight" state?

5. How can the effects of ACEs be buffered? Consider methods other than those that are mentioned in the textbook.

6. Why is it beneficial for pediatric clinicians to screen for ACEs?

Establishing a Nurturing Home Environment

Working in small groups, generate a list of 12 practices that parents (caregivers) can use to help create nurturing home environments. As you work on the list, consider family practices that are appropriate for different age ranges (see the ones listed). Identify simple practices that do not require spending additional money. Perhaps the family can create a routine such as a weekly family game night. Generate four practices for each age range.

1. Early childhood (0–5 years)

2. School age (6–11 years)

3. Adolescence (11–18 years)

Service-Learning Activity: Fostering Quality Family Moments

This is an indirect service activity.

Working independently or in a small group, compile two lists of free and discounted family activities within your community, one for the school year and another for the summer. Take the information and organize it an informational packet or two separate brochures. Contact a local school or community center and arrange for the packet to be distributed to families. Make sure that you check the demographics of the school so that you can have the packet translated into additional languages.

Service-Learning Activity: Helping Children Heal From ACEs

This is a direct service activity.

Based on research, nearly 50% of children are exposed to adverse childhood experiences. Working independently or in a small group, you will design a youth cooking program. Before beginning the project, identify a grade for the program. Make sure the cooking tasks are age appropriate. Also, for younger grades, you may want to incorporate a book that tells a cooking-related story.

1. Explore how cooking is used as a therapeutic method to help people recover from traumatic experiences, such as ACEs.

2. Identify a community partner to work with such as an after-school program, library, school, community center, nonprofit organization, or recreation center. Design a program proposal to present to your community partner.

3. Students, community partner, and instructor should discuss formative and summative evaluation instruments. These instruments can be designed collaboratively to ensure the development of effective evaluation instruments.

4. Plan and prepare four classes. Look for planning resources on the Internet and/or at the library. If you are working with a nonprofit organization, you may be able to access in-kind donations from stores in your community.

5. After each class, you should complete a one-page personal reflection. The reflection should provide an overview of the service, discuss how the service connects to concepts and information from the textbook, and describe how the service made you feel.

6. Review assessment results and share data with the community partner.

References

Berger, K. (2016). *Invitation to the lifespan*. Worth Publishers.

Bethell, C. D., Davis, M. B., Gomojav, N., Stumbo, S., & Powers, K. (2017, October). *A national and across state profile on adverse childhood experiences among children and possibilities to heal and thrive.* https://www.greatcircle .org/images/pdfs/aces-brief-101717.pdf

Centers for Disease Control and Prevention. (2019a). *About the CDC—Kaiser ACE study.* https://www.cdc.gov/violenceprevention/childabuseandneglect/ acestudy/about.html

Centers for Disease Control and Prevention. (2019b). *Behavioral risk factor surveillance system ACE data.* https://www.cdc.gov/violenceprevention/ childabuseandneglect/acestudy/ace-brfss.html

Centers for Disease Control and Prevention. (2019c). *About the CDC-Kaiser ACE study.* https://www.cdc.gov/violenceprevention/childabuseandneglect/ acestudy/about.html

Center for Youth Wellness. (2014). *An unhealthy dose of stress: The impact of adverse childhood experiences and toxic stress on childhood health and development.* Author.

Center for Youth Wellness. (2017a). https://centerforyouthwellness.org/

Center for Youth Wellness. (2017b). *Our work.* https://centerforyouthwellness .org/our-work/

Center for Youth Wellness. (2017c). *Applying universal ACEs screening in the pediatric clinic.* https://centerforyouthwellness.org/advancing-clinical-practice/

Center for Youth Wellness. (2017d). *Working together to educate, engage, and advocate for change.* https://centerforyouthwellness.org/building-a-movement/

Center for Youth Wellness. (2017e). *Decades of scientific investigation guides our work to solve this public health crisis.* https://centerforyouthwellness .org/the-science/

Data Resource Center for Child and Adolescent Health. (n.d.). *The national survey of children's health*. https://www.childhealthdata.org/learn-about-the-nsch/NSCH

Felitti, V. J., Anda, R. F., Nordenberg, D, Williamson, D. F., Spitz, A. M., Edwards, V., Koss, M. P., & Marks, J. S. (1998). Relationship of childhood abuse and household dysfunction to many of the leading causes of death in adults: The Adverse Childhood Experiences study. *American Journal of Preventative Medicine, 14*(4), 245–258.

Health Resources and Services Administration (HRSA), Maternal Child Health Bureau. (2014, June). *The health and well-being of children: A portrait of states and nation 2011–2012*. U.S. Department of Health and Human Services.

Merrick, M. T., Ford, D. C., Ports, K. A., & Guinn, A. S. (2018). Prevalence of adverse childhood experiences from the 2011–2014 Behavioral Risk Factor Surveillance System in 23 states. *JAMA Pediatrics, 172*(11), 1038–1044.

Office of Head Start. (2018, July). *History of Head Start*. https://www.acf.hhs.gov/ohs/about/history-of-head-start

Public Health Management Corporation, Merritt, M.B., Cronholm, P., Davis, M., Dempsey, S., Fein, J., Kuykendall, S.A., Pachter, L., & Wade, R. (2013). Institute for Safe Families. *Findings from the Philadelphia Urban ACE Survey*. https://www.rwjf.org/en/library/research/2013/09/findings-from-the-philadelphia-urban-ace-survey.html

PART III

HOUSING INSTABILITY, HOMELESSNESS, AND SOCIAL EXCLUSION

6

Housing Instability and Homelessness in the United States

THOUGHT QUESTIONS

As you read this chapter, consider the following:

- Why is sustaining stable rental housing a challenge for some working-class and poor people, especially those who live in urban areas?
- What happened to the state of homelessness when the Mental Health Systems Act was repealed in 1981?
- How has the state of homelessness changed from the hobohemia era?
- How does experiencing homelessness affect developing children?
- What approaches are used to help homeless individuals and families regain and sustain stable housing?

Introduction

This chapter explores the social issues of housing instability and homelessness. It begins with a brief overview on the 2007–2009 recession, suboptimal housing, and eviction. The chapter continues with a detailed discussion on homelessness in the United States, which focuses on the political, economic, and social forces that have influenced the existence of homelessness in American society. There is a historical overview of homelessness that starts with the hobohemia era, discusses key legislation that was signed during John F. Kennedy's presidency, and reviews the long-term societal effects that occurred when President Ronald Reagan and Congress repealed legislation that provided federal funding for community mental health centers throughout the United States.

The chapter also discusses single-parent led female families, traumatic stress, and the effects of homelessness on children. Maslow's hierarchy of needs is introduced to provide a theoretical framework for understanding the importance of achieving deficiency needs such as food and safety and stable housing before moving on to higher needs like friendship, confidence, and achievement. Throughout the chapter, research findings are presented and policies are described. The chapter ends with highlighting solutions that can aid in decreasing the number of homeless individuals, families, and children in America.

2007–2009 Recession

During the recession, families across social classes experienced economic and social declines due to a downward shift in the economy. There was a decrease in the gross domestic product (GDP), decrease in consumer spending, high rates of unemployment, and the housing bubble burst, causing the housing prices to plummet. The interest rates on subprime mortgages rose exponentially, and many people were unable to pay increased mortgage payments, resulting in high rates of foreclosures and personal bankruptcy. Low-income and minority families with subprime mortgages were highly susceptible to foreclosures. Many families lost their homes and had nowhere to go. There are many accounts of families becoming homeless. Some families were able to live doubled up with family or friends, while others entered emergency shelters (Bassuk et al., 2014).

Renters felt the effects of the recession too. There was a higher pool of renters across all income levels who were competing for a limited amount of affordable units. The demand was higher than the supply, creating an affordable housing "supply gap" (Bassuk et al., 2014). Low-income individuals and families are at the bottom of the renter pool and immediately priced out of the renter market. Their lack of economic capital decreases their housing pool, which limits their housing options, and this also leads to families living doubled up or becoming homeless.

Housing Instability

Finding affordable housing is a challenging task for the person who makes an average living, which means that it is nearly an impossible task for most low-income wage earners. Even if a low-income individual qualifies for a housing subsidy, they must still undergo an extensive process to receive the subsidy. The process often starts with entering your name on a wait list. Times of wait list vary from several months to a couple of years; however, the average wait time is 2 years (Bassuk et al., 2014).

There is a public myth that most low-income families receive housing subsidies; however, 45 million people are below the poverty line, and only one out of four people receive some form of housing assistance. Three out of four low-income people receive no assistance and must figure out how to make it work on their own (Stanford Center on Poverty and Inequality, 2016). This includes securing and sustaining housing. In larger cities, individuals may experience excessive rental burden due to high rental costs. There are many individuals with low income and limited resources using most of their income to live in the poorest neighborhoods in America.

In America, housing cost estimates show that people should allocate 30% of their income on housing. However, these estimates are not in accord with the cost of living in America. For low-income workers, it definitely is not 30% of their income. The median rental prices increased by 70% over the last 15 years, which has resulted in an increase in poor rental households spending more on housing. According to the 2013 American Housing Survey, only 18% of poor renting households spend 30% or less on housing. Most poor households that fall below the poverty line spend well over 30% of their income on housing and as a result suffer from rental cost burden (Stanford Center on Poverty and Inequality, 2016). A large portion of poor families spend 50% of income on housing, and one in four families spend more than 70% of income on housing costs. Exuberant rental costs have resulted in millions of Americans being unable to afford housing and experiencing eviction due to the inability to pay monthly housing costs (Desmond, 2016).

Suboptimal Housing

The inability to secure affordable housing often results in poor households living in **suboptimal housing**. When families move into suboptimal housing, they often experience overcrowded living environments, exposure to toxins, and increased violence in the community. Long-term living in suboptimal housing and communities can affect child development (e.g., cognition, socialization, etc.) and lead to medical illness. Suboptimal, overcrowded housing can affect children's academic performance. Overcrowded homes tend to be louder, may lack order, and may affect quality of parenting. Children living in these environments experience challenges in focusing and completing schoolwork (Willingham, 2012).

PERSONAL REFLECTION

Imagine if you were a child living in a two-bedroom apartment with six people; would you be able to find a quiet space to do your home-work? Would you be able to concentrate with all the noise in the apartment? How do you think your living conditions would affect your overall academic achievement?

People who live in suboptimal housing conditions may also face health risks. Individuals and families may have exposure to one or more of the following: cockroaches, mice, rats, mold, lead, and tobacco smoke. Exposure to many of these allergens can lead to asthma and other more serious medical issues (Camacho-Rivera et al., 2014; Willingham, 2012). For example, lead exposure can have negative effects on cognition, which eventually affects other functions (Chandramouli et al., 2009).

Suboptimal housing environments are often not safe environments. Violence in communities prevents residents from being able to walk in the community, children are unable to play outside, neighbors may limit socialization with one another, and residents tend to have higher levels of stress. Unfortunately, poor families and children often live in suboptimal housing conditions due to the inability to secure affordable, quality housing. Due to their limited financial resources, they have minimal housing options. Lack of money and resources results in poor families and children living in undesirable, toxic locations. Living in toxic environments is not ideal for anyone and hampers the overall development of adults and children.

Eviction

Harvard Sociologist, Matthew Desmond, provides a glimpse into **evictions** in his unstable housing talk in America's Poverty Course (Stanford Center on Poverty and Inequality, 2016). Evictions occur when a tenant fails to pay rent, engages in criminal activity, causes damage to the property, or violates other terms on the lease. There are formal and non-formal ways to execute an eviction. To formally evict a tenant, the landlord would file a suit against a tenant in civil court. Non-formally, a landlord can ask the tenant to move or pay for the tenant to move. There are numerous other non-formal methods, too. Desmond describes an example of a landlord removing an apartment door. If you live in a poor, undesirable part of town and the landlord removes your door, then you are forced to move immediately. Imagine if you were in this situation; what would you do, and where would you go?

Desmond (Stanford Center on Poverty and Inequality, 2016) found that tenants were often shocked when property owners began the eviction process. In some cases, tenants felt warranted to stop paying rent because of poor living conditions—inoperable toilet, lack of heat, pest issues, and so on. Due to these issues, tenants often believed that they could resolve issues in court. While lack of property maintenance is an issue, in most cities nonpayment of rent still results in eviction. When studying eviction rates in Milwaukee, Desmond discovered the information that is listed in Table 6.1.

TABLE 6.1 Milwaukee Eviction

Milwaukee Eviction Rates
▪ 16,000 people/per year
▪ 45 people/per day
▪ 1 in 30 renter-occupied households is evicted/per year
▪ 1 in 14 inner-city households/year

Source: Stanford Center on Poverty and Inequality, 2016

He also found that most tenants do not show up in court. In Milwaukee, 80% of tenants do not appear at their court date, and they lose due to nonappearance. Those tenants that do attend court often appear without a lawyer. In most cities, 90% of property owners retain lawyers and 90% of tenants appear in court without counsel. Civil court differs from criminal court, and there are no court-appointed lawyers provided (Stanford Center on Poverty and Inequality, 2016). Thus, poor renters who have minimal to no legal experience are left to navigate the legal system on their own.

In eviction courts across the country, there are high rates of single, African American women with children. African American women in poverty-stricken, segregated neighborhoods experience eviction at over two times the rate of men in the same neighborhood (Stanford

Center on Poverty and Inequality, 2016). There is a positive correlation between the high incarceration rates of African American males and high eviction rates of African American females too; Desmond (Stanford Center on Poverty and Inequality, 2016) states, "African American males are getting locked up, as African American women are getting locked out."

Once tenants have an eviction on their record, it limits their housing options. Many property owners will not take tenants who have a recent eviction or criminal record. Due to having limited options, they must take any housing they can find. These individuals occupy the lowest tier of the housing market and end up moving into extremely poor neighborhoods and living in suboptimal housing (Stanford Center on Poverty and Inequality, 2016). In some situations, families may not be able to secure housing at all. When families are unable to secure housing, they are at risk of becoming homeless.

Homelessness

An individual or household becomes homeless when they are unable to secure stable housing. Homeless people become part of the sheltered or unsheltered homeless population. The U.S. Department of Housing and Urban Development (HUD) defines **homelessness** in four categories:

1. People who reside in places that are not suitable living residences such as abandoned buildings, parks, and cars; people who live in transitional housing or emergency shelter; and people who are leaving an institution where they temporarily lived.

2. People who are losing their residence within fourteen days. This includes people living doubled up or in a motel/hotel, and do not have a support system or resources to remain in stable housing.

3. Families with children, or unaccompanied young persons under the age of 25, who lack stable housing. This applies to families who have not had a lease or ownership in a property during the last 60 days or may have moved two or more times during the last 60 days, and families who are likely to remain without stable housing due to disability or employment limitations.

4. People who are escaping or trying to escape domestic violence and lack a support system or resources to secure alternative housing (U.S. Interagency on Homelessness, 2018)

People who experience **chronic homelessness** are homeless individuals who suffer from a disability. HUD defines chronic homelessness as follows:

1. A disabled homeless individual who has one of the following identified conditions: developmental disability, substance use disorder, and/or serious mental illness.

    a. An individual who resides in a place that is not suitable for human habitation, including emergency shelter or a safe haven.

    b. An individual who has been homeless for 12 months or has four separate periods of homelessness during a 3-year period.

2. An individual who lives in an institutional setting, such as a mental health facility or jail for a period of 90 days or less. If prior to entering the facility the individual met the first criteria, the person is chronically homeless.

3. A family with a head of household who is a disabled homeless individual and meets the definition listed in criteria 1 and 2, including families who experience separation from the family unit while the head of household is homeless (U.S. Department of Housing and Urban Development, 2015)

The **McKinney–Vento Assistance Act** is a federal law that ensures that homeless children and youth get appropriate access to education and educational resources. The McKinney–Vento Homeless Assistance Act defines homeless children and youth as the following:

1. Children and youth who are living in a doubled-up situation due to not having stable housing; as a result they may live in motels, trailers, and campgrounds. Children and youth who live in transitional housing or emergency shelters and also youth who have been left by caregivers and lack adult supervision. The definition also includes children who are in the foster care system and are awaiting placement.

2. Children and youth who live in a place that is not meant for human habitation.

3. Children and youth who reside in places that are not suitable living residences such as abandoned buildings, parks, and cars.

4. Migrant children who are living in the conditions that are listed (U.S. Interagency on Homelessness, 2018).

History of Homelessness

The state of homelessness has changed over time. It was once a temporary state of living related to a change in the economy or a disastrous event. In the 1930s, the Great Depression created a downward spiral in the economy and left many people without jobs. This economic shift resulted in an emergence of a hobo population: hobohemia; men from rural and urban areas traveled the United States in search of work. Once the depression ended, the economy improved, job opportunities increased, and people secured stable housing again (Rubin, 2007).

Since this time, there have been many political, economic, and social occurrences that have impacted homelessness. Throughout the text, it has been discussed that American society is highly stratified. Those with high levels of capital have access to opportunities and resources that help them rise to the top of society, while low-income people often have limited access to resources and opportunities. Limitations create barriers and make it more challenging for them to rise out of poverty. For those who lack education or a trade, they are often limited to low-wage jobs that do not produce an income to sustain basic needs. Even working-class individuals struggle to provide for their families because their income does not equate to a living wage. As mentioned in the prior section, urban rental costs are higher than what most low-wage earners can afford. Additionally, lack of employment opportunities and business closures also lead to higher rates of homelessness in communities.

Public policy initiatives have also hugely impacted the state of poverty and homelessness in our society. One policy that significantly affected communities and individuals was the **Housing Act of 1949**. This act was created with the intent of creating safe communities and making home ownership more accessible to all Americans. Cities received funding to clear blighted areas and revitalize them, 810,000 public housing units were erected, and Farmers Home Administration offered mortgage programs to invest in single-family homes in rural areas and "increased authorization for Federal Housing Administration

(FHA) mortgage insurance" (U.S. Department of Housing and Urban Development, 2014).

As cities began to clear slums and renew urban areas, many poor communities were demolished, and poor people were forced out of neighborhoods. While many dilapidated areas were in desperate need of being revitalized, poor residents were not provided the opportunity to be part of the renewal; instead, they were displaced and moved to other poor communities. Public housing was erected in poor communities, but the housing was more for relegating the poor people to specific sections of cities. It was a way to keep the poor contained in undesirable areas, such as near freeways or industrial areas.

Revitalizing poor areas, making them more desirable, bringing in new businesses, increasing rents, and displacing poor residents is a process known as gentrification, and it happens in cities throughout the United States. Low-income and working-class people are unable to afford high rental costs, so they are often left with limited housing options. When individuals and families are unable to secure housing after being displaced, they may experience an episode of homelessness until they can regain stable housing.

Another public policy that has also contributed to the existence of homelessness in our society is the **Community Mental Health Centers Act of 1963**, which was signed into law by President John F. Kennedy. This act was created with good intentions, but there have been many challenges with achieving the initial goals of the act. John F. Kennedy had a personal connection to mental health, as his young sister Rosemary had an intellectual disability. During this time, intellectual disabilities were not a social issue that educators, doctors, or scientists were exploring. People with intellectual disabilities were often housed in institutions, often referred to as "insane asylums," and isolated from the outside world. Kennedy's sister, Eunice Kennedy Shriver, was an advocate for individuals and families who were affected by this issue, and she encouraged her brother to make the issue a priority during his presidency (JFK Presidential Library and Museum, n.d.).

After entering office, Kennedy created the National Institute of Child Health and Human Development. The institute supports and conducts research on child health and human development, maternal health, and intellectual disabilities. In 1961, Kennedy appointed a 27-person panel that included scientists and doctors to discuss and develop a comprehensive federal plan that could be enacted to identify causes and develop preventative measures to help people with intellectual disabilities. The panel generated 100 recommendations, and on February 5, 1963, Kennedy provided an overview of the recommendation to Congress. In October 1963, there were two pieces of legislation signed: the Maternal and Child Health and Mental Retardation Planning Amendment to the Social Security Act and the Community Mental Health Centers Act. The first piece of legislation provided grant resources to states so that they could improve programs for individuals with intellectual disabilities. There was also funding for preventative care for expecting mothers and infants. Many parts of the legislation came from the recommendations that were generated from the President's Panel on Mental Retardation (JFK Presidential Library and Museum, n.d.).

The latter legislation provided funding for the building of facilities that would offer preventative resources, medical treatment, and ongoing care of individuals with intellectual disabilities, specifically facilities such as research centers, university clinics that would provide diagnosis and treatment services, and community-based health centers. Additionally, the act also directed funding toward training special education teachers who worked with children with intellectual disabilities and other special needs (JFK Presidential Library and Museum, n.d.).

Over the last 5 decades, the good intentions of the Community Health Centers Act have been eroded by political, economic, and social forces. Some key historical happenings that have directly impacted this act are the effects from the Vietnam War, the recession that occurred at the beginning of the 1980s, and President Ronald Reagan and Congress repealing a majority of the Mental Health Systems Act in 1981 that was signed into legislation by President Jimmy Carter in 1980. When the act was repealed, the community mental health centers lost federal funding, and mental health became a state and local issue once again (Rubin, 2007).

Mental health had been deinstitutionalized, and there were thousands of individuals in all states throughout America living in communities that could not provide resources to them. There were a limited number of community mental health centers with scarce funds, and the demand was greater than the available resources. Some people were able to live with family, and others went to adult group homes, but many communities had closed state hospitals, halfway homes, and treatment programs. As a result, tens of thousands of people suffering from mental health disorders were left with nowhere to go. For those with severe mental disorders, such as bipolar disorder and schizophrenia, they needed regular monitoring and ongoing care in a residential facility. Without federal funding, facilities, and resources, there became an immediate increase in the number of people experiencing a stable state of homelessness (Rubin, 2007).

Major cities throughout the United States have always had poor neighborhoods and secluded, small pockets of homelessness. These "skid row" areas were home to the poor and those who suffered from substance abuse. In contrast, the current state of homelessness consists of not only "bum" or "hobo" populations who live in hidden homeless enclaves; there are homeless individuals, families and children, youth, veterans, and individuals with mental health disorders who are visible in cities throughout the United States. Across our nation, on any given night there are hundreds of thousands of unsheltered and sheltered homeless people. For some, homelessness is still a temporary experience that is the result of job loss, excessive medical debt, domestic violence, or a natural disaster. After a brief episode of homelessness, these individuals receive resources, work through their challenges, and secure stable housing again (Rubin, 2007). However, for most, homelessness is an inescapable way of life. In cities throughout America (e.g., Los Angeles, Honolulu, and New York), there are densely populated stable, homeless communities where thousands of homeless individuals live in "tent cities" or spaces that are not meant for human habitation. See Chapter 7 for more information on homeless encampments.

How Many Are Homeless?

Each year in January, continuums of care (CoC) conduct a **point-in-time count** of the homeless population across the nation. CoCs are nonprofit providers and government agencies that provide rehousing resources to homeless individuals and families (U.S. Department of Housing and Urban Development, 2020). During the last week of January, the CoCs conduct a count of unsheltered and sheltered homeless people. According to the U.S. Department of Housing and Urban Development, on a single night in 2019 the CoCs counted 567,715 homeless people in the United States (Henry et al., 2020). Slightly less than two-thirds were in a sheltered location (e.g., emergency shelter or safe haven), and close to one-third lived in unsheltered locations.

There are several prominent groups within the homeless population; these groupings are homeless subpopulations. The 2019 Annual

TABLE 6.2 2019 Homeless Subpopulation Estimates

Subpopulation	Estimates
Homeless individuals	567,715
Homeless families and children	172,000 homeless individuals in 54,000 families with children
Unaccompanied homeless youth	35,038
Homeless veterans	37,085
Chronically homeless individuals	96,141

Source: Henry et al., 2020

Homeless Assessment Report (AHAR) to Congress lists the following subpopulations: homeless individuals, homeless families and children, unaccompanied homeless youth, homeless veterans, and chronically homeless individuals. See Table 6.2 for subpopulation estimates. However, the listed counts are only a starting point; the reality is that homeless counts are higher. It is nearly impossible to count all homeless people, especially the unsheltered homeless population who live doubled up (with relatives and friends), in motels, tents, or hidden locations (e.g., in cars, under bridges, or in abandoned buildings).

Single-Parent Female-Led Families

Children under the age of 6 who are being raised by single mothers are more likely to live in poverty in comparison to children living in households with two parents; their likelihood of living in poverty is five times greater. Children living with single fathers also have an increased chance of living in poverty; their potential of living in poverty is two and a half times greater than a child living in a two-parent household. Based on research, there are three factors that place families at higher risk of experiencing poverty:

1. Being a single parent

2. Lack of education

3. Unemployment or part-time employment (Gestwicki, 2016)

Single mothers face many challenges; one parent is solely responsible for nurturing, supporting, and providing for a family. Some single mothers seek support from relatives and friends to assist them with balancing work and raising their children. However, for many single mothers, lack of support and resources, affordable housing, education, and access to living wages make it nearly impossible for them to provide for their families. When single mothers begin to struggle and have nowhere to go for help, they risk eviction from their homes and experiencing an episode of homelessness. If they become homeless, it becomes even harder for them to provide their children with basic needs. Many single mothers have only worked minimum wage jobs, while others have never worked (Bassuk et al., 2014). A homeless single mother with limited education and low-paying work experience does not have many options. If she is unable to turn her life around and provide for her children, she is at risk of losing custody of her children.

Homeless Mothers and Traumatic Stress

In comparison to the total number of women living in the United States, homeless women are two to four times more likely to experience violent acts. Several studies report that 90% of homeless mothers either witness or experience one extreme traumatic stress event. According to the Worchester Family Research Project, 66% of homeless mothers experienced childhood traumatic stresses such as physical violence from a family member or childcare provider. Forty-three percent of the women experienced sexual abuse, typically before the age of 12. In adulthood, almost two-thirds of the sample had been assaulted by an intimate partner, and more than one quarter of the participants needed medical treatment (Bassuk, et al., 2014). The SHIFT study (Hayes et al., 2013) presented findings on homeless families in three housing programs; the study reported the following about maternal trauma: 93% of the mothers experienced trauma, 81% experienced more than one traumatic event, 79% experienced childhood trauma, 56% had more than one traumatic childhood event, 82% experienced adulthood trauma, and 64% experienced more than one traumatic adulthood event. This study also found that sexual assaults were common during childhood, and half of the sample (sample size = 146) reported that they had been assaulted by a family member or person they knew (Hayes et al., 2013).

Homeless Children

Homeless children are categorized as birth to 18 years old and live with one or both parents (caregivers) (Bassuk et al., 2011). The main causes of homelessness for children in the United States are (a) the high rates of families living in poverty, (b) single-parent families, (c) the 2007 recession, (d) lack of affordable housing, and (e) traumatic stress from experiences such as domestic violence (Bassuk et al., 2014). I do want to point out that there is a discrepancy between the number of homeless children reported in the United States. According to the 2014 Annual Homeless Assessment Report (AHAR) to Congress, there were 216,261 individuals homeless in families and 60% were children, which is 129,756. Additionally, there were 194,302 unaccompanied children and youth (under the age of 25) reported (U.S. Department of Housing and Urban Development, 2014). However, based on data from the U.S. Department of Education, there were 1.3 million homeless students enrolled during the 2013–2014 school year. Based on these differences, it is shown that there are greater numbers of families and children living in poverty (U.S. Department of Education, 2016a).

The Effects of Homelessness on Children

Homelessness is especially devastating and traumatic for children. Children who lack stable housing experience high levels of traumatic stress, suffer from medical illnesses, and have challenges in school (Bassuk et al., 2011). Children are dependent on their parents to provide a caring, supportive, and safe home environment. Unfortunately, parents of homeless children are unable to provide these resources to their children. Lack of housing and resources result in homeless families living in toxic environments that are damaging to a child's overall development.

UNSTABLE HOUSING

Homeless families lack stable housing and often move up to three times in a year. Families may "double up" at a relative or friend's house. Doubled-up living situations result in overcrowded homes that lack resources for all occupants. When a homeless family is unable to live doubled up, they will seek out alternative accommodations such as a motel, campground, or sleeping in their car. Once families exhaust all their personal options, their final option is entering a shelter (Bassuk et al., 2011).

Imagine if you were entering a shelter with your family: a spouse and two kids. When you arrive at the shelter, they inform you that men are not sheltered with their families. You are unhappy about the rules, but since you have nowhere else to go, you stay and separate for your family. The shelter is overcrowded, noisy, and unsafe. The food quality is poor, but your family has no other options, so everyone eats it. (Fortunately, when the children re-enroll in school, they will receive free and reduced breakfast and lunch.) The bathrooms are dirty, and the water is so hot that you almost burn yourself when showering. You have no privacy and must always keep all your belongings with you or risk getting them stolen.

Lack of stable housing places families in a chaotic, imbalanced way of living. This one shift leads to numerous other declines that affect the development of children and adults, as well as familial relationships. Regaining stable housing, along with receiving social services and supportive resources, is a crucial necessity for homeless individuals and families. These topics will be discussed more later in the chapter.

TRAUMATIC STRESS

As discussed in Chapter 5, unfavorable early childhood experiences can lead to childhood traumatic stress, which is extremely detrimental for the developing child. When children have ongoing exposure to high levels of stress, without parental, caretaker, or social support to nurture them and act as a buffer against the traumatic experiences, the result is traumatic stress. The excessive stress can damage neural connections within the brain. Traumatic stress in early childhood can lead to changes in brain size and structure, which can harm cognition and memory, emotional self-regulation, behavior, coping skills, and socialization. Research has shown that many American children have experienced a traumatic stress event. According to the National Child Traumatic Stress Network (2008), one out of every four school-age children experience a traumatic event. However, the risk and prevalence of traumatic stress events increase for children who live in poverty. Homeless children, by far, are at higher risks for traumatic stress; they often observe violent acts in their community and among

FIGURE 6.1 Homeless Mother and Child.

Source: https://files.hudexchange.info/resources/documents/2016-AHAR-Part-1.pdf.

family members; lack safe, stable housing; suffer from food insecurity; and are at risk of living separately from their parents/caregivers (Bassuk et al., 2014).

HOMELESSNESS IN CHILDHOOD AND ADVERSE CHILDHOOD EXPERIENCES

Children who experience high levels of traumatic stress often become adults who have poor mental and health outcomes. The adults were children who were exposed to adverse childhood experiences (ACEs). The number of ACEs and repeated exposure negatively affect the development of the child throughout the lifespan. ACEs affect people across social classes, but working-class, poor, and homeless people have higher levels of ACE exposure.

Many children living in poverty suffer from high rates of mental and physical illness (Bassuk et al., 2011). An episode of homelessness is only one of many poverty-related factors that cause these conditions. Other factors include but are not limited to domestic violence, financial struggles, doubled-up living, and parental mental health. Additionally, homeless children are at a higher risk for developing acute and chronic medical issues. They experience hunger insecurity and suffer from hunger two times more than non-homeless children. Traumatic stress, coupled with hunger, often affects brain development. There is a high incidence of developmental delays, behavioral problems, and emotional issues among young homeless children, which is the result of poor brain development. Homeless children also suffer from behavioral and emotional problems, such as depression, withdrawal, and anxiety, at three times the rate of non-homeless children. These factors can influence socialization practices, ability to form long-lasting relationships with adults, and school readiness (Bassuk et al., 2011).

In comparison to other populations, homeless adults have been reported to have more ACEs than non-homeless individuals. Based on findings from a cross-sectional analysis study of data from the 2016 South Carolina Behavioral Risk Factor Surveillance System survey (SC BRFSS), there were higher levels of ACEs reported from those who experienced homelessness in childhood. In the study, there were 7,490 respondents, and 215 experienced homelessness as children. Of the 215 respondents, 68.1% reported exposure to four or more ACEs. In comparison, a significantly smaller portion of respondents (16.3%)

who had not experienced homelessness in childhood reported exposure to four or more ACEs (Radcliff et al., 2019). The "eleven-question ACE module and homeless question included in the 2016 SC BRFSS survey" (Radcliff et al., 2019) are listed in Table 6.3. An overview of all findings from the study is listed in Table 6.4.

TABLE 6.3 Eleven-Question ACE Module and Homeless Question Included in the 2016 SC BRFSS Survey

Childhood Experience	Survey Question(s)
Household dysfunction	
Household mental illness	1. Did you live with anyone who was depressed, mentally ill, or suicidal?
Household substance use 1	2. Did you live with anyone who was a problem drinker or alcoholic?
Household substance use 2	3. Did you live with anyone who used illegal street drugs or who abused medication?
Household incarceration	4. Did you live with anyone who served time or was sentenced to serve time in prison, jail, or another correctional facility?
Parental separation/divorce	5. Were your parents separated or divorced?
Witness household violence	6. Did your parents or adults in your home ever slap, hit, kick, punch, or beat each other up?
Physical and emotional abuse	
Physical abuse	7. Did a parent or adult in your home ever hit, beat, kick, or physically hurt you in any way?
Emotional abuse	8. Did a parent or adult in your home ever swear at you, insult you, or put you down?
Sexual abuse	
Sexual abuse 1	9. Did anyone at least 5 years older than you or an adult try to make you touch them sexually?
Sexual abuse 2	10. Did anyone at least 5 years older than you or an adult try to make you touch them sexually?
Sexual abuse 3	11. Did anyone at least 5 years older than you or an adult force you to have sex?
Homelessness in childhood	
"How often were you homeless when you were growing up? By "homeless" we mean that your family could not afford a place to live."	

*All questions refer to the time period before respondent was 18 years of age and were prefaced with the phrase "Now, looking back before you were 18 years of age …"

Source: Radcliff et al., 2019

TABLE 6.4 Number and Type of ACE Exposure Reported by 2016 SC BRFSS Respondents Who Participated in the ACE Module of Questions, in Total and by Childhood Homeless Status

Aces Exposure in Childhood	Total Sample %	Not Homeless in Childhood % = 95%	Homeless in Childhood % = 4.2%
By number of ACEs:			
Experienced no ACEs	35.8	37.2	2.7
Experienced 1–3 ACEs	45.7	46.5	29.2
Experienced 4 or more ACEs	18.5	16.3	68.1
By type of ACEs:			
Household dysfunction ACEs:			
Household mental illness	16.6	15.4	44.1
Household substance use 1	24.1	22.9	52.2
Household substance use 2	10.8	9.8	34.3
Household incarceration	8.4	7.2	35.7
Parental separation/ divorce	32.1	30.6	66.5
Witness household violence	19.0	17.3	58.3
Physical and emotional abuse ACEs:			
Physical abuse	13.5	12.2	43.9
Emotional abuse	31.7	30.2	66.4
Sexual Abuse ACEs:			
Sexual abuse 1	11.3	10.4	32.7
Sexual abuse 2	8.4	7.6	26.7
Sexual abuse 3	5.2	4.5	22.4

Source: Radcliff et al., 2019

These findings show that adults who experience homelessness during childhood have high rates of exposure to ACEs. As discussed in Chapter 5, children with high numbers of ACEs often become adults who have poor mental and health outcomes. While this study does provide more insight into exposure to ACEs among adults who were homeless during their childhood, it does have a few limitations. The exposure to ACEs is self-reported, and the adults have to recall exposure that occurred during childhood. This retrospective reporting can be biased, and respondents may underreport exposure, which has been seen in other ACE research. The other limitation is that there is no way to know whether the ACEs exposure came before or after the homelessness or possibly caused the homelessness. These are limitations that can be addressed in future studies, as the findings from this study demonstrate the need to further examine the relationship between exposure to ACEs, childhood homelessness, and mental and health outcomes in adulthood. Additional research in these areas will help to strengthen policies, programs, practices, and resources for children and adults who have experienced homelessness and exposure to ACEs.

SCHOOL READINESS

Unstable housing, traumatic stress, and acute and chronic medical illness can all have long-term effects on brain development, which influences how children function and perform in school. Homeless children are four times as likely to have developmental delays, and two times more likely to have learning disabilities. For math and reading proficiency scores, there is a 16% decline among homeless youth. In addition, homeless youth are three times more likely to receive special education resources, eight times as likely to repeat a grade, and two times as likely to have lower standardized test scores (Bassuk et al., 2011).

McKinney–Vento Homeless Assistance Act

The McKinney–Vento Homeless Assistance Act provides homeless youth and children with supportive resources to assist with school enrollment, attending school, and becoming a successful student. The federal law ensures that local educational agencies will provide educational assistance to their homeless students who are at risk of not attending schools. The law helps establish accountability for this vulnerable population of students so that they are guaranteed appropriate access to a free, public education like any other student in the school district. All school districts are mandated to have a homeless liaison to oversee the delivery of educational services (U.S. Department of Education, 2016b). The act requires that

- students have a choice to remain in original school even if they move;

- students can be enrolled into a school without having school records;

- students have a right to be transported to and from school of origin;

- if students are eligible, they may participate in programs or access services;

- unaccompanied youth are allowed to enroll in school; and

- students, parent/caregivers can appeal school eligibility or selection (U.S. Department of Education, 2016b).

The act helps parents (caregivers) advocate for their children and to create stability in the school setting. By offering supportive resources, it helps homeless children and youth feel at ease and comfortable. The act provides transitional resources and helps identify students who may need remediation resources. The goal is to help homeless children and youth feel supported and not isolated (U.S. Department of Education, 2016b).

Maslow's Hierarchy of Needs

Developmental theorist Abraham Maslow developed a framework that describes a humanistic approach to understanding motivation. Maslow believed that people have an innate desire to achieve specific needs. He developed a model that was a hierarchy of needs. Each tier describes a set of needs that must be met before moving on to the next stage.

Maslow's hierarchy of needs has five stages that occur in sequential order. People must climb up the hierarchy starting with the bottom tier—the physiological stage. As people fulfill the needs within each stage, they transition to the next level of the hierarchy and continue to progress through the stages. If people are unable to satisfy the needs

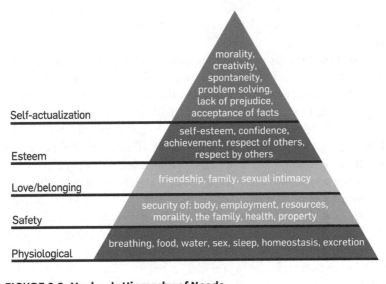

FIGURE 6.2 Maslow's Hierarchy of Needs.

Source: Copyright © 2013 Depositphotos/xprmntl.

of a stage, they may remain in the stage until the needs are met. For example, lacking stable housing can cause a person to not feel safe or secure; therefore, the individual would remain in stage 2: safety until stable in safe, secure housing.

Maslow's hierarchy of needs provides a framework to understand the connections between intrinsic motivation, survival, and homelessness (and poverty). If people are consumed with trying to provide stable, safe housing and basic needs, their motivation is constantly focused on fulfilling the first tiers of Maslow's hierarchy. Once people can obtain and stabilize these needs, then their motivation can shift to fulfilling higher-level needs (Berger, 2016).

Solutions

There are several approaches to alleviating homelessness: **housing first**, **rapid re-housing**, and **permanent supportive housing**. The housing first approach focuses on getting people back into stable, permanent housing (National Alliance to End Homelessness, 2020a). This approach aligns with Maslow's hierarchy of needs, as the individual must first fulfill basic needs before moving on to larger needs (Berger, 2016). Think about how challenging it would be to look for employment while being homeless. It would not be impossible, but there would be challenges.

The housing first approach focuses on helping homeless individuals and families secure their basic needs. All Housing First programs provide the following: help individuals and families quickly return to permanent housing, assistance with obtaining a lease agreement, and provide resources that support housing stability and well-being. Housing first is based on client choice, so all supportive services are voluntary (National Alliance to End Homelessness, 2020a).

Many people only experience homelessness for a short period due to a personal or housing crisis. In some cases, people need supportive services coupled with re-housing. For these individuals, the housing first approach helps them to get quickly re-housed and obtain supportive resources (National Alliance to End Homelessness, 2020a). Being back in permanent housing provides stability so that the individual or family can get through their crisis and move forward with their lives.

Rapid re-housing, like Housing First, is a program that helps people experiencing homelessness return to stable, permanent housing. However, the rapid re-housing approach provides additional housing resources. Rapid re-housing provides housing identification, move-in and rent assistance, supportive services, and case management (National Alliance to End Homelessness, 2020b). The first component helps to identify property owners who are willing to rent to individuals and families experiencing homelessness. Move-in and rent assistance provide people with resources to assist with rental deposits, moving costs, and rental/utility assistance. Case management services provide individuals and families with resources that help them navigate the housing process and secure permanent housing. Such services are assistance with navigating legal issues, locating housing, negotiating lease agreement, crisis resolution resources, and guidance with accessing employment, community, and well-being resources (National Alliance to End Homelessness, 2020b).

Permanent supportive housing (PSH) is also like housing first, but there are differences in implementation. PSH is for individuals and families who experience long-term or repeat episodes of homelessness due to disabilities, substance use disorders, mental health disorders, and chronic illness (National Alliance to End Homelessness, 2016). PSH provides services to people who experience barriers in securing housing and maintaining stable housing without supportive services. This approach provides individuals and families with resources to affordable housing, supportive services, and health care. Like housing first, PSH is also client driven, so clients can choose whether to access voluntary supportive services. The client choice approach is a way of empowering the individual; the power of choice leads to better client engagement in housing programs because the individual wants the services (National Alliance to End Homelessness, 2016).

There is evidence that housing first approaches are effective models to alleviating homelessness. Clients in housing first, PSH, and rapid re-housing programs access housing quicker and have a higher likelihood to remain in stable housing (National Alliance to End Homelessness, 2016). Studies have shown that PSH programs have a retention rate of up to 98% (Montgomery et al., 2013). Other studies have shown that 75–91% of clients remain in stable housing after accessing rapid re-housing resources (Byrne et al., 2015). Additional PSH studies report that clients demonstrate an increase in choice, autonomy, and control in housing programs. Many clients participate in voluntary, supportive services, which often connect them to job-training resources, attending school, discontinuing substance abuse, and having fewer incidences of domestic violence (Tsemberis et al., 2004). Lastly, PSH is a cost-effective way of providing housing to people who are experiencing homelessness. By providing housing to those in need, society, as a whole, saves money. When people are living in stable housing, they are less likely to use emergency services, including hospitals, jails, and shelters. The housing first model offers a preventative method toward alleviating homelessness in communities.

Conclusion

When people experience an episode of homelessness, they lack stable housing and are unable to provide basic needs. Homeless individuals struggle with fulfilling the deficiency needs that occupy the lower levels of Maslow's hierarchy of needs. Since these individuals are concerned with daily survival, the higher tiers of the hierarchy are unmet. In *A Theory of Motivation*, Maslow (1970) states,

> Practically everything looks less important than safety and protection (even sometimes the physiological needs, which, being satisfied, are now underestimated). A man in this state,

if it is extreme enough and chronic enough, may be charac-
terized as living for almost safety alone. (p. 39)

In a country that has so much wealth, Americans should not have
to worry about having safe, affordable, stable housing. Homelessness
is a social problem that needs our attention. It exists in urban and
suburban areas and affects people of all ages, races, ethnicities, social
classes, sexual orientations, and genders. Some people only experience homelessness for a short period, but for others homelessness is
a long-term experience that becomes a way of life. There is not one
explanation for why people experience homelessness; each homeless person has a different story. For some, homelessness stems from
poor personal choices. In other situations, people become homeless
due to an unforeseen economic cause such as a layoff from work or
excessive medical bills. There are veterans who return from war with
post-traumatic stress disorder or with a debilitating disability and
have a difficult time readjusting to civilian life. There are also people
who flee domestic violence situations and have nowhere to go. Additionally, there are people who suffer from substance abuse and mental
health disorders.

Homelessness has vast short- and long-term effects on children.
Homelessness negatively affects children by increasing their stress
levels, undermining their health and well-being, including their
brain development, school readiness, and the quality of parenting
they receive. Homeless children and parents have high levels of stress
due to living in poverty and traumatic experiences such as domestic
violence, childhood neglect and abuse, and loss of safe, stable housing. These experiences affect each family member differently; it may
affect thinking, behavior, social interaction, and how each individual
feels. If children experience frequent exposure to traumatic stress, it
increases the potential of developing behavioral, social, and health
issues in adulthood (Bassuk et. al., 2011).

Homeless children within families are helpless individuals who are
experiencing homelessness because of their parent's decisions and life
experiences. While there are organizations and federally funded programs that offer services for families and children experiencing homeless,
these programs only provide certain resources, some services are voluntary, there are often time limits for programs, and funding is limited.

Take a moment and replace your childhood with that of a homeless
child. Think about how often you move. You live in motels, shelters,

and cars. You are always hungry because your parents do not have money for food. Many of the places you live are crowded and dirty. You attend three different schools in one school year and are behind a grade. You also witness many things that children should never have to see or hear, such as drug use, alcoholism, physical and sexual abuse, crime, and murder. As a society, we must recognize that this is real life for many homeless children (and children living in poverty) and one day these children will become adults. What will be the difference in their lives and our society if we do nothing versus if we do something?

END-OF-CHAPTER ACTIVITIES

Discussion Questions

1. According to Matthew Desmond, what population gets evicted the most? Why? What are your thoughts on the information that he presents?

2. Why is it difficult to get an accurate count of homeless individuals? Explain specific barriers.

3. What are the childhood developmental implications of growing up homeless? What are the short and long-term effects?

4. How can Maslow's hierarchy of needs be used to examine the challenges people endure when living in poverty and experiencing homelessness?

5. Housing First programs offer voluntary supportive services. Client choice is a great feature of the program, but what happens when the client suffers from substance abuse or mental health disorders? Will the individual be able to make a choice that is in their best interest or the best interest of their family? In some cases, should supportive services be mandatory? What should the qualifying factors be?

Homeless Families and Children Case Studies

These case studies are based on my personal experiences working in the Skid Row area of downtown Los Angeles, California. Skid Row has one of the largest stable homeless populations in the United States.

SAMMY'S STORY

On this afternoon, there were many children at the summer program. It was a hot summer day and the center did not have air conditioning. The room was filled with children who were rotating between activity stations. I had a few free minutes before we switched activities, so I quickly went to the bathroom. As I was washing and drying my hands, I could hear two boys talking to each other right outside of the door. The boys were engaged in pretend play. Before I opened the door, I heard Sammy, who was about 8 years old, say to the younger boy, "Hey, do you want to buy some drugs?" I quickly opened the door to investigate, and the boys continued to engage in pretend play. For a moment, I froze because I was in shock by the words I heard Sammy say to the younger boy. I interrupted the boys and asked them about their game. Sammy told me that they were pretending to be people they saw on the street. They both looked at me with such innocent eyes, not understanding why I was interrupting their game. I spoke with the boys about their game and explained why their pretend play characters were not appropriate for them to imitate.

Review Albert Bandura's social learning theory by performing an Internet search on your smartphone, tablet, or computer.

1. Using Albert Bandura's social learning theoretical framework, explain Sammy's pretend play behavior. According to social learning theory, why is Sammy exhibiting this behavior?

2. How can Sammy's parents and caregivers modify Sammy's pretend play behavior?

3. What are the potential long-term developmental effects of being homeless for children, like Sammy? Remember that homeless children often witness traumatic events such as domestic violence, drug exchanges and usage, and prostitution. Consider the social, cognitive, psychological, and emotional effects.

THE RODRIGUEZ SISTERS

After working for a couple of weeks, I noticed there were a core set of kids who came to the program every day. I remember two little girls who were sisters. They were around 7 and 5 years old and very sweet kids. The mom and girls came from Mexico to California, and the mom was having a difficult time finding work. They were immigrants, and she was a single mom. She and the girls had been living at the Union Rescue Mission (URM), but they had recently transitioned from the shelter to voucher housing at a single-room occupancy building near URM.

One morning, she dropped the girls off for the summer program. It was an exceptionally hot day, and it was warm in the learning center. There were many kids playing and having fun. One of the Rodriguez sisters came to me and told me that she had a stomachache. I had her sit down and asked her what she ate for breakfast. She told me Cheetos and fruit punch. Between the Cheetos, fruit punch, and the heat, she ended up throwing up.

When Celine's mom came, I told her what happened. I asked her what Celine had eaten before coming to the program, and she told me that both girls had Cheetos and fruit punch. She explained to me that they had a limited amount of money for meals. Before, they were having meals at the shelter, and now she was using food subsidies. She was getting a low amount and had to make them last. Additionally, since it was summer, they were not receiving free breakfast and lunch at school. While I understood her situation, I suggested that rather than buying Cheetos and fruit punch at the corner store, maybe she could use the money to buy cereal or granola bars. She would be able to save money because the food would last longer, and her daughters could have a more nutritious breakfast. She agreed that the cereal or granola bars were a much better food option. However, the area was a food desert that did not have any grocery stores or healthy fast food eating options. I gave her a bagful of granola bars to help her get started. She was very thankful for the food. She helped her sick daughter stand up and collected her other daughter. As they walked to the door, you could see the remorseful look in her face.

1. When parents have limited money for food and access to quality grocery stores, how does that influence the food that is purchased for their family?

2. How does suffering from hunger affect the developing child?

3. Imagine that you receive a supplemental nutrition assistance program benefit of $100 per week for three people (1 adult and 2 children, ages 4 and 7); what would you buy each week? Make

a food plan for the summer, which means that you need to purchase food for three meals a day, including snacks.

a. Using your tablet, smartphone, or laptop, find a local grocery store sale flier or online grocery shopping portal to make a grocery list.

  i. What type of food choices do you make?

  ii. How much food can you buy? Will it be enough for three people to eat breakfast, snacks, lunches, and dinner for 7 days?

  iii. How do your food choices affect your children's health and well-being?

  iv. How would living in a food desert affect your budget and items that you could purchase?

Service-Learning Activity: Affordable Housing

This is an advocacy activity.

As mentioned in the chapter, one of the root causes of homelessness is a lack of affordable housing in communities. Habitat for Humanity is a global nonprofit organization that helps individuals and families acquire quality, affordable housing. Since 1976, the organization has provided resources to over 10,000,000 people. Habitat for Humanity also encourages others to advocate for affordable housing in their communities. The following are things that people can do to advocate:

- Identify your city councilperson.

- Write or call your councilperson.

- Schedule a face-to-face meeting with your councilperson.

  - Share your feelings on how the lack of affordable housing is affecting your community. Also, express your thoughts on helping working and low-income families achieve homeownership in your community. Lastly, discuss tangible ways to address the issue in your community.

- Communicate with local businesses, community leaders, and realtors.

- Attend local events that focus on addressing the affordable housing issue.

- Respond to an affordable housing article in your local paper by submitting a letter to the editor.

- Volunteer (find your local Habitat for Humanity (2019) affiliate).

You will need to complete one or more items from the advocacy list. After you complete one or more of these items, write a reflection about your experience. Discuss the type of advocacy that you performed, the results of your actions, and how your service connects to topics from the book. If this is an issue of interest to you, how will you continue to advocate for the issue?

References

Bassuk, E. L., DeCandia, C. J., Beach, C. A., & Berman, F. (2014). *America's youngest outcasts: A report card on child homelessness*. National Center on Family Homelessness.

Bassuk, E. L., Murphy, C., Coupe, N. T., Kenney, R. R., & Beach, C. A. (2011). *State report card on child homelessness: America's youngest outcasts 2010*. National Center on Family Homelessness.

Berger, K. (2016). *Invitation to the life span*. Worth Publishers.

Byrne, T., Treglia, D., Culhane, D., Kuhn, J., & Kane, V. (2015). Predictors of homelessness among families and single adults after exit from homelessness prevention and rapid re-housing programs: Evidence from the Department of Veterans Affairs Supportive Services for Veterans Program. *Housing Policy Debate, 26*(1), 252–275. https://doi.org/10.1080/10511482.2015.1060249

Camacho-Rivera, M., Kawachi, I., Bennett, G. G., & Subramanian, S. V. (2014). Associations of neighborhood concentrated poverty, neighborhood racial/ethnic composition, and indoor allergen exposures: A cross-sectional analysis of Los Angeles households, 2006–2008. *Journal of Urban Health, 91*(4), 661–676.

Chandramouli, L., Steer, C. D., Ellis, M., & Emond, A. M. (2009). Effects of early childhood exposure on academic performance and behavior of school age children. *Archives of Disease in Childhood, 94*(11), 844–848.

Desmond, M. (2015). Unaffordable America: Poverty, housing, and eviction. *Fast Focus 22*. Institute for Research on Poverty. https://www.irp.wisc.edu/publications/fastfocus/pdfs/FF22-2015.pdf

Desmond, M. (2016). *Evicted: Poverty and profit in the American city*. Penguin.

Gestwicki, C. (2016). *Home, school, and community relations.* Cengage Learning.

Habitat for Humanity. (2019). *What is advocacy?* https://www.habitatca.org/advocacy/become-an-advocate/

Hayes, M., Zonneville, M., & Bassuk, E. (2013). *The SHIFT study final report: Service and housing interventions for families in transition.* National Center on Family Homelessness.

Henry, M., Watt, R., Mahathey, A., Ouellette, J., Sitler, A., & Abt Associates. (2020). *The 2019 Annual Homeless Assessment Report (AHAR) to Congress.* U.S. Department of Housing and Urban Development. Washington, DC: Office of Community Planning and Development.

John F. Kennedy Presidential Library and Museum. (n.d.). *John F. Kennedy and people with intellectual disabilities.* Retrieved from https://www.jfklibrary.org/learn/about-jfk/jfk-in-history/john-f-kennedy-and-people-with-intellectual-disabilities

Maslow, A. H. (1970). *Motivation and personality.* Harper & Row.

Montgomery, A. E., Hill, L., Kane, V., & Culhane, D. (2013). Housing chronically homeless veterans: Evaluating the efficacy of a housing first approach to HUD-VASH. *Journal of Community Psychology, 41*(4), 505–514. https://doi.org/10.1002/jcop.21554

National Alliance to End Homelessness. (2020a). *Solutions.* http://www.end-homelessness.org/pages/solutions

National Alliance to End Homelessness. (2020b). *Core components of rapid re-housing.* http://www.endhomelessness.org/library/entry/rapid-re-housing2

National Alliance to End Homelessness. (2016). *Rapid re-housing fact sheet: Housing first.* Author.

National Alliance to End Homelessness. (2012). Changes in the HUD Definition of "homeless." Author.

National Child Traumatic Stress Network (NCTN) Schools Committee. (2008). *Child trauma toolkit for educators.* Author.

Radcliff, E., Crouch, E., Strompolis, M., & Srivastav, A. (2019). Homelessness in childhood and adverse childhood experiences (ACEs). *Maternal and Child Health Journal, 23*(6), 811–820.

Rubin, L. B. (2007). Sand castles and snake pits: Homelessness, public policy, and the law of unintended consequences. *Dissent, 54*(4), 51–56.

Stanford Center on Poverty and Inequality. (2016, October 18). Unstable housing: Matthew Desmond [Video file]. https://www.youtube.com/watch?v=NY4Q8XQon6E

Tsemberis, S., Gulcur, L., & Nakae, M. (2004). Housing first, consumer choice, and harm reduction for homeless individuals with a dual diagnosis.

U.S. Interagency on Council on Homelessness. (2018, February). *Key federal terms and definitions of homelessness among youth.* https://www.usich.gov/resources/uploads/asset_library/Federal-Definitions-of-Youth-Homelessness.pdf

U.S. Department of Education. (2016a, July 27). Education releases guidance on homeless children and youth. https://www.ed.gov/news/press-releases/education-department-releases-guidance-homeless-children-and-youth

U.S. Department of Education. (2016b, July 27). *Supporting the success of homeless children and youths.* https://www2.ed.gov/policy/elsec/leg/essa/160315ehcyfactsheet072716.pdf

U.S. Department of Housing and Urban Development. (2014). *Major legislation on housing and urban development enacted since 1932.* Office of Community Planning and Development.

U.S. Department of Housing and Urban Development. (2015, December 15). Homeless emergency assistance and rapid transition to housing: Defining "chronically homeless." *Federal Register, 80*(233) [Docket No. FR–5809–F–01].

U.S. Department of Housing and Urban Development. (2020). *Continuum of care (CoC).* https://www.hudexchange.info/programs/coc/

Willingham, D. (2012). Why does family wealth affect learning? *The American Educator,* 33–39.

7

Social Exclusion

THOUGHT QUESTIONS

As you read the chapter, consider the following:

- How can internalized oppression contribute to the process of social exclusion?
- How has social exclusion evolved from its French origins?
- What are the long-term social and economic consequences of entire areas becoming socially excluded communities?
- Why are foster care youth at risk of experiencing social exclusion?
- What can be done to prevent incarcerated parents' children from experiencing social exclusion as they transition into young adulthood?

Introduction

While some factors leading to social exclusion can be rooted in individual decisions, exclusion can also result from systematic **oppression**, which is also seen in other discriminatory practices such as racism, sexism, ableism, and classism. All forms of oppression are linked, as they are rooted in or supported by economic control and power and share common methods of controlling and limiting people's access to resources and opportunities. Forms of oppression share common elements that start with the idea of the defined norm. The defined norm is not based on what group is the majority in society; however, individuals who are part of the defined norm possess the power and ability to exert control over other groups of people. Those who occupy this position possess economic and institutional power, along with privilege (Pharr, 1988).

According to Research Scientist Peggy McIntosh, the existence of **privilege** occurs when one group of people has an advantage that other groups are denied; the advantage is based solely on social status. The distribution of advantage is not determined on performance or behavior but on social classification. This allocation of privilege is systematically ingrained in our society's culture. It is reinforced in social practices and creates an unequal distribution of power that is socially accepted. The inequalities create a social system that breeds privilege and oppression, and it becomes socially acceptable to value and devalue people based on social class. Placing people in social categories leads to dominant groups being accepted, admired, and included while subordinate groups are rejected, avoided, and excluded (Johnson, 2018)

In extreme cases, oppression can destroy people's lives and lead to social exclusion. Socially excluded people lack social connections with society and over time become socially isolated from the mainstream. In *Homophobia: A Weapon of Sexism*, Suzanne Pharr (1988) discusses the common elements of oppression and explores different aspects of oppression. For example, when a distinct population of society possess power and control, they can control others by limiting access to employment and resources. Often, those with scarce resources are pitted against each other, and society is brainwashed to believe that the "poor" are draining resources. This myth is known as the myth of scarcity. This perception perpetuates stereotypes and causes social divisions in society. It also deters focus from those in power, as they are the ones who consume and destroy resources to increase their economic power (Pharr, 1988).

The distorted image of the poor strips people of their individuality and perpetuates falsehoods of entire groups of people. Further, it dehumanizes people and leads to **blaming the victim** and **internalized oppression**. Those in power use social outlets such as the media to spread the distorted information about "all poor people." Stereotyping can also lead to generalizations about poor people: "They are all on welfare; they are lazy." These types of stereotypes blame the victim for their poor status without taking into consideration social, political, economic, or other factors. It is presumed to be the poor person's fault for living in poverty. In some cases, the repeated negative messages and images lead to a decline in self-esteem among the subordinate group. The ongoing oppression may also become internalized and damage the psyche of the oppressed, which leads to internalized oppression. This oppressive environment is established by dominants to get the subordinates to become compliant, believe that they deserve treatment, and hamper their desire to resist. This weakening of self-pride, self-esteem, and group pride can potentially lead to self-hatred and depression. When people undergo the process of oppression, they experience isolation as part of a group or as an individual (Pharr, 1988). It is a detrimental process that strips people of their sense of belonging to community and pushes people to the outskirts of society.

Defining Social Exclusion

People experience **social exclusion** when they are isolated from society and/or do not participate in society. This concept has French origins; it is rooted in the work of French sociologist Emile Durkheim. Durkheim's theories discuss "social cohesion and solidarity, the importance of collective values and norms, and the risk of social alienation" (anomie) (Jehoel-Gijsbers & Vrooman, 2007, p. 13).

In the 1960s and 1970s, the concept was made popular by Rene Lenoir, the secretary of state for social action, for France. It was used to describe those who experienced social struggles and lacked social resources—the unemployed, physically and mentally disabled, uninsured, and others who were experiencing social and economic deprivations. As social problems grew in France, the definition expanded to include individuals living in isolation. Unlike the concept of poverty, social exclusion focuses on how the individual is isolated from society and lacks the ability to engage in the cultural, social, and economic aspects of society (Evans et al., 2001).

The concept was formally adopted by the European Union toward the end of the 1980s. There was a social divide in how right- and left-wing governments interpreted inequality. The right wing believed that poverty was not an issue in their countries, while the left wing recognized the vast economic inequality in countries. To discuss these issues, both sides agreed on using the term social exclusion. It was a broad concept that allowed both perspectives to be explored (Brown et al., 2018).

Social exclusion became popularized in the 1990s when the United Kingdom's labor politicians used the concept to discuss multiple deprivations and inequality in society. After the general election of 1997, the United Kingdom established the Social Exclusion Unit (SEU). The SEU identified people and geographical areas as experiencing social exclusion when a combination of deprivations occurred, deprivations such as poor health, unemployment, family dysfunction, low income, high levels of crime, and substandard housing (Brown et al., 2018).

In the article "Social Exclusion and Social Solidarity: Three Paradigms," Professor Hilary Silver (1994) discusses three components of social exclusion: solidarity, specialization, and monopoly. With the first paradigm, solidarity, the focus is on the broken bond between the individual and society. This fractured bond is related to a disconnect in culture and morality more so than economics. In the second paradigm, specialization, social exclusion is linked to the type and level of discrimination that the individual encounters in society. The final paradigm, monopoly, identifies how the distributed ideologies and power of the dominant group result in the restrictive access to resources for those who occupy subordinate positions in society (Silver, 1994). Additionally, most perspectives of social inclusion also typically describe four characteristics of social exclusion: lack of participation, multidimensional, dynamic, and multilayered.

1. Lack of participation: The level of social exclusion varies and is relative to the society.

2. Multidimensional: Social exclusion is related to income poverty, but it encompasses other deprivations such as lack of employment.

3. Dynamic: Promotes probing into the process and causes of social exclusion.

4. Multilayered: The causes of social exclusion are ingrained in multiple levels in society: institutional, community, household, and individual (Brown et al., 2018).

As discussed, the concept has evolved since it was first conceptualized. The two main interpretations of the concept are rooted in Anglo American and French scientific traditions. These two perspectives have different foci: (a) the Anglo American approach focuses on economic-structural exclusion (distributional dimension), while (b) the French approach focuses on social-cultural exclusion (relational dimension) (Jehoel-Gijsbers & Vrooman, 2007).

The first approach discusses distributional aspects: nonmaterial and material characteristics. Socially excluded people experience material deprivation due to a lack of economic resources. Without a sufficient income, they are unable to afford basic needs and material items. Lack of economic resources leads to the inability to maintain a stable and sufficient lifestyle to exist in society (in a way that any given society considers desirable or functional). Income, material, and lifestyle deprivation, coupled with limited access to public assistance resources, lead to a decline in social rights and an eventual deterioration of inclusion in society (Jehoel-Gijsbers & Vrooman, 2007).

The second approach discusses relational aspects: social relations, cultural norms, and values. People who experience social exclusion lack social integration within society. They suffer from inadequate participation in formal and informal social networks. Concurrently, socially excluded people fail to adapt to social norms and values; there becomes a distance between themselves and larger society. Insufficient social and cultural integration results in people becoming socially isolated from society (Jehoel-Gijsbers & Vrooman, 2007).

Excluders and the Excluded

The *process* of social exclusion is multidimensional and is influenced mostly by structural factors; it includes both social and economic aspects of disadvantage. Over time, different dimensions of social and cultural integration slowly degrade, leading to social alienation. This process involves the active interaction between two agents: the excluders and the excluded. Those who occupy the role of excluders occupy important social positions and, in turn, possess power in society. They use their position and power to create and sustain a social hierarchal system within society. The excluders use their social position to limit (and often deny) the disadvantaged access to resources (Silver, 2007).

Without access to resources and opportunities, the disadvantaged are slowly pushed to the lower stratum of the hierarchal system. Eventually, the disadvantaged become socially excluded from society. The combination of being oppressed, loss of social recognition, and downward descent in social class often leads people to more permanently occupy the role of "excluded." In some situations, the excluders actively push the disadvantage into this role by using their power to manipulate structural forces. In other cases, people may withdraw from society due to mistreatment and low levels of capital (Silver, 2007). Regardless of how people become excluded, it is important to recognize that the process of social exclusion is a result of "actively" being excluded (by excluders) from social involvement, networks, and institutions; it is the process of being socially isolated from society.

Social Exclusion and Poverty

Social exclusion and poverty share many commonalities; however, the concepts are fundamentally different. Both concepts are multidimensional, dynamic processes that are rooted in the social relations and categorization of stratified social systems. Social exclusion and poverty are both context dependent and relate to institutional and cultural factors (Silver, 2007).

A consequence of poverty is social exclusion. It encompasses the aforementioned commonalities, but it transcends poverty and connects the nonmaterial and material and social and economic multidimensional aspects of disadvantage. Similar to poverty, social exclusion also relates to social relations and access to resources, but it focuses on the relationship between the excluder and the excluded. It also focuses more on "horizontal" social ties (a sense of belonging), while poverty emphasizes "vertical" mobility and distribution (Silver, 2007). The following list provides a comprehensive overview on the differences that are often discussed in literature:

Horizontal ties versus vertical distribution: Social exclusion is focused on "horizontal" social ties that establish a sense of belonging. Poverty is concerned with social mobility: Are people moving up or down the social hierarchy (Silver, 2007).

Relative concept versus absolute: There is not a distinct point of "absolute social exclusion." The concept is understood by using social comparison. It is rooted in social relations. However, when people experience poverty, there is an absolute (and measurable) inability to provide basic needs (Jehoel-Gijsbers & Vrooman, 2007).

Multidimensional versus unidimensional disadvantage: When people experience social exclusion, it involves limitations and deficiencies in multiple dimensions. These deficiencies are connected to the person's ability to be fully engaged in society, such as lack of education, stable housing, income, and/or access to health resources. If someone is identified as living in poverty, there is a lack of income to provide resources (Jehoel-Gijsbers & Vrooman, 2007).

Relational versus distributional focus: This conceptual framework reviews the difference between nonmaterial versus material. Social exclusion has a relational focus; it is concerned with sociocultural and social relational aspects of society. In contrast, poverty focuses more on the distributional aspects of disadvantage. The concept relates more to income deprivation and inability to acquire material resources (Jehoel-Gijsbers & Vrooman, 2007). For example, a low-income worker may struggle to provide basic needs for family members due to their low wages.

Exogenous versus endogenous agency: The term **agency** refers to the ways that people express their power. It is the process of how people think, act, and make choices. People exercise their free will through their thoughts and actions, which, in turn, allows them to exercise their personal power. The process of social exclusion is often connected to limited access to communal resources, which is connected to exogenous factors. If the main employer in a town leaves, how does that affect residents in that area? Lack of communal resources and opportunities can lead to inactivity in social networks, lack of presence in social institutions, and withdrawal from society. Individuals possess capital, and access to resources decreases; this lack of power results in the excluded having minimal to no control over exogenous factors. For those who are poverty stricken, they too lack access to resources and opportunities. However, the concept of agency is more centralized to the individual. When analyzing poverty, agency is reviewed from an endogenous level—lack of individual income and financial resources results in the inability to provide basic needs (Jehoel-Gijsbers & Vrooman, 2007).

While the comparison list does highlight many differences, it is important to remember that social exclusion and poverty are not static concepts. They are both multidimensional dynamic concepts, which makes it challenging to provide concrete definitions for each term. Each listed difference does provide a framework for understanding and can be supported, but they can also be challenged due to numerous variables like geography and socioeconomic shifts in society, culture, and time.

It is also important to remember that we do not live in a static world: Our society is constantly evolving, so our sense of being changes too. It is hard to measure things in absolute, concrete terms because we live in a changing world that exists based on relativity. When discussing concepts such as social class, inequality, poverty, and social exclusion, it is important to remember that each person has a unique experience and journey through life that is influenced by endogenous and exogenous factors. In the end, concepts are grounded in theory but often evolve over time.

Socially Excluded Communities

Alternative communities take different forms. In some situations, like-minded people come together to create an egalitarian community and engage in communal living. Communes have been around since the turn of the century; these early communes tended to be religious and secular communities. The concept of communes became popular in mainstream culture in the 1960s and 1970s during the hippie era. Communal living had never ceased to exist, but the hippies provided a revival to communal living. Hippies created communities that provided open membership, accepted drug use, rejected mainstream culture, and welcomed sexual exploration (Miller, 1992).

Of course, every commune had its guiding principles, but the one commonality across these types of communes is that people were *choosing* to reject mainstream culture. They were not being pushed into social exclusion; however, they chose to step away from mainstream society and explore an alternative way of living. At any time, they could choose to reenter society because they had not been stripped of resources, been oppressed, or been pushed to the edge of society. In present day, there has been an emergence of socially excluded populations and communities. These are not new-age communes, but they are communities filled with socially excluded people who have minimal, if any, access to opportunities and resources.

Adams County, Ohio

In November 2016, shortly after the election of Donald Trump, Dayton Power & Light informed state officials that it would be closing two coal-firing burning plants, Stuart and Killen, in the summer of 2018. The J.M. Stuart plant opened in 1970 and, at that time, was one of the largest facilities in the country. The Killen station opened 12 years later in 1982, and both plants were thriving, as the state of Ohio obtained

FIGURE 7.1 J.M. Stuart Plant Located in Adams County, Ohio.

80% of electricity from coal-fire burning plants. In 2011, Dayton Power & Light was purchased by AES Corp., a global energy company based in Arlington, Virginia (MacGillis, 2018).

The Stuart and Killen Stations were the primary employers and largest tax contributors in Adams County. Even with this industry supporting the county, the area was still identified as the poorest county in the state. Toward the end of 2016, Adams County began to experience profound effects from the planned closures. The valuation for Stuart and Killen decreased by $56 million due to the impending closure (MacGillis, 2018). Once the closures took place in May 2018, the county experienced a major financial decline. The county lost millions in salaries and tax revenue (Dennis & Mufson, 2019).

Prior to the plant closures, county officials were scrambling to make budget cuts. There were county offices sharing employees, and the County Sherriff's office was operating with only 22 officers to monitor 583 square miles. The jail was frequently overcrowded with up to 75 inmates, when it was only designed to hold 33, and there was often only one officer to oversee 60 or more inmates. The school district also experienced major budget cuts.

So, what does all of this mean for Adams County? The residents are forced to make a big decision: Do they stay or relocate to someplace new? They could commute to one of the big cities, such as Cincinnati, but traveling to another area for work would not help the community. People are being placed in a very challenging situation. They are having to contemplate moving away from their families, home, friends, and community. Many of the residents have spent their whole lives in Adams County, and it is emotionally difficult for them to simply pack up and relocate. In a study by MacGillis, one of the residents discussed his attachment to the community by describing his version of the American dream. He wants to live close to his parents and have his children grow up near his family. Some residents have no desire to relocate for greater opportunity; they are happy in their town and want to persevere their community (MacGillis, 2018). However, there are some that left to seek job opportunities in other states (e.g., Oregon, Washington, Florida, Colorado, Idaho, and Wyoming). These departures have led to a decline in school enrollment and position cuts (Dennis & Mufson, 2019).

It is hard for small towns to thrive when the main employer leaves. Over time, large numbers of people leave, with no influx of people moving into the area. There are many towns throughout America that have a similar story: Bridgeport, Connecticut; Detroit, Michigan; and more. When industry leaves or companies close, there becomes a huge opportunity gap between areas with a thriving economy and areas without economic opportunity.

The social and economic divide between urban areas and small towns and cities is fueled by factors such as economic concentration, globalization, technology, and green business practices (MacGillis, 2018). Deindustrialization causes major social and cultural changes in communities; it often causes small towns to suffer massive declines, which leads to areas that become socially excluded from urban areas. While the urban areas thrive, the remote areas experience a gradual demise.

In addition to the economic impact, there are environmental impacts to consider. The Killen and Stuart Stations are two of sixteen plants that closed in 2018. Many of the plants are in remote areas where they were the main employer for the town. Coal-burning plants are facing mass closures due to government regulations on carbon emissions and the cheaper power source alternative of using natural gas. Coal-burning plants also produce large amounts of coal ash. In Adams County, there is land near the plants that is used to store coal waste; the waste is accumulated into large ash ponds (MacGillis, 2018).

According to the U.S. Environmental Protection Agency (2018), coal ash, which is also known as coal combustion residuals, is produced by burning coal at power plants. There are several different byproducts that are produced: fly ash, bottom ash, boiler slag, and flue gas desulfurization material. All coal ash byproducts contain contaminants (e.g., arsenic, mercury, and cadmium) that are associated with serious health issues such as cancer. Coal ash can be disposed of in dry form by creating large ash ponds or in large reservoirs that contain a combination of coal byproducts and water, which is called coal slurry. Without proper disposal, monitoring, and regulations, contaminants can seep into groundwater and enter drinking water sources or blow into the air in dust form. Also, if coal impoundments are not properly constructed, they can break and cause detrimental effects to the environment and to residents who live near the area (U.S. Environmental Protection Agency, 2018).

The plants in Adams County have landfills with ash ponds, and county officials were not informed about how the company or state would handle the waste. Technically, fly ash is not identified as hazardous, so the ash ponds could remain after the plants closes (MacGillis, 2018). The plants close, unemployment increases, tax revenue declines, county resources and social services decline due to budget cuts, and large piles of "nonhazardous" waste are left behind near the river. When communities are left in this state, a huge gap between thriving cities and struggling cities widens. Struggling cities enter a downward decline and may become socially excluded from cities that are experiencing development and economic growth.

Homeless Encampments

People who are homeless experience an extreme type of social exclusion. They experience multiple deprivations that extend past simply lacking material needs. Homeless individuals who lack access to resources and temporary housing in shelters becoming part of the unsheltered homeless population. These individuals often seek housing in locations that are not meant for human habitation. In some cases, homeless people will gather with other homeless individuals and set up living spaces that are known as **homeless encampments**. There has been an emergence of "tent cities" throughout the United States. The growth of tent cities is discussed in a 124-page report entitled "Tent City, USA: The Growth of America Homeless Encampments and How Communities are Responding" (National Law Center on Homelessness and Poverty, 2017.) The following are the national trends that were reported in the document:

1. There were 19 reported encampments in 2007 and 255 encampments reported by mid-2017. Two-thirds of the increase

occurred after the recession ended. Over the 10-year period, homeless encampments had increased by 1,342%.

2. Homeless encampments were identified in all 50 states and the District of Columbia. California had the greatest number of encampments; states such as Michigan, Oregon, and Iowa had significant numbers reported too.

3. Most of the reported encampments were medium to large. About 50% had populations of 11–50 people, while 17% had populations of a 100 or more people.

4. Homeless encampments were becoming semi-permanent communities in cities. Two-thirds of reported encampments had existed for over a year, and over one-quarter had existed for over 6 years.

5. Most of the homeless encampments were illegal and residents were at risk of eviction. Seventy-five percent were reported to be illegal, 21% were semi-legal, and only 4% were actually legal. Additionally, 35% of the encampments were being shut down through eviction or were scheduled to receive evictions. Evicted residents often had no where to go, as the homeless encampments were their only housing option (National Law Center on Homelessness and Poverty, 2017).

FIGURE 7.2 This is an Example of a Tent City. Tents Line the Streets in the Skid Row Area of Downtown Los Angeles, California.

The United States is one of the richest countries in the world, yet people are socially excluded in homeless encampments across every state and in the District of Columbia. The drastic increase in homeless encampments reflects the overall growth in the homeless population across the United States, due in part to the severe affordable housing shortage in many parts of the country. According to a 2017 report by the Federal Home Loan Mortgage program (Freddie Mac, n.d.), there was a 60% decrease in affordable apartments for low-income individuals throughout the United States from 2010 to 2016. In rapid-growth cities such as Los Angeles, a 5% hike in rental prices can result in an additional 2,000 people becoming homeless (Freddie Mac, n.d.).

The Tent City study reported that California had the highest number of homeless encampments. The state of California should be building 180,000 new housing units annually, but the state has built less than 50% of this target figure. Consequently, most renters in California allocate more than 30% of income to rent, and one-third of renters spend more than 50% of income on rental costs. These figures demonstrate how many *employed* Americans are at risk of becoming homeless. Imagine if you were in this situation and you missed one paycheck, had a medical emergency, or needed an expensive car repair; you could easily fall behind in paying your rent and face eviction. If you did not have any housing alternatives, you could very easily become homeless (National Law Center on Homelessness and Poverty, 2017).

A multitude of health issues confront people living in places that are not meant for human habitation. No access to running water and sanitation facilities results in inability to maintain proper hygiene. Lack of access to water and bathrooms lead to open urination and defecation. In March 2017, a **Hepatitis A** outbreak started in San Diego, California. The outbreak was detected in March, but it originated in late 2016. Nineteen people died, and 588 people were infected statewide during the epidemic; almost every person was homeless (Warth, 2018). Hepatitis A is transmitted by ingesting something that has been exposed to fecal matter of a person who is infected with the disease. Some of the symptoms are fever, nausea, abdominal pain, vomiting, and fatigue. The symptoms are usually short term; however, if the disease infects people who have poor health, the effects can be more serious and may lead to death. The main way to prevent infection is through vaccination. Additionally, it is important to properly wash hands after using the restroom, changing diapers, and prior to making or eating food (Centers for Disease Control and Prevention (CDC), 2018).

On June 15, 2018, there was a memorial service on Commercial Street underneath the I-5 freeway in San Diego, California, where homeless people often congregate. Close to 30 people gathered to recognize the 20 people who died from the Hepatitis A outbreak. Twenty candles were lit for each of the nameless victims by the memorial organizer, Jack Fitzgerald (Warth, 2018). Fitzgerald commented on the symbolism of the nameless victims: "It boils down to how a community treats its lowest members" (Warth, 2018). Fitzgerald organized the candlelight vigil to acknowledge the victims in a dignified manner, which is something that Fitzgerald felt that the county failed to do when they did not release the victims' names. Since the victims were nameless, people shared small bits of information about the individuals and prayed for each victim (Warth, 2018).

At the memorial, people discussed how the county and city failed to respond quickly to the Hepatitis outbreak. Eventually, the county provided portable handwashing and toilet units to decrease the spread of the disease (as well as washing the inhabited areas with bleach solutions), but the epidemic had already affected so many (Warth, 2018). Further, this was a temporary fix to a much larger social issue, which is the existence of homelessness and homeless encampments. At the vigil, the people discussed the ongoing neglect of the area and the unsanitary conditions. Even at the gathering, the street smelled of urine. One of the attendees commented that the city council and mayor should visit the site, pray, and take a deep inhale of the smell. Another person commented that the smell is symbolic of the injustice that people in the area endure, while another hoped that the death of the 20 people would spark change in the area (Warth, 2018).

At the memorial, one of the attendees shared a quote by St. Pope John Paul II: "Human persons are willed by God; they are imprinted with God's image. Their dignity does not come from the work they do, but from the persons they are" (Warth, 2018). Regardless of one's religious faith, there is a powerful message in this quote. It is important to recognize that everyone has a different life story and journey. Some people face more challenges and obstacles than others, but it does not make them any less of a person. All people deserve equal access to resources, opportunities, and basic needs.

In Chapter 6, I discussed the hobohemia era and how the state of homelessness has changed over the years from a temporary state of existence to becoming a more stable and permanent way of life for people across the United States. The permanence of homelessness in our society can be seen in the emergence of stable, homeless encampments across the United States. In extreme cases, socially excluded people may find themselves becoming homeless and seeking refuge in "tent cities." Tent cities are not a solution to alleviating homelessness, nor are they helping to address the root causes of homelessness. Homeless encampments are not viable long-term options for people, and many social issues need to be addressed in order for there to be a decrease in homeless encampments

Child Welfare System

When children are removed from their homes and enter the child welfare system, they are at risk of experiencing social exclusion. At times, the removal process is temporary, and the child (children) returns to their home once the familial issue is resolved. In some cases, children enter the system and are adopted. Then there are others who may spend their entire lives going in and out of the system as they are placed in different foster care homes, and they eventually age out of the system. For those who age out of the system, there is a high probability that some may experience an episode of homelessness. According to the U.S. Department of Health and Human Services (2018), over 20,000 children age out of the foster care system each year. The National Center for Housing and Child Welfare reports that 25% of these youth will experience an episode of homelessness during the first 4 years of being out of the system, and a high percentage of the remaining youth have challenges keeping stable housing (U.S. Department of Housing and Urban Development, 2019).

Children enter the foster care system for many different reasons—abuse, neglect, child abandonment, incarcerated parents, and other reasons that result in the child lacking safe, stable housing. Table 7.1 lists the conditions that lead to the removal of children from homes and result in a foster care placement.

Once the child is removed from the home, there is an immediate focus on making sure the child is safe and finding permanent housing (Auspitz, 2017). According to the Adoption and Foster Care Analysis and Reporting System report for FY 2018, there were 437,283 children in foster care (U.S. Department of Health and Human Services, 2019). Each year, the child welfare system spends nearly $30 billion on the following:

1. Conducting investigations on child neglect and abuse

2. Preventative and supportive services to help parents/caregivers support and nurture their children

TABLE 7.1 Conditions That Caused Removal of Children from Homes

Conditions	Percent	Number
Neglect	62%	163,543
Drug abuse (parent)	36%	94,386
Caretaker inability to cope	14%	35,802
Physical abuse	13%	33,672
Housing	10%	27,323
Child behavior problem	9%	22,868
Parent incarceration	7%	19,719
Alcohol abuse (parent)	5%	13,871
Abandonment	5%	12,088
Sexual abuse	4%	9,894
Drug use (child)	2%	6,468
Child disability	2%	4,339
Relinquishment	1%	2,733
Parent death	1%	2,389
Alcohol abuse (child)	0%	1,032

Source: U.S. Department of Health and Human Services, 2019

3. Temporary housing for children who need to be removed from homes due to safety issues

4. Supporting permanent housing placement; reunification with parents/caregivers, adoption, or transitioning children into independent living (Ringel et al., 2017)

On average, youth spend about 1 year in foster care. About 50% of youth will reunify with parents/caregivers, one fourth will get adopted by families, and around 20,000 will remain in foster care and eventually age out of the foster care system when they are 18 or 21 or when they complete high school (varies by state). When youth have a greater length of stay in foster care, there is a greater likelihood that they will move between multiple foster homes. This instability exacerbates the child's stress levels and results in the child displaying socioemotional challenges. The shifting between homes, peers, relatives, schools, teachers, and other social figures causes constant disruption in the formation of stable relationships. The moves may also result in changes in caseworkers and legal officials involved in cases, which can potentially affect obtaining stable housing and the children's overall well-being (Williams-Mbengue, 2014).

Lesbian, gay, bisexual, transgender, and queer (LGBTQ) youth in foster care face greater challenges than heterosexual youth. They are often removed from home due to mistreatment by caregivers. Unfortunately, the mistreatment often continues once they are placed in the foster care system. They experience prejudicial attitudes and discrimination and experience many adverse situations. In comparison to their heterosexual peers, they are more frequently sent to group homes where many LGBTQ youth report being victims of violence. The continual mistreatment causes re-traumatization and social exclusion (Berg, 2016).

The consequence of living in an unhealthy environment, being removed from home, and entering foster care often results in children developing socioemotional challenges. Children who are placed in foster care due to child maltreatment may suffer from behavioral and cognitive impairments. In the home setting, children may have experienced physical, medical, emotional, or educational neglect; sexual abuse and/or physical abuse; or lack of parental supervision. Other reasons for removing a child from their home include exposure to domestic violence and/or substance abuse. Additionally, many children from low SES backgrounds have lived in poverty-stricken areas and witnessed community violence (Williams-Mbengue, 2014).

When children live in unsafe conditions that affect their health, they often suffer from high levels of stress. Children in the foster care system often experience **complex trauma**, which involves long-term exposure to multiple invasive, traumatic events, such as child maltreatment, physical abuse, and violence. As discussed in chapters 4 and 5, stress affects the developing brain, all aspects of development, and social relationships. If the stress is not buffered by a caring adult, the effects can remain through the adulthood years (Williams-Mbengue, 2014). Children may experience long-term effects such as post-traumatic stress disorder and social exclusion due to depression and anxiety.

Adverse Childhood Experience and Foster Children

Researchers have been working to further understand the effects of trauma on foster children. They have used the Adverse Childhood Experiences Scale to assess children's exposure to traumatic events.

People who receive a high adverse childhood experience (ACE) score are at greater risk of social, emotional, and health problems. If a person receives a high score, then they are at great risk for developing ACE-related health issues. An ACE score of 4 or higher is of concern (Stevens, 2017). Fifty-one percent of children in foster care who have taken the ACE questionnaire have received a score of 4 or higher, while 13% of non-foster care children had similar scores (Alvarez, 2018). This difference reinforces that children in the child welfare system have a greater likelihood of being exposed to adverse childhood experiences.

Table 7.2 list the potential health risks associated with ACEs. These risks were identified in the adverse childhood experiences study. This was a longitudinal study that examined the health outcome of adults who were exposed to traumatic life events and high levels of toxic stress due to events such as child maltreatment or abandonment, experiencing a parent being incarcerated, witnessing domestic violence, having parents who suffer from a substance abuse, or residing in a home with a caregiver who suffers from a mental health disorder (Williams-Mbengue, 2014).

TABLE 7.2 Health Risk Associated With ACES

Behavior-Related Health Risks	Physical and Mental-Related Health Risks
Lack of physical activity Smoking Alcoholism Drug use Missed work	Severe obesity Diabetes Depression Suicide attempts Sexually transmitted diseases Heart disease Stroke Chronic obstructive pulmonary disease Broken bones

Source: Starecheski, 2015

Foster Care Prevention

To keep children out of the child welfare system, it is important that policy efforts focus on prevention, family preservation, and **kinship care**. By offering preventative services, such as home visits, resources could be offered to families and children who are at risk of experiencing abuse and neglect. Preventative resources support family preservation by offering families treatment (e.g., counseling, basic needs resources, help with substance use disorders) rather than splitting the family apart. When children must be removed from the home, it helps when children can be placed in kinship care, which is in the care of a relative. Placing the child with a relative minimizes the out-of-home placement trauma because the child is placed in a familiar setting (Ringel et al., 2017).

In February 2018, the **Family First Prevention Services Act** (FFSPA) was signed into law. FFSPA is administered by the Administration for Children and Families, which operates under the U.S. Department of Health and Human Services. FFSPA focuses on keeping families together by providing funding to states that will support preventative treatment services and resources to support family foster care. The goal of FFSPA is to support strengthening the family so that children will not have to enter the child welfare system (Alvarez, 2018).

Prior to the passing of the FFSPA, some states had implemented programs that offered preventative treatment services. The state of New Jersey has family success centers that are offered through the Department of Children and Family Services. These centers provide preventative treatment resources to at-risk families before a crisis emerges in the family. They offer parenting resources, life skills classes, employment services, housing assistance, referrals to external resources, access to advocate assistance, and other family programs and services (State of New Jersey, 2018). As states utilize the FFSPA funding, hopefully there will be an emergence of programs like the family success centers, and there will be a decline in the number of children in the child welfare system.

Incarceration as a Form of Social Exclusion

The criminal justice system in America socially excludes mass amounts of youth, men, and women criminal offenders from society. Across the criminal justice system, there are a total of 2.3 million inmates housed in 3,163 small local jails, 1,852 juvenile detention centers, 1,719 state prison facilities, 102 federal prison facilities, and there are 80 jails on Indian reservations. There are also people being held in psychiatric medical institutions, military prisons, immigration holding facilities, and prison facilities in United States territories (Wagner & Sawyer, 2018).

Jails are often the gateway into a cycle of incarceration. After people are arrested, they are placed in jails, which function as a temporary holding facility. People are detained in jail for several reasons:

1. They are unable to post bail and must wait until trial to receive their punishment.

2. The person receives a conviction for a minor crime and a jail sentence of 1 year or less.

3. The inmate has been convicted and is processed to a state prison.

4. The person has violated either probation or parole and is being held until their hearing.

5. The inmate faces federal charges and is being held until trial because there are no available beds in a federal facility.

6. The inmate needs to be transferred to another jurisdiction.

7. The person is an immigrant who is detained until review of violations or deportation (Subramanian et al., 2015).

Jails were originally created to house criminal offenders and people who were potential flight risks before trial. In present times, jails have become overcrowded facilities that house poor people who are unable to post bail and unmanageable people with medical conditions (e.g., mental health and substance abuse disorders) who are too sick to exist and to remain stable in mainstream society. Unfortunately, when people are held in jail, it can increase their chances of being jailed for longer periods of time. If inmates are convicted and face longer sentences, they are transferred to state or federal prisons to serve their prison sentence (Subramanian et al., 2015).

Once people become inmates in the incarceration system, there can be long-term negative effects to their lives. There is a greater chance of them becoming repeat offenders, it decreases employability, and longer-term incarceration can have negative effects on existing medical conditions (Subramanian et al., 2015). Additionally, nearly 70% of all incarcerated men in prison lack a high school degree (Howard, 2018). Inmates who do not have high school diplomas or a general education development (GED) credential are required to attend a program to obtain their GED or attend 240 hours of adult literacy instruction. However, many inmates are not obtaining their GEDs. In 2017, there were 16,013 prison inmates enrolled in a GED program and only 2,667 earned their GED (Bureau of Prisons, 2018).

Lack of education creates a multitude of additional challenges for inmates, especially people of color, to overcome during their **reentry** back into society. Imagine being a high school dropout with a criminal record and returning home after you serve your jail sentence. When people get out of jail, they may return to the same environment and peer group. Often, they become re-immersed in the environment and return to engaging in deviant behavior. Also, it can be challenging for parolees to obtain work, so they return to engaging in deviant behavior and illegal activity, as it is more lucrative than getting a minimum wage job, which can be a contributing factor to a cycle of incarceration.

Parental and maternal incarceration can also have exclusionary effects on their children. Studies have shown that the incarceration of parents can contribute to their children experiencing social exclusion as they transition into young adulthood. Researchers have used the National Longitudinal Study of Adolescent Health to examine how a father's incarceration affects the social exclusion of children as they transition into young adulthood (Foster & Hagan, 2007). The survey analyzed the transition of children into young adulthood and included questions that asked youth participants about parental incarceration, bonds with parents, parental income, parent's involvement in the home, presence of substance use in the home, parent's level of educational attainment, child's education, childhood experience with neglect and abuse in the home, parent's rate of delinquent behavior and arrests, and young adult's experience with homelessness, political disengagement, and lack of health coverage. Research findings indicated that fathers' incarceration led to young adults experiencing social exclusion through homelessness, poor educational outcomes, lack of health coverage, and political disengagement. Daughters of incarcerated fathers were found to be at high risk of becoming homeless due to fleeing abuse and neglect in the home (Foster & Hagan, 2007).

Additional research was performed using the National Longitudinal Study of Adolescent Health to determine how maternal and paternal incarceration contributed to social exclusion in young adults in their later 20s and early 30s, focusing on four outcomes in young adulthood: (a) personal income, (b) household income, (c) perceived socioeconomic status, and (d) feelings of powerlessness (Foster & Hagan, 2015). Parental incarceration reduced personal and household income and perceived socioeconomic status while maternal incarceration reduced perceived socioeconomic status and feelings of powerlessness. Findings again demonstrated that paternal incarceration was a significant contributing factor to social exclusion. College completion was shown to buffer the social exclusion effects caused by paternal and maternal incarceration (Foster & Hagan, 2015). A college education was a pathway toward upward mobility for young adults and provided a means for youth to overcome social exclusion.

More research is needed in this area to further explore the linkage between parental incarceration and the social exclusion of children as they become young adults. Progress in this area will help generate key questions to address intergenerational social exclusion and inequality that stems from the incarceration of parents. This research will also inform other issues that are related to social exclusion and poverty—social detainment, poor educational outcomes, health disparities due to being uninsured, abuse and neglect, and homelessness.

Conclusion

We live in a world that is constantly evolving. Deindustrialization, globalization, and technological innovation are driving many of these changes. These changes are affecting the economy, social practices, geographical landscape, climate, culture, employment opportunities, and the housing market. Some of these changes are beneficial while others create challenges and further social division among people in society.

The economic and social gap between dominant and subordinate groups is becoming wider. Based on 2016 data from the Survey of Consumer Finances, an analysis performed by the Pew Research Center, upper-income households possessed 75 times more wealth in comparison to low-income households. In 1983, upper-income families only had 28 times greater wealth than low-income families (Kochhar & Cilluffo, 2017). As the world evolves, marginalized populations are being left behind while dominant groups experience growth and prosperity. Unfortunately, many people are unable to achieve their version of the American dream and instead they find themselves struggling to exist in society.

In some situations, people get pushed to the edge of society because they lack economic resources to maintain stable housing and provide basic needs. Or, people turn against society because they feel that they will never get ahead, and so they become involved in deviant behaviors that result in them being physically and socially excluded.

When people experience social exclusion, they may begin to distrust people, the community, institutions, and government. Instead, they become focused on individuality and survival, which creates fractured communities that breed chaos. This chaos leads to the ongoing cycle of social problems such as social and educational detainment, homelessness, incarceration, and the existence of poverty-stricken areas.

END-OF-CHAPTER ACTIVITIES

Discussion Questions

1. What are the similarities and differences between social exclusion and poverty?

2. What are some of the psychosocial effects of being socially excluded?

3. Why has there been an increase in homeless encampments across the United States?

4. How can preventative resources help families avoid having children removed from their care and being placed in the foster care system?

5. What types of resources can make the reentry process into society easier for those who have been incarcerated?

The Decline of the Coal Industry

Identify an area that has been affected by the closing of coal plants. Review information about the area, community, and the closing of the plant. Answer the following questions:

1. How is the community handling the loss of jobs, changing job roles, or relocation?

2. Are there signs of traumatic stress from people in the community? If so, what are some of the signs?

3. What is the coal company doing to help people transition?

4. Are there other companies/industries coming into the area?

5. Are community members staying or leaving? Try to locate personal stories/anecdotes to provide background on people's choices.

Transitioning People From "Tent Cities"

You will work in a small group to complete this activity. Your group is working with a city planning group to develop a strategic plan to decrease the number of homeless encampments in your community. Your group is creating a proposal that details how to transition homeless individuals from tent living into temporary shelters. As you complete this activity, your group will need to identify instrumental resources and potential challenges. For example, most shelters have limited storage for personal belongings. Where will the people's personal items be stored?

Develop seven recommendations and provide detailed steps on how to achieve each one. Create a PowerPoint that describes your recommendations. Consider using Google Docs to complete this activity so that your group members can work collaboratively on the PowerPoint.

Service-Learning Activity: Care Packages

This is an indirect service activity.

Each year thousands of children age out of the foster care system. Some of these young adults transition on to college. Once they are there, they begin a new journey of being a college student. Many college students receive care packages from family members with personal care items and goodies to let them know that their loved ones are thinking about them.

Foster Care to Success developed a care package program so that foster youth could also receive care packages like their peers. The program sends 7,500 care packages to students each year. For this service project, you will need to host a care package drive to collect items to donate to the program. The needed care package items are listed. It is also recommended that you visit their website to review a current list of items that are needed, and you can read about the other ways that you can support the Care Package program. The Foster

Care to Success Care Package program website is www.fc2success.org/programs/student-care-packages/

Contribute items (500 minimum of each item)

- School supplies

- Snacks

- Motivational items or keepsakes

- Health and personal care items

- Small toys or electronics

- Gift cards to national chains

After you complete the service project, write an overview to reflect on the service that you performed and discuss how the service connects to the information that you have read in the chapter.

*If you would like to explore other ways to get involved, visit the Children's Bureau in the U.S. Department of Health and Human Services. May is National Foster Care month, and their website lists other ways to create awareness and perform service. The website is www.childwelfare.gov/fostercaremonth/

References

Alvarez, F. (2018, December 1). *Understanding childhood trauma: ACES and foster children*. Foster Care Newsletter. http://foster-care-newsletter.com/understanding-childhood-trauma-aces/#more-608

Auspitz, Z. (2017). The American child welfare system: The inconspicuous vehicle for social exclusion. *University of Miami Race & Social Justice Review, 7* (1), 60–78.

Berg, R. (2016, October 14). A hidden crisis: The pipeline from foster care to homelessness for LGBTQ youth. Chronicle of Social Change: Children and Youth, Front and Center. https://chronicleofsocialchange.org/child-welfare-2/hidden-crisis-pipeline-foster-care-homelessness-lgbtq-youth/21950

Brown, G., McLean, I., & McMillan, A. (2018). *A concise Oxford dictionary of politics and international relations*. Oxford University Press.

Bureau of Prisons. (2018). *Federal Bureau of Prisons program fact sheet*. U.S. Department of Justice. Bureau of Prisons. (2018). *Federal Bureau of Prisons program fact sheet*. U.S. Department of Justice.

Centers for Disease Control and Protection (CDC). (2018, June 11). *Outbreak of Hepatitis A virus (HAV) infections among persons who use drugs and persons experiencing homelessness*. https://emergency.cdc.gov/han/han00412.asp

Dennis, B. & Mufson, S. (2019, March 28). *In small towns across the nation, the death of a coal plant leaves an unmistakable void*. Washington Post. https://www.washingtonpost.com/national/health-science/thats-what-happens-when-a-big-plant-shuts-down-in-a-small-town/2019/03/28/57d62700-4a57-11e9-9663-00ac73f49662_story.html

Evans, P., Bronheim, S., Bynne, J., Klasen, S., Magrab, P., & Ranson, S. (2001). *Social exclusion and children—creating identity capital: Some conceptual issues and practical solutions*. Organisation for Economic Co-operation and Development, Centre for Educational Research and Innovation (OECD/CERI).

Foster, H., & Hagan J. (2007). Incarceration and intergenerational social exclusion. *Social Problems, 54*(4), 399–433.

Foster, H., & Hagan, J. (2015). Maternal and paternal imprisonment and children's social exclusion in young adulthood. *Journal of Criminal Law and Criminology, 105*(2), 387–430.

Freddie Mac. (n.d.). Rental affordability is worsening. https://mf.freddiemac.com/docs/rental_affordability_worsening.pdf

Howard, K. (2018). *Recommendation to rescind anti bias guidance for school discipline will harm students and reduce school safety*. First Focus, Making Children and Families the Priority. https://firstfocus.org/blog/recommendation-to-rescind-anti-bias-guidance-for-school-discipline-will-harm-students-and-reduce-school-safety

Jehoel-Gijsbers, G., & Vrooman, C. (2007). *Explaining social exclusion: A theoretical model tested in Netherlands*. Stichting Publicatie.

Johnson, A. (2018). *Privilege, power, and difference*. McGraw Hill.

Kochhar, R., & Cilluffo, A. (2017, November 1). *How wealth inequality has changed in the U.S. since the Great Recession by race, ethnicity, and income*. Pew Research Center. http://www.pewresearch.org/fact-tank/2017/11/01/how-wealth-inequality-has-changed-in-the-u-s-since-the-great-recession-by-race-ethnicity-and-income/

MacGillis, A. (2018, May 28). No one is coming to save Adams County, Ohio: Why do Americans stay when their community has no future? *Bloomberg Businessweek*, 40–57.

Miller, T. (1992). The roots of the 1960s communal revival. *American Studies, 33*(2), 73–93.

National Law Center on Homelessness & Poverty. (2017). *Tent City, USA: The Growth of America's Homeless Encampments and How Communities are Responding*. Author.

Pharr, S. (1988). *Homophobia: A weapon of sexism*. Chardon.

Ringel, J. S., Schultz, D., Mendelsohn, J., Holliday, S. B., Siek, K., Edocie, I., & Davis, L. (2017). Improving children's lives: Balancing investments in prevention and treatment in the child welfare system. RAND.

Silver, H. (2007). *The process of social exclusion: The dynamics of an evolving concept*. Brown University Press.

State of New Jersey, Department of Children and Families. (2020). Family success centers. https://www.nj.gov/dcf/families/support/success/

Starecheski, L. (2015, March 2). *Take the ACE quiz—and learn what it does and doesn't mean*. NPR. https://www.npr.org/sections/health-shots/2015/03/02/387007941/take-the-ace-quiz-and-learn-what-it-does-and-doesnt-mean

Stevens, J. (2017). *Got your ACE, resilience scores?* ACES Connection. https://www.acesconnection.com/blog/got-your-ace-resilience-scores

Subramanian, R., Delaney, R., Roberts, S., Fishman, N., & McGarry, P. (2015). *Incarceration's front door: The misuse of jails in America*. Vera Institute.

U.S. Department of Health and Human Services. (2019). *Adoption and foster care analysis and reporting system FY 2018 data*. Author. https://www.acf.hhs.gov/sites/default/files/cb/afcarsreport26.pdf

U.S. Department of Housing and Urban Development. (2019, July 26). *HUD launches initiative to prevent and end homelessness among young people aging out of foster care: "FYI" initiative to offer housing vouchers to at-risk young people facing homelessness*. https://www.hud.gov/press/press_releases_media_advisories/HUD_No_19_111

U.S. Environmental Protection Agency. (2018). *Frequent questions about the 2015 coal ash disposal rule*. https://www.epa.gov/coalash/frequent-questions-about-2015-coal-ash-disposal-rule#1

Wagner, P., & Sawyer, P. (2018, March 14). *Mass incarceration: The whole pie 2018*. Prison Policy Initiative. https://www.prisonpolicy.org/reports/pie2018.html

Warth, G. (2018, June 13). Memorial held in Sherman Heights for 20 hep A victims. *San Diego Union-Tribune*. https://www.sandiegouniontribune.com/news/homelessness/sd-me-hepa-memorial-20180611-story.html

Williams-Mbengue, N. (2014). *The social and emotional well-being of children in foster care*. National Conference of State Legislatures.

PART IV

SUPPORTIVE RESOURCES AND CREATING CHANGE IN COMMUNITIES

8

Programs and Resources for Families and Children in Poverty

As you read the chapter, consider the following:

- How did teaching influence President Johnson's views on poverty?
- What types of resources do federal programs provide to low-income individuals and families?
- Why should long-term supportive services be included in some federal programs for low-income individuals?
- How does the cradle-to-prison pipeline contribute to the cycle of poverty that is prevalent in certain low-income communities?
- Why are nonprofit and community-based organizations important resources for low-income individuals and families?

Introduction

When John F. Kennedy campaigned in 1960, he traveled to different parts of the United States. During his campaign, he had the opportunity to see how Americans across social class levels lived. He visited urban and rural areas; some were representative of middle-class American living, and others were populated with people struggling to provide basic needs.

After visiting low-income communities, President Kennedy was able to associate images and people's stories with the issue of poverty. These experiences, along with reviewing books and articles by journalists, economists, and activists, motivated him to further research the issue of poverty. Michael Harrington's (1962) book, *The Other America*, especially caught the attention of President Kennedy. In his book, Harrington discussed "the invisible poor," people such as poor minorities in urban areas, elderly living in remote areas, and migrant farmworkers. He also discussed the struggles of people living in depressed factory towns and areas with high unemployment rates (e.g., coal-mining areas). Harrington's book revealed that toward the end of 1950 there were 40 to 50 million Americans living in poverty (Mangum et al., 2003).

Researching poverty made him more aware of the adversities people in poverty face each day. President Kennedy directed his Council of Economic Advisers to conduct a study on poverty in the United States. President Kennedy wanted to use this research for his 1964 presidential campaign. He planned to take a stance on poverty and present an antipoverty initiative, but his desire to address this social issue never happened, as Kennedy was assassinated on November 22, 1963 (Mangum et al., 2003).

The work that Kennedy started was pursued by President Lyndon B. Johnson when he transitioned from vice president to president in 1963. Johnson had personal connections with poverty, and he decided to tackle the issue during his presidency (Mangum et al., 2003). At the age of 20, Johnson worked as a teacher to help pay for his college education. Johnson taught fifth, sixth, and seventh grade in Cotulla, Texas, which had a large poor, Mexican American population due to the area being primarily farmland (Lyndon B. Johnson Museum, 2018). Many children of the migrant farmworkers attended Wellhausen School where Johnson was a teacher. Johnson witnessed the daily poverty-related struggles that his students faced each day. There were minimal resources at the school, but he also noticed that many students suffered from hunger; he witnessed students digging in the trash and sucking on grapefruit rinds in order to get juice (Block, 2014).

During his time at the school, Johnson worked tirelessly to provide resources and opportunities for the youth who attended the school. He created experiential learning projects for his students and established special programs at the school—spelling bees, debate, and physical education. He also used his personal money to purchase sports equipment for the physical education program (Lyndon B. Johnson Museum, 2018).

The superintendent recognized Johnson's efforts and promoted him from teacher to the school's principal. Unlike Johnson, many of the school's teachers were not attentive to the students. While Johnson was very committed to creating positive change at the school and learning opportunities for the students, he noticed that other teachers were not invested in helping the students learn. Johnson pushed the teachers to become more engaged in the school and students, which was not received well by the teachers. However, his persistence pushed the teachers to engage with the students during recess. He also continued to promote and support extracurricular activities at the school. Even though Johnson spent a short period of time working at the school, his work experiences impacted his views on poverty and influenced his desire to create a more equitable America (Lyndon B. Johnson Museum, 2018).

President Johnson's War on Poverty

In January 1964, President Johnson gave his State of the Union address, and he shared his vision to create a "great society." Johnson was determined to push legislation that would improve life for Americans of all socioeconomic backgrounds. He presented reforms to address racial discrimination, illiteracy, and poverty. During his address, he announced a **war on poverty**. He declared that the federal government would actively work toward solving the root causes of poverty so that the issue could be removed from society (Bailey & Duquette, 2014).

FIGURE 8.1 Lyndon B. Johnson.

Source: https://history.house.gov/People/Listing/J/JOHNSON,-Lyndon-Baines-(J000160)/.

Congress supported Johnson's political agenda and passed legislation that created much needed change in the areas of healthcare, environment, education, and civil rights issues. Johnson was also an advocate for the environment. He advocated for urban parks, creating nature preserves, and developing policy measures and research protocols to monitor water and air pollution (Bailey & Duquette, 2014; Caro, 2012).

President Johnson's goal of alleviating and eventually ending poverty was ambitious and not attainable during his presidency. However, Johnson did make poverty a major focus. There were several federal programs for low-income individuals, children, and families that were established while he was in office, and he pushed for revisions to older federal safety net programs too.

This is a comprehensive list of all programs that were established during his presidency:

1. Economic Opportunity Act

2. Head Start program

3. Supplemental Nutrition Assistance program

4. Medicare and Medicaid

5. Department of Housing and Urban Development

6. Voting Rights Act

7. Civil Rights Act

8. National Foundation of the Arts and Humanities Act (Caro, 2012; Mangum et al., 2003)

Economic Opportunity Act

After President Lyndon B. Johnson declared a war on poverty on January 8, 1964, the government introduced initiatives to alleviate poverty in the United States. There were four core pieces of legislation that were passed during this time: the Economic Opportunity Act of 1964, the Food Stamp Act of 1965, the Social Security Amendments of 1965, and the Elementary and Secondary Education Act 1965. There were many programs that were created from these acts, many of which were for low-income individuals, programs such as Medicare, Medicaid, the Title I program that subsidizes schools, Job Corps, and the Head Start program (Matthews, 2014). Johnson's war on poverty increased federal expenditures on education, health, and welfare programs significantly. By 1970, 15% of the total federal budget was allocated to these areas, which was triple the amount that was allocated prior to the implementation of the programs (Bailey & Duquette, 2014).

Johnson's goal was to empower poor people with skills so that they could rise out of poverty. He felt that directing funds toward creating training and employment programs was an important approach to successfully combat poverty. In 1964, Congress approved the **Economic Opportunity Act**, and there were several programs funded under it. The Neighborhood Youth Corps offered work opportunities to low-income youth, and the Job Corps program used nonoperational forestry and military buildings as job training centers for disadvantaged youth (Matthews, 2014).

The Community Action program was designed to help poor community members become involved in the local government. This program provided a way for residents to voice their concerns and take an active role in policy-making decisions. The Manpower Development and Training Act of 1962 was updated to provide trainings for individuals who had experienced job loss due to declines in the economy and technological changes in certain industries. Through this program, individuals received educational remediation and training in a new field (Mangum et al., 2003).

The Head Start program was also introduced under the Economic Opportunity Act (Mangum et al., 2003). The program gave low-income youth access to free preschool; it provided early school experiences for youth and offered numerous resources to families. It also gave parents a safe environment to send their children while they attended school, participated in job training, and/or went to work.

Head Start

The **Head Start** program was one of many intervention programs that were developed in the 1960s and 1970s to provide low-income populations with supportive resources for families, parents, and youth. The program was conceptualized to help dismantle the cycle of poverty by providing low-income families access to comprehensive supportive services and opportunities to take on leadership responsibilities within their child's school (Office of Head Start, 2019). Head Start provides free early childhood education to low-income children, along with emotional, psychological, health, nutritional, and social services for the family (U.S. Department of Health & Human Services, 2018). A key feature of the program is that parent involvement is mandated for programs that receive these funds. The focus on parental involvements encourages families to become invested in the program. Their participation is valued and important to the success of the program. Parental involvement helps to create strong family-school partnership ties and creates a sense of community among the school, teachers, families, and students (Gestwicki, 2016).

FIGURE 8.2 Lady Bird Johnson Visiting a Project Head Start Classroom in 1966.

Source: https://commons.wikimedia.org/wiki/File:Lady_Bird_Johnson_Visiting_a_Classroom_for_Project_Head_Start_1966.gif.

THE PERRY PRESCHOOL PROJECT

The Perry Preschool project, located in Michigan, is another early childhood program that was started in the 1960s. The project began in 1962 as part of a research study that was led by psychologist Dr. David Weikart in partnership with Charles Eugene Beatty, the principal of the Perry Elementary School; 123 African American, preschool children were participants in the longitudinal study. They were studied from childhood through adulthood to determine how a high-quality preschool education impacted children with high risk factors for low educational attainment. The children were placed in two groups; the children in group one received a high-quality preschool education while the children in group two did not receive a preschool education. The participants were studied through the year that they turned 40 (HighScope Educational Research Foundation, 2020).

The project lasted for 5 years, 1962–1967, and it led to a longitudinal study. The findings from the long-term study showed that participants who attended the quality preschool program performed well socially and academically. Participants had the following:

- Less remedial education

- Twice the rate of high school graduation

- Twice the postsecondary education

- Twice the successful work history

- Fewer arrests

- Fewer teenage pregnancies

- Less dependency on safety net programs

- Low level of behaviors that pose challenges to family and community

- More likely to be married, own homes, engage in volunteerism, and have stable employment (Gestwicki, 2016)

INVESTMENT IN EARLY CHILDHOOD

Investment in early childhood programs directly benefits children and their families, but there are benefits for our entire society. Since these programs support the healthy development of children, those who participate often avoid grade repetition, special education, early parenthood, and incarceration. Each of these outcomes results in excessive costs for the government and taxpayers (Center for High Impact Philanthropy, 2015).

According to a 2009 study of the Perry Preschool program, there was an estimated return of $7 to $12 for every $1 that was invested in the program (Heckman et al., 2010). This return to society by far outweighs the potential costs of resources and services for children who do not attend early childhood programs. Early childhood programs help to decrease the need for intervention programs later in life. Studies have reported that parents and children (later in life) who are part of high-quality early childhood programs tend to have higher rates of employment, which allows them to be productive citizens and consumers who can contribute to the economy (Center for High Impact Philanthropy, 2015).

The Food Stamp Program

The Food Stamp program (1939) was a government program that was developed to address the hunger issue that many unemployed Americans experienced as a result of the Great Depression. Many Americans suffered from food insecurity and lacked access to quality food. As discussed in Chapter 4, food insecurity can lead to nutritional deficiency and high levels of stress and negatively affect the overall health of an individual. The Food Stamp program began as a temporary program to address food insecurity by providing food vouchers to low-income individuals. People receiving relief were eligible to purchase orange and blue stamps. Orange stamps allowed people to purchase any type of food, and blue stamps could purchase food identified as surplus by the Department of Agriculture. The program operated for 4 years and provided food resources to 20 million Americans. Once the economy improved and unemployment rates declined, the temporary program ended in 1943 (U.S. Department of Agriculture, 2018)

Eighteen years later, the program was piloted between 1961 and 1964. The program was reviewed and revised before being signed into law as the Food Stamp Act (1964). Since 1964, the program has undergone additional changes and evolved into the **Supplemental Nutrition Assistance program (SNAP)** (U.S. Department of Agriculture, 2018). SNAP is the biggest government program that provides assistance to those in need. Like the Food Stamp program, SNAP also focuses on ending food insecurity in the United States. SNAP resources can potentially alleviate the effects of lacking access to fresh and healthy foods. Gaining access to food can prevent people from suffering from hunger and experiencing negative health outcomes (Nguyen et al., 2015).

Researchers examined data from National Health and Nutrition Examination Survey, years 2003 through 2010. They analyzed dietary intake data from 8,333 adults and examined whether receiving SNAP food subsidies altered the relationship between food insecurity, weight, and dietary intake. Researchers used the Healthy Eating Index 2010 to analyze dietary intake. They also reviewed empty calories, solid fat, and daily caloric intake. Results indicated that SNAP recipients with some marginal food insecurity possessed smaller body mass index (BMI) and less probability of being obese. Receiving SNAP benefits and marginal, low, or really low lack of access to adequate food was connected to better dietary intake and decreased BMI. Thus, a lower incidence of obesity was connected to SNAP participants who experienced marginal food insecurity (Nguyen et al., 2015).

Other research has shown that those that experience food insecurity often eat foods that are more energy-dense rather than healthy. Healthier foods often cost more and will perish faster than packaged and canned foods, which are less expensive. Also, low-income individuals may not have easy access to stores with adequate foods due to lack of stores with quality food in their neighborhoods and/or transportation challenges. This research shows that if people do not make healthy food choices (or have access to healthy food) when they use SNAP food resources, then using food subsidies can still lead to food-related, health challenges (Nguyen et al., 2015).

Medicare and Medicaid

During his presidency, President Johnson also addressed the need for elderly and poor populations to have access to health care. Johnson pushed Congress to approve the healthcare legislation so that poor and elderly could have access to health insurance, and his efforts were successful. In 1965, **Medicare** and **Medicaid** programs were signed into law. Medicare provides medical insurance to people over the age of 65; it consists of two parts: hospital insurance (Part A) and medical insurance (Part B). Since the programs were passed, there have been changes. The two parts are referred to as "original Medicare"; more people qualify for coverage, and the program includes additional benefits like coverage for prescriptions (Centers for Medicare and Medicaid Services, 2020).

Medicaid provides medical insurance to low-income Americans, and it is funded collectively by the state and federal government. Initially the program provided coverage to people who were receiving cash subsidies. Over time, the program expanded to provide health coverage to people with disabilities, people who require long-term care, pregnant women, and low-income children and families (Centers for Medicare and Medicaid Services, 2020). As of 2019, Medicaid provides over 70 million people with health coverage. Many of these Medicaid recipients are part of a working family. People may qualify for Medicaid even if they are employed, but their wages must be low. Due to their low wages, they are often unable to afford private health insurance, so Medicaid is the only way for them to acquire medical insurance (Centers for Medicare and Medicaid Services, n.d.a.). Other programs have spawned from Medicare and Medicaid. The Children's Health Insurance program (CHIP) (1997) provides health coverage to 11 million children who are uninsured in America. Since 1997, states have expanded the CHIP so that more children can receive health insurance. All states provide coverage to children if their family's income is within 200% of the poverty guideline. In 2010, the Affordable Care Act was signed into law, and it created a place where the uninsured could access private health insurance. Starting in 2014, the act was expanded to provide coverage to individuals 65 and younger living in families whose income was below 133% percent of the poverty guideline (Centers for Medicare and Medicaid Services, n.d.b.).

Summary

Johnson signed many historic laws during his presidency. He tackled issues like racial discrimination, healthcare, education, and poverty. Under his presidency, the Civil Rights Act and the voting rights laws were passed. Johnson advocated for marginalized Americans and provided much needed economic, social, and health resources to people living in poverty with the formation of programs such as Head Start, the Supplemental Nutrition Assistance program (formally known as the Food Stamp program), Medicare, and Medicaid.

Federal Programs for Low-Income Individuals

There are many federally funded programs for low-income individuals and families. However, to qualify for benefits, individuals must meet specific eligibility factors. One of the main qualifying factors for low-income programs is that income and income eligibility levels are based on the federal poverty measure. Departments that administer low-income programs use the poverty guidelines to determine if people qualify to receive program benefits (U.S. Department of Health and Human Services, 2020). As mentioned in Chapter 1, the U.S. Department of Health and Human Services (HHS) formulates annual poverty guidelines based on the poverty thresholds, which are also issued annually by the Census Bureau (U.S. Department of Health and Human Services, 2020).

The funding for health- and human service–related low-income programs is administered through HHS. Each social service area is allocated an annual budget that is funneled into another government office that oversees the funding for programs and resources. Some of the HHS programs are offered through the U.S. Department of Agriculture and Administration for Children and Families.

Other low-income programs are offered through the Department of Education, Department of Housing and Urban Development, Federal Communications Commission, Department of Labor, Social Security Administration, and Internal Revenue Service. Table 8.1 provides an overview of many federal programs for low-income individuals and

TABLE 8.1 Federal Programs for Low-Income Individuals

Program Name	Department	Qualifying Factors	Description of Benefit
Supplemental Nutrition Assistance Program (SNAP)	U.S. Department of Agriculture	Must meet gross and net monthly income limits Gross income cannot exceed 130% of poverty guidelines, net income cannot exceed 100% of poverty guidelines	Nutrition assistance in the form of food subsidies
Free and Reduced School Meals	U.S. Department of Agriculture	Reduced meal benefit, gross income cannot exceed 185% of poverty guidelines Free meal benefit, gross income cannot exceed 130% of poverty guidelines	National school lunch program School breakfast program Special milk program Children and adult care food program Summer food program
Women, Infants, and Children (WIC)	U.S. Department of Agriculture	Categorical: Women, infant, or child Residential: Must reside in state where they submit application Income must be between 100 and 185% of poverty guideline Nutrition risk; this is determined through a health screening	Food subsidies Nutrition education Social and health services
Medicaid, children's health insurance program	U.S. Department of Health and Human Services	Eligibility level based on modified adjusted gross income and poverty guidelines; eligibility levels fluctuate by state	Medical insurance for low-income individuals
Early Head Start Head Start	Administration for Children and Families, Office of Head Start	General requirement; at or below poverty guidelines Local requirements; contact local office	Access to early childhood education program and resources for children under 5 and their caregivers
Office of Child Care	Administration for Children and Families, Office of Child Care	Eligibility factors vary by state	Childcare subsidies to assist paying for childcare program

(continued)

Program Name	Department	Qualifying Factors	Description of Benefit
Temporary Assistance for Needy Families (TANF)	Administration for Children & Families, Office of Family Assistance	Eligibility factors: citizenship, income, assets, age, resources, and additional factors	Temporary cash aid for families with children
Home Energy Assistance (LIHEAP)	Administration for Children and Families, Office of Community Service	Program has income guidelines	Energy bill assistance Emergency assistance Weatherization improvements and repairs
HUD public housing	Department of Housing and Urban Development	Citizenship status Income limits Good references Apply through local public housing agency	Housing subsidies
Pell grants	U.S. Department of Education	Complete free application for federal student aid	Grant money to pay for college costs
Federal trio programs	U.S. Department of Education	Taxable income cannot be greater than 150% of poverty guideline	Outreach and student services programs for middle school- to college-aged students
Earned income tax credit	Internal Revenue Service	File tax return Meet certain requirements	Decreases amount of tax owed. Taxpayer may receive tax refund
Social Security income	Social Security Administration	Categorical: 65 and older, blind, and disabled Income limits; limited income and resources.	Cash subsidies to provide basic needs
Lifeline	Federal Communications Commission	If an individual receives benefits from another low-income program, they may automatically qualify Income no more than 135% of poverty guidelines	Discounted rates on phone service

Sources: Benefits.gov, n.d.; ChildCare.gov, 2018; Federal Communications Commission, 2019; Federal Register, 2018; Head Start, 2018; Internal Revenue Service, 2019; Medicaid, n.d.; Social Security Administration, n.d.; State of California, 2020; U.S. Department of Agriculture, 2019a, 2019b; U.S. Department of Education, 2015, 2019; U.S. Department of Health and Human Services, 2014

provides the name of the program, the department that oversees the program, qualifying/eligibility factors, and a brief description of the benefit. All applicants must complete the application process to receive final determination of their eligibility status and benefit award amount.

There were many training and employment programs that were created under the Economic Opportunity Act that are still in existence today. Since they were established, some of the programs have undergone changes and others no longer exist. For those that remain, the programs continue to focus on achieving equity in employment opportunities across classes and providing resources to low-income individuals and communities. For example, **Job Corps** (2018) provides free job training programs for individuals aged 16 to 24 and assistance with completing high school or a GED program. The **Volunteer in Service to America program** (VISTA) is offered under the AmeriCorps program, and it continues to train volunteers to serve with nonprofit organizations that are dedicated to combatting poverty in America (Corporation for National and Community Service, n.d.).

Federal- and state-funded programs offer many resources for low-income individuals and families. Even when people access these benefits, they may still struggle to provide basic needs. Some programs have waitlists (e.g., housing subsidies), income levels may be slightly too high to qualify for benefits, or the benefit amount may not cover all expenses. This gap in resources can provide additional strain on many low-income households and result in sliding deeper into poverty. When low-income individuals and families need additional resources, they often seek help from nonprofit and community-based organizations. These organizations help many low-income families with obtaining access to educational, housing, health, and other human service–related resources.

Long-Term Supportive Services and Community-Based Resources

Allocating private and/or public funding toward social issues such as homelessness and education resources for at-risk youth are beneficial; however, when funded resources include long-term supportive services, this makes a vast difference in the effectiveness of resources— services such as social workers, therapy, mentorship, and other types of long-term supportive resources. Earlier in the chapter, I discussed the effectiveness of Head Start and the early childhood programs. By educating parents on child development and providing supportive parenting services, programs can empower parents with knowledge that helps them become effective parents, educational advocates for their children, and active community members. As discussed, the research on early childhood programs demonstrates the tremendous influence on program participants and community. Poverty is being addressed simultaneously among older and younger generations by educating parents and children and mandating parental engagement in programs.

The Cradle-to-Prison Pipeline

Poor people and families often live in poverty-stricken areas with limited opportunities and resources. Poor communities often become socially excluded enclaves that have high levels of crime, gang presence, and drug trafficking. Poverty, lack of resources, and living in areas with high levels of violence and crime can foster areas that contribute to the **cradle-to-prison pipeline.**

Exposure to social culture plays a significant role in people's overall development. Through socialization, people learn gender roles, become racialized, and acquire culture. Repeated exposure to unhealthy behaviors, gang life, crime, and violence can potentially lead to enculturation through social interactions. Over time, people become normalized to everything that is around them. In poor communities, the cradle-to-prison pipeline contributes to the cycle of poverty that is apparent in cities across America.

When states, lawmakers, and communities make sustainable investments in low-income neighborhoods and youth, they can begin to dismantle the cycle of poverty and rebuild crime-ridden neighborhoods into thriving communities that empower community members. Through efforts such as charitable trust funds and promise neighborhoods (see Chapter 9), it is possible to save communities and youth from becoming included in poverty statistics. In the following section, the First Chance Trust Fund is discussed. Pennsylvania is creating a public trust to provide educational and social resources for children who live in areas with increased school dropout, crime, and incarceration rates. This is how Pennsylvania is addressing the cradle-to-prison pipeline.

The First Chance Trust Fund

Pennsylvania governor, Tom Wolf, and Pennsylvania Department of Corrections secretary, John Wetzel, worked collectively to create change in the Pennsylvania State Corrections System. Since Wetzel took office in 2011, there have been steady declines in the prison population. In 2017, the Pennsylvania State Corrections System experienced a 1.8% decline in inmates. The prison population decreased from 49,301 (2016) to 48,438 (2017) (Commonwealth of Pennsylvania, 2018).

In 2017, Wetzel was able to request less funding for the state prison system budget, which reduced taxpayers' dollars being allocated toward funding prisons. Wetzel has spoken candidly about the prison decline efforts and redirecting money toward creating employment and education opportunities. Improvement in these areas helps to decrease crime, which lowers prison population rates (Pennsylvania Government, 2016). The prison system is quite costly; there is an annual cost of about $41,000 for each inmate, so a steady decline in the number of inmates results in a decrease in prison costs.

In fall 2017, **the First Chance Trust Fund** measure was signed and passed into law by Governor Wolf. The measure was written by Senators Vincent Hughes, Pat Browne, Jay LaCosta, and Richard Alloway. The charitable trust fund provides funding for scholarships and programs that service children living in communities with high crime, dropout, and incarceration rates in the state of Pennsylvania. This measure has been needed for quite some time, as 65% of Pennsylvania inmates are parents. In the state of Pennsylvania, there are close to 81,000 children with parents in jail (Pennsylvania Department of Corrections, n.d.). Consider the developmental implications of having a parent or parents incarcerated during any point in childhood. Children often express externalizing or internalizing behaviors when they experience traumatic stress such as the absence of a parent. Parental absence can lead children to have behavioral problems, challenges in school, and criminal behavior (Senator Vincent Hughes, 2017). Unfortunately, most children do not know how to discuss what they are feeling; instead, they act out or withdraw from people.

The First Chance Trust Fund provides education and supportive services for children. The fund receives funding by three methods: there is a 1% surcharge to vendors who have contracts in excess of $5 million with the Corrections department. Additional agencies can also allocate a portion of their contract to the fund, and private, tax-deductible donations are accepted. The fund is expected to generate $500,000 to $1 million annually. Funds will be directed to communities that have increased rates of at-risk youth and students who drop out of high school (Pennsylvania Department of Corrections, n.d.).

Being that it is the first state in the country to adopt this type of fund, the state of Pennsylvania is trailblazing the path for other states to follow. By providing resources to at-risk communities, the fund directs money into communities that need resources the most. Additionally, educational resources, coupled with supportive services, deters the cycle of poverty and crime among at-risk youth. The fund will also protect communities from becoming undesirable, crime-ridden neighborhoods (Pennsylvania Department of Corrections, n.d.).

Empowerment Theory

Poor people need access to valuable resources and education so that they can become empowered participants in their communities and countries. When people become empowered, they have more control over their environment and life, which leads to better life opportunities and equitable access to resources. According to research, once people become empowered, they begin to recognize the social stratification system that organizes society. With this new perspective, research states that people begin to recognize how their communities are affected by the unequal distribution of power. They also come to realize how this has affected their lives and social standing in society (Zimmerman, 2000).

Professor Lorraine Guiterrez has studied **empowerment** in Chicano communities in the southwest United States and Chicago, Illinois. Through her research Guiterrez identified three cognitive components of empowerment: (a) group identification, (b) stratum consciousness, and (c) self and collective efficacy. Group identification occurs when people identify with the collective. They can identify with others' experiences and commonalties that exist among the group. Stratum consciousness is a concept that describes how individuals learn about the social hierarchies in society. Individuals learn that society is organized by levels of power, which determine one's social status and access to resources. The final concept is self and collective efficacy. This is the stage when individuals believe that they are in control of their lives and that they possess the power to make changes in their lives and communities (Guiterrez & Lewis, 1999).

In the section that follows, nonprofit and community-based organizations will be discussed. These types of organizations provide resources that help people increase their economic, social, and cultural capital, which, in turn, increases their human capital. If people can cultivate resources, they can potentially become empowered and make progress toward their goals.

Nonprofit Organizations

Nonprofit organizations are created to address social issues and engage in charitable work. These tax-exempt organizations use profits to further support the organization's mission and goals. Each day non-profit organizations provide resources to millions of people. They provide shelter to those without homes, food to people who suffer from hunger, health resources to people in need of medical care, educational resources to youth living in struggling school districts, and many other resources to families and individuals in need.

The nonprofit sector is the third largest employment industry in the United States (Salamon, 2018). Based on data from the Bureau of Labor Statistics, nonprofit organizations provided 12.3 million jobs across the United States in 2016 (U.S. Bureau of Labor Statistics, 2018). This figure increased since 2012. At that time, there were 11,460,870 individuals employed by nonprofit organizations, which had increased from the 2007 reported amount of 10,534,183. This data shows that more people are choosing to work in the nonprofit sector (U.S. Bureau of Labor Statistics, 2014).

Across America, many communities and community members depend immensely on the work of nonprofit organizations. In states throughout America, people are creating grassroots movements and organizing through nonprofit and community-based organizations to create change in communities. Without the presence of nonprofits, many areas and people would experience greater struggles and no access to resources. Nonprofits strive to create change for public benefit, create employment opportunities, and support economic growth in local communities, along with contributing to the overall American economy (National Council of Nonprofits, n.d.).

Community-Based Organizations

Community-based organizations (CBOs) are nonprofit organizations that help to improve communities. They are a valuable resource in all communities but provide much needed resources in low-income communities. They are comprised of people who are invested in the community: community leaders, local businesspeople, public officials, and community members. Most community-based organizations have regular meetings to discuss local issues and strategize on how to address issues. Occasionally, CBOs collaborate with other organizations to address larger issues. By mobilizing resources, the organizations can potentially have a greater impact in the communities that they serve.

Without CBOs many low-income communities would have limited access to resources and opportunities. Community members would have lower levels of capital and greater struggles. CBOs provide opportunities for people to increase their social and cultural capital, which can potentially strengthen their economic capital and local economy. Imagine if communities did not have CBOs that offered educational resources such as tutoring, mentoring, extracurricular activities, after-school and summer programs. Youth in those communities would have limited access to resources that middle- and upper-class parents often access for their children. Many CBOs help to challenge these types of inequities, create equal access across communities of all classes, and help sustain access to continual resources for community members. As they help to strengthen and rebuild communities, they also empower community members to create positive change in their communities.

Conclusion

History seems to have a cycle that includes challenges, uprisings, triumphs, and losses, and the Johnson era is another piece of American history that displays this cycle. More than a half century after Johnson's State of the Union address, we are entering yet another cycle and revisiting challenges that our society has experienced before. Over 50 years later, racial and class discrimination is still prevalent in our society. There are differences across class and race lines that create an unequal society for many Americans. There are places where people struggle to provide basic needs for their family, communities where people experience difficulties trying to vote because of their skin color, and neighborhoods that have failing schools.

Alleviating poverty and other social ills that are deeply embedded in our society is an ongoing process. Since 1959, the poverty rate has gone from 22.4% to 12.3% (UC Davis, 2018; U.S. Census Bureau, 2018). While there are still many political, social, and economic hurdles to overcome in America, the foundation for change was formed to give future generations their rights as American citizens. With these rights, Americans continue to help shape the political, economic, and social structure of our society.

END-OF-CHAPTER ACTIVITIES

Discussion Questions

1. How do individuals qualify for federally funded low-income programs?

2. How do early childhood programs, like Head Start, increase parents' cultural capital?

3. In what ways do the safety net programs (family- and children-related programs) buffer against children being exposed to adverse childhood experiences?

4. Based on the information presented in the chapter, what is the relationship between poverty, federal programs, and empowerment theory?

5. Since 2007, what type of employment trend has happened in the nonprofit sector? Why do you think that this employment trend has occurred?

Head Start Programs

The Head Start program is discussed in this chapter. There are two other types of Head Start programs: Early Head Start and Migrant and Seasonal Head Start. Each program provides resources for low-income children. Research the programs and answer the following questions:

1. What specific population does the program serve?

2. What are the eligibility requirements?

3. What services and resources does the program provide to children? Provide a summary.

4. What types of parenting resources are offered? Provide a summary.

Research a Local Community-Based Organization

For this assignment, you will need to find an organization in your community that works to help low-income families and individuals. You will need to research and summarize the following information:

- When was the organization established? Provide an overview on the history of the organization.

- What types of resources and services does the organization offer?

- What are the qualifying factors? How long do recipients receive resources?

- How many families and/or individuals does the organization serve annually?

- How is the organization funded?

- What are some of the challenges that the organization experiences?

- What are some of the accomplishments that the organization has achieved?

- What is your reaction to the work that the organization does?

- What type of volunteer opportunities are available?

- What do the recipients think of the program? Try to find program reviews.

Service-Learning Activity: Head Start

This activity requires that students conduct research.
For this project, you will need to partner with a local Head Start program. You will need to obtain approval from the director to conduct research. You will need to submit a research proposal to the school and institutional review board at the university. Visit the Human Subjects Research site to review the institutional review board process. The focus of your research will be to obtain parents' opinions on the services and resources that the Head Start program offers. Sample survey questions are listed:

- Have the parenting resources helped to strengthen your parenting skills?
- Have you noticed any developmental differences in your child (children) since starting the program?
  - Have you noticed any physical changes?
  - Have you noticed any emotional changes?
  - Have you noticed any social (i.e. socialization) changes?
- What resources have been the most beneficial to you, your child (children), and the family?

References

Bailey, M. J., & Duquette, N. J. (2014). How Johnson fought the war on poverty: The economics and politics of funding at the Office of Economic Opportunity. *Journal of Economic History, 74*(2), 351–388.

Benefits.gov. (n.d.). *HUD public housing program.* https://www.bencfits.gov/benefit/863

Block, M. (2014, April 11). *LBJ carried poor Texas town with him in civil rights fight.* NPR. https://www.npr.org/2014/04/11/301820334/lbj-carried-cotulla-with-him-in-civil-rights-fight

Caro, R. A. (2012). *The years of Lyndon Johnson, the passage of power.* Random House.

Center for High Impact Philanthropy. (2015). *High return on investment.* Author.

Centers for Medicare and Medicaid Services. (2020). *History.* https://www.cms.gov/About-CMS/Agency-Information/History/index.html?redirect=/History/

Centers for Medicare and Medicaid Services. (n.d.a.). *Fifty years of Medicaid, from the director.* https://www.medicaid.gov/about-us/program-history/ennsylv-50th-anniversary/?entry=47687

Centers for Medicare and Medicaid Services. (n.d.b.). *Program history.* https://www.medicaid.gov/about-us/program-history/index.html

ChildCare.gov. (n.d.). *Paying for childcare.* https://childcare.gov/consumer-education/paying-for-childcare

Commonwealth of Pennsylvania. (2018, January 22). *Governor Tom Wolf announces prison inmate population drops for fourth consecutive year after record reduction.* https://www.governor.pa.gov/governor-wolf-announces-prison-inmate-population-drops-fourth-consecutive-year-record-reduction/

Corporation for National and Community Service. (n.d.). *AmeriCorps Vista.* https://www.nationalservice.gov/programs/americorps/americorps-programs/americorps-vista

Federal Communications Commission. (2019). *Lifeline program for low-income consumers.* https://www.fcc.gov/general/lifeline-program-low-income-consumers

Federal Register. (2018, May 8). *Children nutrition program: Income eligibility guidelines.* https://www.federalregister.gov/documents/2018/05/08/2018-09679/child-nutrition-programs-income-eligibility-guidelines

Gestwicki, C. (2016). *Home, school, and community relations.* Cengage Learning.

Guiterrez, L., & Lewis, E. (1999). *Empowering women of color.* Columbia University Press.

Harrington, M. (1962). *The other America: poverty in the United States.* Macmillan.

Head Start, ECKLC. (n.d.). *Applying for the Head Start program.* https://eclkc.ohs.acf.hhs.gov/how-apply

Heckman, J. J., Moon, S. H., Pinto, R., Savelyev, P. A., & Yavitz, A. (2010). The rate of return to the HighScope Perry preschool program. *Journal of Public Economics, 94*(1–2), 114–128.

HighScope Educational Research Foundation. (2020). *Perry Preschool project.* https://highscope.org/perry-preschool-project/

Internal Revenue Service. (2019). *Earned income tax credit.* https://www.irs.gov/credits-deductions/individuals/earned-income-tax-credit

Job Corps. (2017). *About the program.* https://www.jobcorps.gov/

Lyndon B. Johnson Museum. (2020). *LBJ in Cotulla.* https://lbjmuseum.com/lbj-in-cotulla/

Mangum, G. L., Mangum, S. L., & Sum, A. M. (2003). *The persistence of poverty in the United States.* Johns Hopkins University Press.

Matthews, D. (2014, January 8). Everything you need to know about the war on poverty. *Washington Post.* https://www.washingtonpost.com/news/wonk/wp/2014/01/08/everything-you-need-to-know-about-the-war-on-poverty/

Medicaid. (n.d.). *Medicaid, Children's Health Insurance program, and basic health program eligibility levels.* https://www.medicaid.gov/ennsylv/program-information/ennsylv-and-chip-eligibility-levels/index.html

National Council of Nonprofits. (n.d.). *What is a "nonprofit"?* https://www.councilofnonprofits.org/what-is-a-nonprofit

Nguyen, B. T., Shuval, K., Bertmann, F., & Yaroch, A. L. (2015). The Supplemental Nutrition Assistance program, food insecurity, dietary quality, and obesity among US adults. *American Journal of Public Health*, 105(7).

Office of Head Start. (2019). *History of Head Start.* https://www.acf.hhs.gov/ohs/about/history-of-head-start

Pennsylvania Department of Corrections. (n.d.). *First chance trust fund.* https://www.cor.pa.gov/family-and-friends/Pages/First-Chance-Trust-Fund.aspx

Pennsylvania Government. (2016, January 19). *Pennsylvania State Prison population records largest decrease in 40 years.* https://www.governor.pa.gov/ennsylvania-state-prison-population-records-largest-decrease-in-40-years/

Salamon, L. M. (2018). *Nonprofits: America's third largest workforce.* John Hopkins Nonprofit Economic Data Project.

State of California. (2020). CALWORKS. http://www.cdss.ca.gov/CalWORKS

Senator Vincent Hughes. (2017, October 31). *Lawmakers applaud measure creating trust fund for youth impacted by the prison system.* http://www.senatorhughes.com/lawmakers-applaud-measure-creating-trust-fund-for-youth-impacted-by-prison-system/

Social Security Administration. (n.d.). *Understanding supplemental security income SSI application process and applicants' rights.* https://www.ssa.gov/ssi/text-apply-ussi.htm

U.S. Bureau of Labor Statistics. (2014, October 21). *Nonprofits account for 11.4 million jobs, 10.3 percent of all private sector employment.* https://www.bls.gov/opub/ted/2014/ted_20141021.htm

U.S. Bureau of Labor Statistics. (2018, August 31). *Nonprofits account for 12.3 million jobs, 10.2 percent of private sector employment, in 2016.* https://www.bls.gov/opub/ted/2018/nonprofits-account-for-12-3-million-jobs-10-2-percent-of-private-sector-employment-in-2016.htm

U.S. Census Bureau (2018, September 12). *Income and poverty in the United States: 2017.* https://www.census.gov/library/publications/2018/demo/p60-263.html

U.S. Department of Agriculture. (2018). *A short history of SNAP.* https://www.fns.usda.gov/snap/short-history-snap

U.S. Department of Agriculture. (2019a). *Supplemental nutrition assistance program.* https://www.fns.usda.gov/snap/eligibility

U.S. Department of Agriculture. (2019b). *Women, infants, and children*. https://www.fns.usda.gov/wic/wic-eligibility-requirements

U.S. Department of Education. (2015). *Federal Pell grant*. https://www2.ed.gov/programs/fpg/index.html

U.S. Department of Education. (2019). *Federal trio programs*. https://www2.ed.gov/about/offices/list/ope/trio/index.html

U.S. Department of Health and Human Services. (2020, January 8). *Poverty guidelines*. https://aspe.hhs.gov/poverty-guidelines

U.S. Department of Health and Human Services. (2014, December 15). *Help with paying for heating and cooling*. https://www.acf.hhs.gov/ocs/resource/help-with-paying-for-heating-or-cooling

University of California, Davis (UC Davis). (2018, October 15). *What is the current poverty rate in the United States?* Center for Poverty Research. https://poverty.ucdavis.edu/faq/what-current-poverty-rate-united-states

Zimmerman, M. A. (2000). Empowerment theory. In J. Rappaport & E. Seidman (Eds.), *Handbook of community psychology* (pp. 43–63). Springer.

9

Parent and Family Involvement and Cradle-to-Career Approach

THOUGHT QUESTIONS

As you read the chapter, consider the following:

- What are the different roles that parents (caregivers) occupy, and how do they manage all of these roles?
- How can ecological systems theory be used to explain the multidimensional aspects of poverty and the effects of poverty on children and family dynamics?
- What are the key goals of the cradle-to-career approach?
- Why is parent and family involvement a key component of the Harlem children zone model?
- How has the promise zone initiative helped to transform low-income communities?

Introduction

You may have heard the phrase, "It takes a village to raise a child." The village is a community of people who live in an area and provide supportive resources to community members. In turn, the community supports not only developing children, but the community members also support one another. When parents have support from family and their community, it helps lessen the stress of occupying numerous parental roles, such as provider, nurturer, worker, and educator. This shared responsibility within a community transcends working together not only for the betterment of children, but to strengthen the community so members mobilize and collectively create change for the entire community.

Parenting and Social Change

The world is constantly changing, and parents juggle numerous roles in order to provide for their children. *Home, School, and Community Relations* (2016) discusses seven complex roles that most parents try to manage as they raise their children. Parents nurture their children by providing affection and attention and attending to their physical and emotional needs. As parents tend to their children, they also try to satisfy their personal needs. Concurrently, parents (caregivers) and children experience developmental changes as they progress through life, which, at times, can be a lot for parents to manage.

Many parents juggle personal developmental milestones, as they try to support and guide their children through developmental stages. It is important for parents to take care of themselves so that they can nurture their family and fulfill their other roles. For example, if the parent is in a relationship, then they must also allocate time to nurture their relationship with their partner, while still tending to their individual needs and addressing their children's needs. Parents must also manage the role of being a worker. Many times, the stage in life when people decide to become parents coincides with when they are also investing in career growth. The investment in career can often place strain on the family and marital happiness may decline. For these reasons, it is important to achieve work-life balance, which can be challenging for those who may not have resources or high levels of capital. In some instances, people are unable to foster work-life balance because their focus is solely on being a worker and provider.

Amid working and caring for their children, parents must also find time to manage their household. Parents pay bills, purchase groceries, and buy items for all family members. Additionally, they may also need to coordinate child-related tasks such as child care, extracurricular activities, and summer camps. Another role that parents often occupy is educator. Parents are expected to be active in their children's education, which is not always doable for everyone. They need to provide them with educational tools, assist them with homework, advocate for their child (children), and be active in the school community. Parents may also find themselves becoming active in their local community, especially if they are members of a religious institution or their children attend after-school programs, play sports, or engage in other extracurricular activities (Gestwicki, 2016). Table 9.1 lists the roles that many parents manage daily.

TABLE 9.1 Parenting Roles

Seven Parenting Roles
1. The parent as nurturer
2. The parent as an individual
3. The parent in an adult relationship
4. The parent as a worker
5. The parent as a consumer
6. The parent as an educator
7. The parent as a community member

Source: Gestwicki, 2016

ECOLOGICAL SYSTEMS THEORY

The stress of living in a modern society can be overwhelming. Managing numerous roles, along with changes in laws, social and political issues, and the economy, can place a great strain on all members of the family unit and greatly affect children. Urie Bronfenbrenner's **ecological systems theory** discusses how children are centered around interrelated social systems. Bronfenbrenner was a developmental researcher who believed in ethnographic research, studying people in their natural environments as they go through their day-to-day lives. His theory states that the connectivity between systems shape the child's environment and affect the child's development. The five systems are *microsystem, mesosystem, exosystem, macrosystem,* and *chronosystem* (Berger, 2008).

The microsystem consists of relationships the child has with immediate family and experiences that occur within the child's personal surroundings. Examples are familial relationships, school, community programs, and religious institutions. The mesosystem is the connections between the people, programs, and structures that are part of the child's microsystem. This includes family-school partnerships and the relationship between the school and surrounding community. The exosystem system is the factors that the child is not directly in contact with; however, the factors are connected with structures in the child's microsystem, such as their adult caregivers' work and/or school schedule. Some people work multiple jobs or work and attend school

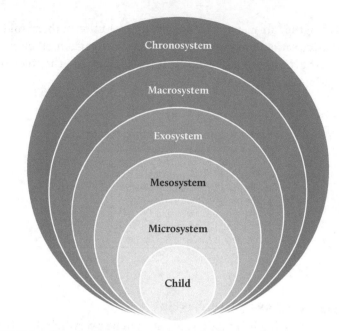

FIGURE 9.1 Bronfenbrenner's Ecological Systems Theory.

Source: Carol Getswicki, "Bronfenbrenner's Ecological Systems Theory," Home, School, and Community Relations. Copyright © 2016 by Cengage Learning, Inc.

in addition to having a family. Their schedule and lack of parental presence affects the developing child. The macrosystem is the framework of one's social environment. It is the traditions, social norms, cultural beliefs, and laws that affect varying aspects of the family unit. An example is the amount of paternal and maternal leave provided to care for a newborn child. The chronosystem describes how social conditions and components within the system change over time, such as the timing of when a parent starts school and graduates (Berger, 2008).

Bronfenbrenner's theory helps to understand the effects of living in a changing society that is affected by social, economic, and political forces. Modern living can be stressful as parents juggle multiple roles and work to provide for their families. The cost of living in many places forces parents to work more than a 40-hour work week. When parents work more, the amount of time they spend with their family decreases, and there is an imbalance between work and home. As a result, children often spend time in after-school care, with a nanny or family member, or may be at home alone. Parents find themselves working so much that they realize they have limited to no quality time with their children, and a parental time deficit develops. This is a deficit that occurs across social classes. Middle- and upper-class parents may have economic resources to actively cultivate their children through extracurricular activities, but the consequence of occupying a higher class standing is that they might be paying a nanny to take children to activities or depending on a grandparent to take on parental roles so that they can spend more time at work. For working-class and poor parents, they too will often seek the help of relatives or identify afford-able or subsidized child care, or children may be at home unattended.

It is important that families allocate time to spend together. Cul-tivating parent-child and familial relationships helps to strengthen relationships and support the healthy development of all family mem-bers. Busy work and personal schedules can often be a barrier to having family time, but dedicating time to nurture relationships is a simple and free way to help a family become closer, which can increase the overall well-being of all family members. Also, by spending time together, parents actively cultivate their children by engaging in conversation and shaping their socialization practices.

QUALITY MOMENTS

Resources, opportunities, and high levels of capital can make a huge difference in life experiences; however, studies have also shown that there is high value in simple moments that parents spend with their children. Often, in a parent's quest to take care of their family, fulfill work duties, and "get it all done," they can forget the importance of simply spending time with their kids. Quality time is free and only requires that parents engage with their children in an activity for an uninterrupted period of time without any distractions. The term "**qual-ity time**" originated in the 1970s when parents began to work more and spend less time with their families (Kremer-Saldik & Paugh, 2005).

Researchers Tamar Kremer-Saldik and Amy Paugh, from the Center on Everyday Lives of Family at the University of California, Los Angeles, began studying the concept of quality time and found that families had challenges trying to schedule quality time with their families. There were often obstacles that prevented having routine quality time, such as long work days and children's activities. When Kremer-Saldik and Paugh reviewed video that showed daily interactions of families, they noticed that the families had numerous moments during the day that resembled quality time. They called these interactions "**quality moments**." These were unscheduled moments that occurred in places like riding in the car, standing in a check-out line at the store, or organizing laundry. These moments provided time for parent-child

FIGURE 9.2 Family Members Can Have a Quality Moment When Doing Laundry.

Source: Copyright © by ryan harvey (cc by-sa 2.0) at https://flic.kr/p/pS1W3m.

interactions (Kremer-Saldik & Paugh, 2005). While the moments were brief, they allowed for parents and children to engage with each other. The researchers also found that these moments could happen with only a few family members present, which allowed for parents with multiple children to engage with them at separate times. When family members have separate quality moments, it helps to strengthen the overall family unit. Quality moments do not replace families having a set period of quality time, but these moments do allow families with busy schedules several moments throughout the day to communicate and connect with their children so that they can build a strong parent-child relationship (Kremer-Saldik & Paugh, 2005).

Varying levels of human, social, economic, and cultural capital influence the life experiences of all families. High levels of capital can provide greater resources and opportunities, but it can also result in middle- and upper-class families needing to spend time away from the family to work more hours. In contrast, working-class and poor caregivers often work more hours to help provide basic needs, and they may not get the benefit of greater resources and opportunities. Parents' daily personal and work experiences affect stress levels, which then affects psychosocial relationships with children and childrearing techniques used. As people move busily through their day-to-day lives, it is important to embrace the simple moments. Regardless of social class, when parents take the time to engage in quality moments with their children, the parent-child relationship and family bond are strengthened.

History of Parent Involvement

The parent-child relationship can also become strengthened when parents become involved in their children's school. Parental involvement helps establish a family-school relationship and shows children that parents are invested in their schools, which helps children become more comfortable in the school setting. By becoming more involved in the school, parents gain knowledge that helps them better support their child's education and advocate for their child's needs.

Early models of effective parent involvement were seen in parent cooperative nursery schools. Cooperative schools were mostly popular in middle-class communities, such as suburban and university towns. In these schools, parents and staff worked collaboratively on making decisions and maintaining the school. Parents were actively involved in the school—from creating the philosophy to daily practices, to school maintenance (Getswicki, 2016). Parent cooperative nursery schools began in 1917 when a group of University of Chicago faculty wives needed time to complete Red Cross work, provide their children with peer socialization, and obtain parent educational resources for themselves (Parent Cooperative Preschools International, n.d.a). Parent cooperatives reached their peak in the 60s and continue to operate in present times.

Cooperative schools also provide opportunities for parents to receive training to become a paraprofessional in the classroom. This allows parents to assist classroom teachers and enrich their own learning so that they can support their child's education. When parents are active in their child's school, it helps to establish a strong family-school partnership that benefits the child, teacher, parent(s), and the family unit (Getswicki, 2016).

Early models of low-income parental involvement were seen in nursery schools and child care centers that were established by the government for families after the Great Depression. The schools provided health care and nutritional resources to low-income families who needed resources due to the social and economic effects from the Great Depression. Years later, during World War II, there were childcare centers supported by the government and private employers. The Lanham Act child centers provided child care to parents with war-related jobs. Even during war times and being from culturally and ethnically diverse backgrounds, these parent populations were very receptive to educators who provided parent development courses at the centers. It took close to 20 years before the field of early childhood education experienced another surge of growth, driven largely by a surge of women entering the workforce out of choice or necessity. When reinterest sparked, there was renewed interest in parental involvement in schools (Getswicki, 2016).

Motives for Parent and Family Involvement

Just as there are different perspectives on how to approach educating youth, there are different reasons to support family and parent involvement in schools. Research data is one motive that has guided involvement. Research studies indicate that there is a positive correlation between parental involvement and the social and cognitive development of children (Getswicki, 2016).

Another motive that guides family involvement is the requirement to follow laws that mandate parent involvement in programs. As previously mentioned, Head Start is a program that mandates parent involvement. If a child participates in a Head Start Program, the parent(s) is required to participate in the program. This regulated involvement helps to establish a link between the family and school (Getswicki, 2016).

A third motive is the need for the community to become more active in their local schools. By encouraging parental involvement, schools are creating opportunities for families to become more invested in the school community. This helps to strengthen the culture of the school, improve the school community, and provide support to the family structure. It is difficult for progressive transformation to happen in declining schools when there is not a system in place to support the change. When parents become invested in schools, they can be the catalyst to guide change and support the educational, social, and psychological development of their children (Getswicki, 2016).

Dr. Joyce Epstein, a scholar in family-school partnerships, identifies six areas of involvement: parenting, communicating, volunteering, learning at home, decision making, and collaborating with the community. Epstein finds that effective programs consists of all six types of parent involvement:

1. Parenting: Schools provide supportive resources to help families with parent and childrearing techniques. They offer parent development opportunities that educate parents on child development and how to support their child's learning. For this type of involvement to be successful, schools must become familiar with the population of families and students the school serves.

2. Communicating: Schools utilize various modes of communication to exchange information with parents about their child's progress and student events.

3. Volunteering: Schools devise methods to strengthen trainings, recruitment, and opportunities for families to volunteer with the school.

4. Learning at home: Schools provide parents with educational resources that will aid them in helping children with curriculum-related activities such as homework.

5. Decision making: Schools provide leadership opportunities for parents to become active in the school community, opportunities such as parent-teacher associations, advisory councils, and other types of school governance committees

6. Collaborating with the community: Schools access resources from local businesses, nonprofits, and agencies. Also, schools provide resources to the local community, creating a cyclical relationship of support that establishes a linkage between school and community entities (Getswicki, 2016).

Schools with effective family-school partnerships work to incorporate all six types of involvement. Even if the school is not achieving all six, most schools try to achieve as many as possible. Some schools are more successful than others at adapting each type of involvement. All schools are not created equal, and there are schools that struggle to establish and sustain family-school partnerships due to staffing, low parental involvement, funding, and limited resources.

Parent involvement is known to be a contributing factor to development across the school years, but it is highly important during the early years. During the early years, children are acquiring the building blocks of learning. When they have experienced traumatic stressors associated with poverty, those blocks are cracked and damaged. Parent involvement can help to lessen the effects of poverty by providing parents access to supportive resources. Parents who get involved in their child's school often have access to free parent trainings and leadership roles within the school, and they learn how to best support their child's learning.

These acquired skills and knowledge help to empower parents, which can lead to an increase in cultural, social, and economic capital. It may also benefit the community if members are invested in strengthening their community. This is highly important in low-income communities because empowered community members can help create an empowered community.

The Harlem Renaissance, Decline, and Rebirth

The Harlem neighborhood of New York City has experienced at least three distinct periods of transition during the early, middle, and late 20th century, with differing economic impacts. From the year 1910 to the 1930s, there was a mass migration of African Americans from southern states to northern cities. There were also many African Americans emigrating from the West Indies too. Scholar and activist W.E.B. Dubois was one of the prominent African American figures who led this great migration movement (Campbell et al., 1987). By the year 1920, nearly 300,000 African Americans emigrated from southern states to northern states. Most people were drawn to big cities to find work opportunities, and Harlem was one of the most desirable cities (Watson, 1995).

From the 1910s to 1930s, Harlem experienced a cultural, social, and artistic boom. Originally this era was called "the New Negro Renaissance," but it was later referred to as the Harlem Renaissance. During this time, Harlem became home to many up-and-coming Black intellectuals and artists, such as W.E.B. DuBois, Alain Locke,

James Weldon Johnson, Jessie Faucet, and Charles S. Johnson. Harlem became an African American artist mecca overflowing with creative energy from writers, poets, singers, dancers, musicians, painters, and other types of artists who flocked to the area to share their talents (Watson, 1995).

March 21, 1924 was a pivotal turning point for the movement. On this date, prominent White literary publishers and writers gathered with Harlem intellectuals and writers at the Civic Club, which admitted both White and African Americans to their dining room. This event was organized to introduce the White literary crowd to the "new Negro movement" that was happening uptown in Harlem. The night was a huge success; shortly after the event, magazines such as *Harper's* published works by Harlem writers and featured articles that discussed the Harlem Renaissance (Watson, 1995).

At the beginning of the Harlem Renaissance, the target audience and people invested in the movement were primarily African American. After the Civic Club meeting, Harlemania began, and White artists, publishers, and philanthropists became captivated with Harlem (Watson, 1955). This movement also embodied more than just literature and art; it also created a space to address topics such as racial integration, race building, progressive politics, freedom of expression through music, and sexual freedom.

Over time Harlem became known for literature, art, and musical entertainment, and people of all races flocked to Harlem to visit the night clubs and see performers such as Duke Ellington and Cab Calloway at the Cotton Club. It was an electrifying time for Harlem, and the area evolved into a creative forum and safe haven for many African American artists, such as Claude McKay, Langston Hughes, Zora Neal Hurston, Josephine Baker, Countee Cullen, and Paul Robeson (Campbell et al., 1987).

With the stock market crash in 1929, followed by the end of the prohibition era in 1933, Harlem began to experience a decline, and many White people no longer had a reason to visit the Harlem clubs for illegal alcohol. Additionally, many of the intellectuals who were integral forces in the new Negro movement were leaving the area; Alain Locke took a faculty position at Howard University, Charles Johnson accepted the director of social sciences position at Fisk University (he later became the university's first African American president), and James Weldon Johnson and Aaron Douglas moved to Nashville to teach at Fisk University (Watson, 1995).

With the onset of the Great Depression, the area worsened, and stable, long-term residents moved out and new migrants from the South moved in. Many moved with barely any resources, which boosted a need for public assistance among the new migrants. The downward transformation continued throughout 1935 when a riot broke out in the area, resulting in millions of dollars of damage, fatalities, and hundreds injured. The riot signified the end of the Harlem Renaissance.

In the decades that followed, Harlem became a declining urban enclave that was plagued by crime, drugs, and violence. The area felt the effects of many significant historical happenings—job loss from the Great Depression, deindustrialization after World War II, the crack epidemic in the 1970s to 1980s, and gang violence of the 1980s. The area that was once a vibrant light with intoxicating energy became a physically and socially depressed place.

Harlem Children Zone

In the 1990s, the area began to experience a rebirth because of the work of Geoffrey Canada and his vision for the **Harlem Children Zone** (HCZ). Canada grew up in a poor neighborhood within the South Bronx. Even though his surroundings were deleterious, Canada did not let his depressed community deter him from achieving his goals. He pursued his undergraduate studies at Bowdoin College and graduate studies at the Harvard Graduate School of Education. After leaving Harvard, Canada began working in poor communities, helping to educate and empower children and families (HCZ, 2019h).

Canada decided to target one specific area, Harlem, New York, to test out a communal-educational, psychosocial health approach to address generational poverty. In 1990, Canada developed a pilot program that was focused on ending the cycle of generational poverty that plagued the area for decades (HCZ, 2019a). Canada wanted to revitalize the community, increase **civic engagement**, and create opportunities for children and families in Harlem. The community had experienced massive declines over the years, and the community members were suffering from lack of resources and low-performing schools. What had once been an African American artist mecca had deteriorated into a poverty-stricken community.

Canada created a cradle through college pipeline approach to the address the problem (see the HCZ pipeline in Figure 9.3). He wanted to transform the community by creating community-building programs,

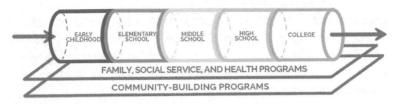

FIGURE 9.3 Harlem Children Zone Supports Families and Youth From Cradle Through College.

Source: https://hcz.org/about-us/pipeline/.

access to social services, and health resources. He believed that these types of changes would help to empower residents and help them become agents of change in their communities. He also believed that strong communities could support the developmental and academic growth of youth, from cradle to career (HCZ, 2019a).

In 2000, HCZ announced a 10-year plan that would help them expand their programming and provide resources to more of the Central Harlem area. The Harlem children zone area grew from the one-block pilot to 27 blocks, then increased to 60 blocks, and now the area encompasses 97 blocks (HCZ, 2019a). This growth has been supported by public and private funding sources. HCZ's budget is a combination of 70% private funding and 30% government funding. Additionally, the organization allocates 90% of its funding toward programming and 10% to administrative costs (HCZ, 2013)

On July 1, 2014, Geoffrey Canada passed his chief executive officer (CEO) duties on to Anne Williams-Isom, who was the chief operating officer of the HCZ. Canada had occupied the roles of CEO and president for 3 decades, from 1990–2014. CEO Anne Williams-Isom is leading Harlem Children Zone into the future by strengthening the Central Harlem community, supporting families, and cultivating the next generation of innovative thinkers. HCZ provides programming and supportive resources to 25,000 families and children in the zone area. The organization invests in the community by providing numerous community-building programs. HCZ supports families and youth with an array of educational, social, cultural, physical, health, and emotional programs and resources. HCZ families have access to services that provide support from birth through adulthood. CEO Williams-Isom has continued to direct HCZ to accomplish the goal of supporting families and children while strengthening the community. To accomplish the organization's mission, she is supported by 2,000 staff members, a dedicated board of directors, and Geoffrey Canada, who continues to serve as president of HCZ (HCZ, 2019i). HCZ continues to flourish not only because of great leadership, but also because of the government and private funding that they receive. To combat generational poverty, it takes collective investment to create and sustain transformative changes in depressed communities.

The Cradle-to-Career Approach

The **cradle-to-career approach** provides supportive resources for youth from birth through college. Youth and families receive access to social services and health resources. When families have access to supportive services, they do not have to worry about surviving; instead, they can focus on strengthening the family unit and supporting their children through every stage of development. With this approach, resources are also funneled into the community to strengthen families, community ties, and the community as a whole. The cradle-to-career approach encourages high levels of family engagement to support children's educational and developmental outcomes. By strengthening families and communities, community members become invested in community and communities begin to thrive. Also, youth are supported throughout their education and often become more civically engaged in their communities. This cradle-to-career pipeline is very similar to building a home. In order for a house to remain intact, it must be supported by a strong foundation. If a home lacks a proper foundation or the foundation is cracked, then the home will eventually begin to shift and fall. If low-income youth, families, and communities do not have supportive resources, then communities begin to struggle, educational attainment rates decrease, unemployment rises, and crime and violence increase.

Harlem Children Zone's Programs

The early years are important for establishing a strong and healthy foundation for the developing child. Throughout the text, we have discussed the potential consequences of not properly nurturing a child during pivotal periods of development. It can affect them socially, emotionally, and physically. Experiences during the early childhood years can also have long-lasting effects on the developing person. Many parents need support as they take on the new role and added responsibilities. Early childhood programs are instrumental in educating children and families during the child's years of learning. Knowing the importance of early childhood education, Canada started his pipeline approach with early childhood programs.

The cradle-to-college pipeline begins with the early childhood programs: the Baby College, the Three-Year-Old Journey, and Harlem Gems. These programs were created to provide supportive services to families during the early stages of development. To access the programs, families must live in the 97-block area of the HCZ. For the Baby College program, expecting parents must complete an application that will determine their eligibility for the program. The Three-Year-Old Journey and Harlem Gems programs are part of the charter school pipeline. Parents/caregivers apply for the admittance to the Promise Academy for Kindergarten 2 years prior to their child's start date. If the child is admitted through the lottery process, the child receives placement into the Three-Year-Old and Harlem Gems programs (HCZ, phone conversation, October 15, 2018).

The Baby College program provides expecting parents (or caregivers) and parents with children ages 0–3 a 9-week training series that educates them on child development and parenting skills. The course covers topics such as health and nutrition, child behavior, language and brain development, communication, and child safety. The course also includes home visits to help reinforce learning over the 9-week term and provide support to the parents as they integrate learned concepts into their homes. Classes are offered in several languages, and families have access to the other social services that the Harlem Children Zone offers. The Baby College program helps to build community among the participants and strengthens the community by providing resources to parents (HCZ, 2019b). In 2010, HCZ started the Guardians Responding and Developing Strategies (GRADS) Early Head Start Program. This 0–3 program supports and deepens the knowledge that families obtain in the Baby College program. The GRADS program provides education, social, and health resources for the children, along with social support resources for their caregivers. Since the program is affiliated with Head Start, applicants must meet low-income eligibility requirements to participate (HCZ, 2015).

The Three-Year-Old Journey program continues to educate parents on child development and encourages community building. As the parents participate in workshops, their children learn socialization skills as they engage in play, arts and crafts, and story time in supervised child care offered by HCZ. The workshops also give parents a safe space to exchange ideas, ask questions, and reflect on their parenting practices. As parents progress through the early childhood programs, they begin to meet other families and build relationships with people in their community (HCZ, 2019b).

The last early childhood program is Harlem Gems. Harlem Gems is a quality, full day, pre-kindergarten program that is offered year-round. The program services an average of 240 kids at four different sites throughout the Harlem neighborhood. One of the main goals of the program is to ensure that children are properly prepared to enter kindergarten so that they can thrive and experience success in school. To achieve this goal, the program keeps a low child-to-adult ratio, 4:1. The low-class ratio provides children more one-on-one opportunities with teachers and allows for more individualized interactions. The program emphasizes literacy skills, teaches students beginning Spanish and French vocabulary, stimulates learning through exploration, and introduces children to health and nutrition. The program continues to support family involvement and community building, which further strengthens the link between home, school, and community (HCZ, 2019b).

The Harlem Children Zone's early childhood programs have experienced great success. In 2017, 100% of the Harlem Gems students tested ready for school. Additionally, since the year 2000, there have been 6,000 Baby College graduates. Take a moment and really consider the significance of this number. The HCZ program has created positive change for 6,000 young lives through their Baby College (HCZ, 2019b). This number does not reflect the family members and communities that were empowered with supportive services, so the figure could easily be doubled. This figure also highlights one program of many that are offered by HCZ. The HCZ intervention programs and charter school have created tremendous change for the people and community of Harlem.

HCZ'S OTHER PROGRAMS AND SERVICES

HCZ also offers a kindergarten through 12th grade charter school, specialized school programs, and extracurricular activities for school members. HCZ continues to support their high school graduates as they pursue and attend college. HCZ sets high expectations for college attendance and provides supportive services to students through their college experience to ensure that students graduate.

HCZ provides numerous family and community resources too. These resources are available to school members' families and families who live within the Harlem Children's Zone area. Resources include community centers that provide family and youth activities, childcare, enrichment programs, and cultural events. Other resources include tax preparation services, community service opportunities, and family strengthening programs to prevent children from entering the foster care system. The zone also offers three programs that support healthy living: Healthy Harlem, Harlem Armory, and HCZ Food Services.

HEALTHY HARLEM

Healthy Harlem provides youth and families with nutrition education and physical education activities. As of 2018, the program is offered at 20 sites and serves more than 4,000 youth. The program was designed to address the high rates of obesity among children and within the community of Harlem. Over two-thirds of Harlem residents are obese or overweight, and 40% of zone students are also obese or overweight. HCZ is committed to decreasing the rates of obesity among community members. To help youth participants adapt a healthy lifestyle, HCZ records body mass information, guides children through a health plan, and offers exercise services (HCZ, 2019c).

For children to fully adopt a healthy lifestyle, the zone encourages parent involvement. As of July 2018, the zone works with close to 3,000 parents and residents of the Harlem Zone area. Healthy Harlem offers workout classes, farmer's markets, cooking instruction, and family programming such as Family Fit. In this program, families exercise and learn about healthy lifestyles together (HCZ, 2019c).

HARLEM ARMORY

The Harlem Armory is the second component of HCZ health program. The Armory is a 50,000 square-foot athletic facility that offers services to 1,000 HCZ youth each week—preschool to high school youth. Participants can play a wide range of sports including volleyball, gymnastics, track, basketball, and soccer. The armory is also open to adults who live in the surrounding community. During non-school hours, the armory offers classes for youth, adults, and families. Hundreds of community members take yoga, Zumba, and other classes at the armory. The armory provides a great service to the community, as many people would not have access to the health resources. The armory's services are integral resources in helping the HCZ combat obesity in the community (HCZ, 2019d).

HCZ FOOD SERVICES

The Harlem children's zone knows the importance of providing nutritional meals to developing children. For these reasons, the zone has a Food Services Department run by a professional chef. The Food Services Department makes 96% of meals from scratch. Annually, the Food Services Department prepares 1.45 million meals (HCZ, 2019e).

The food team makes meals for students at two HCZ charter schools and four kindergarten programs. They serve 2,000 students breakfast, lunch, and an afternoon snack. The team creates menus with food items that have low amounts of sugar, salt, and fat. They also work diligently to provide culturally diverse menus with lots of variety, and the two charter school sites have a daily salad bar with fresh vegetables and different side dishes that are made fresh every day. Additionally, the Food Services Department offers activities such as cooking instruction for students, families, and community members (HCZ, 2019e).

RESEARCH

In 2017, Mathematica policy research evaluated the Healthy Harlem initiative. There were two components to the comprehensive evaluation: an implementation study and an impact study. The implementation study reviewed the implementation process of Healthy Harlem into each of the after-school sites. The study also evaluated how students, parents (caregivers), and HCZ and Healthy Harlem staff reacted to the program. The impact study evaluated the program's impact on student participants' body mass index, fitness levels, nutritional understanding and attitudes, and available social support for physical activity and nutritious diet (Malbi et al., 2017).

Since its inception, Healthy Harlem has provided resources to 9,000 HCZ youth participants. The research findings revealed that the program had a positive impact on student health outcomes. There was an increase in student participant knowledge on nutrition and accountability in relation to exercise. The findings also showed that there was an overall increase in participants' levels of exercise and a decrease in rates of overweight and obese participants enrolled in Healthy Harlem (Malbi et al., 2017).

Harlem Children Zone Results and Replicating the Model

To ensure that the zone is accomplishing its mission and goals, HCZ tracks goals, gathers data, and reviews results for all programs across the organization. Each year the organization tracks 600 goals, and the following is an excerpt of the data collected from the year 2017:

- The organization provided services to 27,573 adults and children; 13,447 were youth 0 to 23 years old and 14,126 were adults.

- Since 2000, there have been 6,059 graduates from Baby College.

- 100% of pre-kindergarteners displayed school readiness when tested.

- There was a 97% college acceptance rate among the HCZ student population.

- Nearly 3,000 families in the Harlem Children Zone program received $4,700,000 in tax refunds through the organization's free tax services program.

- As of 2017, there were 861 Harlem Children Zone alumni attending college.

- Over 1,200 families have remained together due to receiving HCZ foster care preventative services

- Nearly 500 United States and 175 international visitors have participated in workshops offered through the Practitioners Institute since 2005 (HCZ, 2019f)

The program is putting data to good use by helping other organizations create similar change in their communities. In 2003, the Harlem children's zone developed the Practitioners Institute. The institute provides groups with the opportunity to learn about the organization's pipeline approach and best practices and discuss all aspects of its work. The institute is a resource for organizations throughout the United States and across the globe who want to address social issues in their communities, issues such as high rates of poor health, violence and crime, struggling schools, and poverty. Each community has its own personal struggles, and the institute helps groups to identify specific issues within their communities and develop a plan to address the issues using effective, sustainable, long-term methods (HCZ, 2019g).

HCZ has experienced success with their approach and offers educational workshops to organizations that would like to replicate their methods. The organization currently offers two fee-based workshop options: a 3-hour workshop and a 3-day series of workshops and activities. For over a decade, the institute has offered workshops to community leaders from the United States and other countries such as Singapore and Indonesia. (HCZ, 2019g).

A Strengthened Community

Canada's vision for Harlem was not an abnormal desire for a community. His vision describes how communities should function; they should be safe environments with community resources where families can live and children can develop in a healthy environment. While this should be a norm for all communities, plentiful resources and good schools are more often a norm in middle- and upper-class communities and failing schools with scarce resources are a norm in low-income communities. Due to the social class structure and social inequities in our society, children who live in low-income and poverty-stricken communities are at a disadvantage because of their parent's social class standing and residential zip code. The cradle-to-career approach is a way to empower communities and provide youth with opportunities and resources they deserve.

Overview of Promise Neighborhoods

During his 2008 presidential campaign, Senator Barack Obama spoke of Geoffrey Canada's success with the Harlem children's zone model. The Harlem Children Zone programs and school were instrumental in transforming the Harlem area by reducing crime, improving access to educational resources, providing access to health care, increasing employment opportunities, and empowering residents within the zone area. HCZ experienced great success with their pipeline approach, and President Obama spoke openly about wanting to replicate the HCZ model in other struggling communities across the United States. President Obama wanted low-income communities to receive supportive resources to assist communities with rebuilding, creating opportunities, and improving developmental and educational outcomes. Obama was inspired by Geoffrey Canada's success with the Harlem children's zone and worked with his administration to create the **Promise Zone Initiative** (HCZ, 2018h).

In 2010, President Obama's Administration announced the Neighborhood Revitalization Initiative. The initiative was developed to address the increase in poverty throughout country. The initiative consisted of three centerpiece programs: Bryne Criminal Justice Innovation, Choice Neighborhoods, and Promise neighborhoods. All of the programs are based on a theory of change: the Bryne Criminal Justice Innovation program helps neighborhoods develop community-based methods to decrease violence and crime; the Choice Neighborhood program was designed to help communities remediate distressed homes to stimulate neighborhood revitalization; and the Promise Neighborhoods program is structured to help distressed communities with decreasing poverty by rebuilding communities and empowering community members by targeting the areas of health, education, social services, and community building (White House, President Barack Obama, n.d.).

The Promise Neighborhood grant program is administered by the U.S. Department of Education. The program began in 2010 to provide federal funding and resources to struggling, distressed, low-income communities. The funding for the program is administered through the Fund for Improvement of Education program (FIE) (U.S. Department of Education, 2018).

Institutions of higher education, nonprofit organizations, and Indian tribes are eligible to access Promise Neighborhood program funding. The goal of the Promise Neighborhoods program is to rebuild distressed communities and improve developmental and educational outcomes for youth. The program helps struggling areas improve schools and provide supportive community and family resources. With educational and familial resources, Promise Neighborhood program youth are supported throughout their stages of development. Their social network and resources prepare them for college, provide support through the college years, and assist with transitioning into a career (U.S. Department of Education, 2018). In order to provide effective support that results in achievement at each stage of this process, the program supports transformative change in communities by the following:

- Creating a large pool of eligible entities

- Offering comprehensive academic, educational, and familial cradle-to-career resources

- Coordinating interaction between programs and establishing effective communication channels to guide the solution implementation process

- Designing systems to support local infrastructure that will provide solutions across Promise Neighborhood program areas, as well as in surrounding communities

- Assessing the impact of the program, strategies utilized, and educational outcomes through rigorous evaluation methods (U.S. Department of Education, 2018)

The Promise Neighborhoods program began disseminating awards in 2010. During the 2010 award period, 21 communities were awarded 1-year planning grants to support the Promise Neighborhood program development process. The following year (2011) there were 15 additional planning grants awarded and five implementation grants given to communities that applied in 2010. A third set of planning and implementation grants were awarded in 2012. During this award cycle, there were 10 planning grants and seven implementation grants awarded (U.S. Department of Education, 2018).

Promise Neighborhoods Institute at PolicyLink

The Center for the Study of Social Policy, Harlem children's zone, and **PolicyLink** work collectively to mobilize resources for developing and sustaining promise neighborhoods. PolicyLink is an organization that focuses on research in the areas of economic and racial equality. The organization also provides advocacy, engagement, and implementation resources. The Center for the Study of Social Policy works with community organizations, private businesses, the government, and philanthropic partners to improve communities and create public policy solutions. The center conducts research studies to produce research-driven results; it uses data to guide the organization's work, gather information on social issues and risk factors, and develop accountability measures (Promise Neighborhoods Institute, n.d.).

Their collective efforts are organized under the Promise Neighborhoods Institute at PolicyLink. Before the institute was established, the organizations, along with Child Trends, collaborated on a recommendation paper in 2009 for the Promise Neighborhoods federal initiative. The document was instrumental in guiding the discussion on Promise Neighborhoods program results and helped during the development process of the initiative (Promise Neighborhoods Institute, n.d.).

After undergoing a rigorous planning, development, and implementation process, the first set of promise zones achieved designation status in 2014. The five zones were in south eastern Kentucky, San Antonio, Philadelphia, Los Angeles, and the Choctaw nation of Oklahoma. Each zone area received federal funding and resources to support them in achieving their zone goals. From 2014 to 2017, there were a total of 22 designated promise zones. Each zone area had specific goals for their community; however, all zone communities do the following:

- Employ accountability measures

- Have access to federal resources

- Receive AmeriCorps members from the Corporation of National Service

- Invest in effective methods

- Offer tax benefits for businesses in promise area (U.S. Department of Agriculture, 2014)

In 2016, President Obama announced the final nine promise zone areas: South Los Angeles, California; San Diego, California; Nashville, Tennessee; Atlanta, Georgia; Evansville, Indiana; southwest Florida; Eastern Puerto Rico; Turtle Mountain Band of Chippewa Indians, North Dakota; and the Spokane Tribe of Indians, Washington (White House, President Barack Obama, 2016).

There has been much progress made in all the promise zone areas. In zone areas, there has been an increase in graduation rates, college acceptance rates, number of AmeriCorps members providing educational and social resources to youth, job training and placement services, and colleges connecting to the local community and community members. There has also been a decrease in crime and acts of violence in many of the promise zone areas. Additionally, there has been geographical restructuring in cities by increasing access to public transit, revitalizing business districts, and enacting blight remediation (White House, President Barack Obama, 2016).

The funding helped neighborhoods improve community and family building, give access to health resources, and increase educational attainment outcomes among youth. The grant program focused on similar improvement areas that the HCZ cradle-to-career pipeline targets. Like the HCZ pipeline model, the grant program was designed to create transformative change in low-income communities (National Neighborhood Indicators Partnership, 2016).

Conclusion

When poverty-stricken areas are ignored, the state of poverty worsens and the cycle of poverty proliferates. In some communities, poverty becomes a normalized state of existence. To combat the cycle, seeds of change have to be planted in the community. These seeds come in the form of early childhood programs and community-based organizations. While these programs are unable to reverse the effects of poverty, they can provide resources and forms of capital that can potentially empower low-income individuals. As mentioned in this chapter, low SES parents who lack knowledge on child development and parenting practices can gain beneficial information by becoming involved in their child's school and participating in parent education classes. By increasing parents' cultural capital, their overall human capital also increases. They gain information that increases their knowledge and ability to affect their child's development in positive and supportive ways.

Community-based organizations can also help guide positive change throughout a low-income community. The Harlem children's zone (HCZ) model is a community-based initiative, which empowers residents to make a difference in the life of the community. HCZ focuses on supporting community, family, education, and access to health resources. By focusing on these areas, the organization can provide supportive resources to the surrounding community and school members because of the numerous programs that are offered by HCZ. Since the program began, it has helped strengthen families, educate children, and revitalize the community. The success of the program has been recognized and replicated through the Promise Zone Initiative. Over the last 20 years, HCZ has grown from a one-block pilot program to a national model for breaking the cycle of poverty. HCZ and the promise neighborhoods are creating transformative change in depressed communities and providing families and children with access to resources and opportunities.

END-OF-CHAPTER ACTIVITIES

Discussion Questions

1. How might living in poverty affect a parent's (parents') ability to fulfill the seven parenting roles that are discussed in the beginning of the chapter?

2. Why are quality moments important for families across social classes?

3. Why is parent and family involvement a key component of the Harlem Children Zone model?

4. How do the Harlem Children Zone model and promise neighborhoods increase the social, cultural, and economic capital of the children, families, and communities that the organizations serve?

5. What other cities have a similar history to that of Harlem (it was once a bustling city and then experienced an economic and social decline)? What is the current state of the city, and are there revitalization plans for the city?

Six Types of Parent Involvement

Contact one of the elementary schools in your community and ask about the different types of parent involvement opportunities at the school. Create a checklist using Epstein's six types of parent involvement to assess the parent involvement opportunities at the school. Record examples of the different types of parent involvement. After you complete your interview, research the neighborhood and school demographics. You can conduct an Internet search engine and/or visit greatschools.org to help you with obtaining neighborhood and school information. When you have compiled all your research, you can compare your findings with your classmates.

Promise Neighborhoods

In this chapter, you learned about the Promise Zone Initiative. Choose one of the 22 promise zone areas to research and answer the questions:

- How has the area changed since becoming designated as a promise zone? List and discuss five changes.

- How did the community react to the changes? Have there been any challenges reported?

- How are community members preserving community history and culture?

Service-Learning Activity: Backpack Drive

This is an indirect service activity.

Once summer comes to an end, families return to their fall routines. To prepare for the school year, children often need new clothes and shoes, backpacks, lunch bags, and school supplies. Some parents can easily buy these items for their children, but there are others who struggle to provide these items. In lots of communities, groups organize back-to-school backpack drives so that they can provide resources (i.e., cultural capital in the form of educational and cultural tools) to youth.

For this activity, you should work in groups to complete the service project. First, you will need to partner with a local after-school program that needs back-to school-supplies for their youth participants. Make sure to obtain information to help you compile a wish list of items, such as how many participants and grades of participants. It is also recommended that you inquire about children with any type of special need or disability or children whose first language is not English. If possible, make specialized backpacks and incorporate any specialized items that they may need.

Make arrangements to host a back-to-school supply drive on your college campus, place of employment, or religious institution, or host a digital backpack drive and have items shipped to your home. Once you have all the items, you will need to coordinate a time to make the backpacks with additional volunteers, if needed. After the backpacks are done, coordinate a time to drop them at the after-school program. Last, write a reflection about your experience. Include the following and any other pertinent comments:

- Overview of the service project

- How the experience made you feel

- How it connects to information discussed in the book

References

Berger, K. (2008). *The developing person through the life span*. Worth Publishers.

Campbell, M. S., Driskell, D., Lewis, D. L., & Ryan, W. (1987). *Harlem Renaissance: Art of Black America*. Harry N. Abrams.

Gestwicki, C. (2016). *Home, school, and community relations*. Cengage Learning.

Harlem Children Zone. (2013). Harlem's children zone: A national model for breaking the cycle of poverty with proven success. Author. https://hcz.org/wp-content/uploads/2014/04/FY-2013-FactSheet.pdf

Harlem Children Zone. (2015) The Harlem children's zone GRADS Early Head Start 2015 annual report. Author. https://hcz.org/wp-content/uploads/2016/01/HCZ-EHS-2015-Annual-Report.pdf

Harlem Children Zone. (2019a). *About us.* https://hcz.org/about-us/

Harlem Children Zone. (2019b). *Early childhood.* https://hcz.org/our-programs/

Harlem Children Zone. (2019c). *Healthy Harlem.* https://hcz.org/our-programs/healthy-harlem/

Harlem Children Zone. (2019d). *Harlem Armory.* https://hcz.org/our-programs/harlem-armory/ https://hcz.org/our-programs/healthy-harlem/

Harlem Children Zone. (2019e). *HCZ food services.* https://hcz.org/our-programs/hcz-food-services/

Harlem Children Zone. (2019f). *Our results.* https://hcz.org/results/

Harlem Children Zone. (2019g). *Spreading the model.* https://hcz.org/spreading-the-model/

Harlem Children Zone. (2019h). *Geoffrey Canada.* https://hcz.org/about-us/leadership/geoffrey-canada/

Harlem Children Zone. (2019i). *Anne William-Isom.* https://hcz.org/about-us/leadership/anne-williams-isom/

Kremer-Saldik, T., & Paugh, A. (2005). *Working families matter.* UCLA Center on Everyday Lives of Families.

Malbi, J., Bleeker, M., & Fox, M. K. (2017). *The impact of healthy Harlem on the prevalence of child overweight and obesity and contributing factors: Interim evaluation report.* Mathematica Policy Research.

National Neighborhood Indicators Partnership. (2016, September 21). *NNIP resources for promise Neighborhood Initiative.* https://www.neighborhoodindicators.org/library/guides/nnip-resources-promise-neighborhood-initiatives

Parent Cooperative Preschools International. (n.d.) *The early co-op preschool movement.* https://www.preschools.coop/our-history

Promise Neighborhoods Institute. (n.d.). *About PNI.* https://www.promise-neighborhoodsinstitute.org/cradle-to-career-movement/about-pnihttp://www.promiseneighborhoodsinstitute.org/about-the-institute/background

U.S. Department of Agriculture. (2014, January 9). *Obama Administration announces the first five promise zone designees.* https://www.usda.gov/media/press-releases/2014/01/09/obama-administration-announces-first-five-promise-zone-designees

U.S. Department of Education. (2018, March 5). *Promise neighborhoods.* https://www2.ed.gov/programs/promiseneighborhoods/index.html

White House, President Barack Obama. (2016, June 6). Obama Administration announces final round of promise zone designations to expand access to opportunity in urban, rural, and tribal communities. https://obamawhitehouse.archives.gov/the-press-office/2016/06/06/obama-administration-announces-final-round-promise-zone-designations

White House, President Barack Obama. (2016, June 6.). *Neighborhood Revitalization Initiative.* Office of Urban Affairs. https://obamawhitehouse.archives.gov/the-press-office/2016/06/06/obama-administration-announces-final-round-promise-zone-designations

Watson, S. (1995). *The Harlem Renaissance: Hub of African-American, culture 1920–1930.* Pantheon.

10

Researching Poverty and Civic Engagement

THOUGHT QUESTIONS

As you read the chapter, consider the following:

- How does the Institute for Research on Poverty share the responsibility of supporting poverty research and facilitating poverty policy with other university-based research centers?
- In what ways does community organizing strengthen and empower low-income communities?
- Why can gentrification be damaging to low-income communities and community members?
- How is the Obama Foundation helping to increase local, regional, national, and global civic engagement?
- How can civic engagement decrease poverty in low-income communities?

Introduction

Universities support learning, creativity, and innovation through special initiatives and programs. They have a long history of educating the public on medical, environmental, and social issues that exists in our society. These institutions support the research and scholarly work of their academics and offer multiple platforms for scholars to share work with the public. In the last decade, universities have become more involved in researching the causes and consequences of poverty. Poverty and inequality are being recognized more as serious social issues that need to be studied.

As universities make efforts toward researching poverty, it is equally important for communities to make local efforts toward combatting the issues within their neighborhoods. When community members mobilize and voice their opinions in a collective, organized manner, they can create change within in their communities. Community organizing and increased civic engagement help to strengthen communities and empower citizens to take on leadership roles within their communities. In these roles, individuals can advocate on behalf of their community and become active participants in the formation of laws and policies that affect their neighborhoods.

The Institute for Research on Poverty

The **Institute for Research on Poverty** (IRP) at the University of Wisconsin-Madison received a $9.5 million contract to serve as the only national poverty research center in the United States that is federally funded. This is a 5-year agreement (2016–2021) with the U.S. Department of Health and Human Services (HHS). Specifically, the cooperative agreement is with the Office of the Assistant Secretary for Planning and Evaluation (ASPE), which is an office within HHS (Institute for Research on Poverty, 2020a).

IRP functions as a hub for policy research and training; the institute also produces reports, fact sheets, and informational materials that provide current poverty data that aids in developing policy questions, informs policy researchers, and shapes poverty-related policy and legislation. The IRP's cooperative agreement with ASPE results in all information being directed to the secretary of HHS, as the ASPE is the lead advisor on policy and legislation, policy research, strategic planning, economic analysis, and policy evaluation (Institute for Research on Poverty, 2020a).

As part of the cooperative agreement, ASPE supports the initiatives offered through the national research center. This includes the U.S. Collaborative of Poverty Centers, Annual Poverty Research and Policy Forum, extramural small research grant competitions, graduate research fellows program, IRP summer research workshop, and "Focus, Fast Focus, and Poverty" fact sheets (Institute for Research on Poverty, 2020a).

The **U.S. Collaborative of Poverty Centers** (CPC) is a network of university poverty centers. The IRP established this formal network to work with other university-based centers to study poverty and inequality. Poverty is a multifaceted topic that cascades into many other social issues, so it is more effective for a group of poverty centers to develop policy-related programs, trainings, and disseminate poverty research. There are 10 member organizations in the Collaborative of Poverty Centers:

1. Institute for Research on Poverty, University of Wisconsin-Madison

2. Center on Poverty and Social Policy, Columbia University

3. Center on Race and Wealth, Howard University

4. Poverty Solutions, University of Michigan

5. Stanford Center on Poverty and Inequality, Stanford University

6. Center for Poverty Research, University of California, Davis

7. Center for Poverty Research, University of Kentucky

8. West Coast Poverty Center, University of Washington

9. Wilson Sheehan Lab for Economic Opportunities, University of Notre Dame

10. Center for Population, Inequality, and Policy, University of California, Irvine (Institute for Research on Poverty, 2020a)

The goals of the CPC are to facilitate communication between research communities and policy makers, influence poverty-related policy to help decrease poverty and inequality (along with the effects of poverty), produce and support research, and distribute poverty research findings. The IRP works collectively with CPC to support the research networks. The five national research networks were formed to guide, create, and advance research and policy in specific thematic areas (Institute for Research on Poverty, 2020a). The research networks are listed and described in Table 10.1.

Each thematic network consists of practitioners, policymakers, and researchers who work collectively to explore a diverse range of approaches that informs current discussion on poverty-related policy and influences research and practice. These intellectuals contribute varied professional and policy views, which provides the research networks with highly skilled, diverse leadership. Collectively, the leaders

TABLE 10.1 Research Networks

Research Network	Description
Poverty and geography	This explores the connections between poverty, inequality, and geographic location. This network also explores the specific locational approaches to best address inequality and poverty.
Poverty and family functioning	This network focuses on the interconnection between human development over the life span, family function, inequality, and poverty. It identifies programs and policies that support healthy families and promote the development of human capital.
Poverty, employment, and self-sufficiency	This network reviews dynamics and characteristics of labor markets; the relationship between race, poverty, and self-sufficiency; and strategies, along with policies, that promote work in order to reduce material deprivation and poverty.
Poverty and the transition to adulthood	Key issues that are studied include how poverty impacts health as individuals transition into the adult years. Other topics that are explored are family formation, educational attainment, and participation in the labor force. The network also identifies key strategies that promote healthy youth development for those from disadvantaged backgrounds.
Poverty, tax, and transfer policies	The focus is on how tax and transfer policies can support healthy family development, decrease poverty, and generate participation in labor markets.

Source: Institute for Research on Poverty, 2020b

guide each thematic area to inform programs and policy that respond to key issues related to the causes and effects of inequality and poverty in the nation (Institute for Research on Poverty, 2020b).

Summary

It is important for universities, organizations, and communities to take an active role in helping to create solutions to social issues. Poverty affects all races, ages, genders, and people of all sexual orientations. It has no geographic boundaries and affects people in urban, suburban, and rural areas. A great portion of the U.S. middle class is sliding into poverty due to limited economic opportunities and resources. Even though poverty statistics reveal one set of information, the reality is a greater number of the U.S. population lives in poverty or is at risk of living in poverty. Research on poverty and inequality must continue so that policymakers can be well informed on the current state of poverty in communities across our nation.

Civic Engagement

As organizations, nonprofits, colleges, schools and school districts, and other community partners, along with support from the federal government, work toward creating change in low-income communities, it is important for community members to be engaged in the change process that is occurring in their community. If people are not active participants, they may not be aware of the changes that will be occurring in their community and how the changes will affect the culture and landscape of the community. Further, they may not agree with every change that is being presented for their community.

Civic engagement is an important tool for creating change in poverty-stricken communities. When community members communicate, organize, work together, and mobilize resources, low-income communities have the potential to make great strides toward progress. Community members can utilize their knowledge and strength of community ties to create change for the overall community. By working together rather than individually, the community can mobilize their capital and power. The unification provides a once marginalized community with power—power to voice their concerns and be heard, power to take control of their destiny, and power to create change. Once community members become empowered agents of change, they can transcend into becoming leaders. As they make progress, they can occupy roles of power, work toward modifying policy that oppresses subordinate groups, and create economic, social, and political opportunities for other marginalized populations.

The Political Sector: Inclusive Representation

When Hillary Clinton did not win the 2016 presidential election, it left many people questioning whether America was ready to embrace a female president. It also prompted people to consider the future of women in politics (Glatter, 2017). One year after the presidential election, there was a resurgence of women running for political positions, and many of them were triumphant. While the glass ceiling was not broken during the 2016 presidential election, there was a definite shift in the political arena, and women were creating a political renaissance across the United States. In 2017, the website workingmother. com featured 16 working moms who were victorious during the 2017 elections. Many of the women were either the first female or person of their ethnic or racial heritage to be elected to their position. See the list of women:

1. Idaho: Holli Woodings, Boise City Council

2. Iowa: Mazahir Salih, Iowa City Council

3. Louisiana: LaToya Cantrell, mayor of New Orleans

4. Massachusetts: Kim Janey, Boston City Council

5. New Hampshire: Joyce Craig, mayor of Manchester

6. New Jersey: Jessica Salinas, Bloomfield School Board

7. New York: Laura Gillen, Hempstead town supervisor

8. North Carolina: Vi Lyles, mayor of Charlotte

9. Texas: Sue Deigaard, Houston School Board

10. Virginia: Jennifer Carroll Foy, Virginia House of Delegates

11. Virginia: Kathy Tran, Virginia House of Delegates

12. Virginia: Hala Ayala, Virginia House of Delegates

13. Virginia: Elizabeth Guzmán, Virginia House of Delegates

14. Virginia: Danica Roem, Virginia House of Delegates

15. Washington: Jenny Durkan, mayor of Seattle

16. Washington: Manka Dhingra, Washington State Senate (Bodgas, 2017)

During the 2017 elections, history was made in the city of Boston. There were six women elected to city council, and all of them were women of color. Four of the six women had served the previous term. Lydia Edwards and Kim Janey were newly elected; Michelle Wu, Annissa Essaibi George, Andrea Joy Campbell, and Ayanna Pressley served the previous term. Eight years prior, Pressley was the first women of color on the council. Additionally, Pressley was the only woman on the council in 2011 (Glatter, 2017). Since 2009, the council experienced a major shift. The board is comprised of close to 50%

women, and several of them are working mothers. So, despite the outcome of the 2016 presidential election, other countries have already been led by women (many times over the course of hundreds of years), and the U.S. is beginning to recognize their contributions in local and regional politics.

Community Organizing: An Urban Case Example

My daughters and I had the opportunity to canvas with Kim Janey during her 2017 campaign for Boston City Council. I met Janey in 1999 when we worked at a nonprofit organization, Parents United for Child Care, in downtown Boston. Parents United for Child Care was a wonderful nonprofit organization with dedicated employees who supported the organization's mission of creating access to affordable, quality childcare throughout the city of Boston and surrounding areas. I was one of several **AmeriCorps** members at the organization. My service term was for a 1-year period, and I worked on different service projects, along with helping staff members when needed. Janey was a **community organizer**, so she was always in and out of the office, as much of her work was done in the field. A community organizer mobilizes community members so that the community can address prominent social issues that affect their neighborhood. Community organizers work diligently to bring together community members to increase communication and civic engagement within neighborhoods.

During my AmeriCorps year, I had the opportunity to work with several after school programs, help with projects, and attend many events and meetings in the community. Attending meeting with community organizers provided great learning experiences. You were able to engage with community members, hear concerns, listen to community members exchange ideas and share resources, and develop plans of action.

Nearly 20 years later, Janey and I, along with my daughters, were walking through the streets of Roxbury, canvassing for her upcoming election. As we walked through Roxbury with Kim, she pointed out houses and streets where family members and friends lived. It was great to have the opportunity to accompany her and listen as she responded to questions and discussed community issues with residents. As we made our way up and down the streets, we occasionally would see people walking, driving, or parking their car who would wave and speak to Janey. She always took a moment to chat, remind people of the upcoming election, and ask if she could count on their votes.

Throughout the afternoon, we chatted about her community and decision to run for city council. Kim is a fourth generation Roxbury resident. Her father's grandparents moved to Roxbury nearly 100 years ago, and six generations later she and her family still reside in the neighborhood. Janey also has a connection to the South End. Her mother's grandparents migrated from the South to Boston and settled in the South End. Kim grew up in Roxbury but also spent a good portion of her childhood in the South End. Over the generations, the Janey family has been very active in their community. Janey's family consists of educators, artists, entrepreneurs, activists, and community organizers (Janey, 2018a). Janey's work in community organizing and advocacy has impacted many neighborhoods across Boston, including Roxbury and South End. Over the last 20 years, Janey has worked toward creating change on issues such as racial justice, equity in education, economic inequality, and community empowerment. Janey helped facilitate the development of schools, create educational policy that promotes diversity and inclusion in schools, coordinate panels and town halls for public officials and community members to discuss social issues, and mobilize community members to become empowered residents that promote change in their local schools and communities. (Janey, 2018a).

As we canvassed through her community, I asked her how people responded when she asked them for their vote. She told me that people often asked, "Why should they vote for her? What would be different if they voted for her? What was she going to do once she took office?" She shared her stance on social issues, would listen to their concerns, but she also kindly told people that she could not accomplish everything on her own. She often reminded people that she alone could not create change, but that "we" can work together and create change in "our" community.

Kim Janey retired her canvassing tennis shoes on the day of the election. By the end of her campaign, Janey personally knocked on 10,000 doors (personal interview, June 11, 2017). Janey's tenacious drive and love for her community led her to victory in the 2017 Boston City Council election. Councilor Kim Janey is the first woman to represent District 7, which includes Roxbury and sections of Dorchester, South End, and Fenway. On February 14, 2018, at the Boston City Council meeting, Councilor Janey gave her maiden speech, discussing the challenges and opportunities that small business owners face in her district as well as throughout the city of Boston.

She discussed the quest for the American dream and how many people are struggling to achieve their version of the dream due to racial injustice and income inequality. She spoke of how communities suffer when community members experience economic and social struggles. She also mentioned that when people can build wealth through homeownership and small business, it helps to provide growth to the community (Janey, 2018a). In her speech she also discussed that at the core of thriving communities are successful businesses, which create economic growth with employment opportunities, increase the tax revenue of a city, and make the communities desirable to homebuyers.

Think about the concept of the "Main Street" in villages and towns: The main street houses small businesses for community members to access, and the residential community is built around the main street. When small businesses on the main street are bustling, it increases the value of the community. In contrast, when there are empty storefronts and limited economic opportunity in the area, the area often experiences an economic, social, and residential decline. To prevent neighborhood declines, there are two things that lead communities toward economic prosperity: thriving businesses and homeownership. These are two points that Janey discussed in her maiden speech:

> We need communities where people can live, work, and play. Our local business districts need to be places where you can work in an office, dry clean your clothes, enjoy a meal in a sit-down restaurant, buy a cute outfit for yourself or a gift for a friend, catch a performance in a theater, and shop for healthy, affordable groceries for your family. This is a vision within our reach, and together we can make it a reality. (Janey, 2018a)

Janey speaks of a community where community members are residents, work in the local business district, and enjoy local entertainment. The places that she speaks about are realistic features of a community, but in many low-income communities these types of resources are unavailable. When areas have high rates of crime, violence, and drugs, they become undesirable, poverty-stricken areas with struggling business districts. Occasionally, investors are attracted to decaying neighborhoods because low-income neighborhoods that undergo **gentrification** typically return a high profit on investment. Investors purchase for low prices, invest in revitalization, and sell at high costs. The neighborhood experiences an increase in residential and commercial rent costs, property values increase, and new businesses move into the area. As these community improvements occur, long-time community residents and business owners who rent are often pushed out. Typically, they are pushed to another undesirable area where they can afford to rent, and the **cycle of poverty** continues. Nothing is solved for the poor population who occupies the area; poverty is simply relocated to another area.

When people do not invest in their community—economically and socially—it is easy for outsiders to invest and exert control over the community. Lack of community investment is what makes gentrification—as well as foreign ownership of business and property—possible in communities across America. If people want to see growth in their communities and to preserve them, they must become civically engaged in the community and take an active role in being part of the communal growth. Civic engagement and community organizing by community members are two tools that can create transformative, positive change in communities.

2018 Midterm Elections

There were many historic victories on the night of the 2018 midterm elections. Across many news outlets, it was called "the night of firsts." It was a night that represented the diversity of America, as women, Muslims, Native Americans, and LGBT candidates celebrated their wins. It was also a night that showed the power of civic engagement and transformative change, as many elected officials made history with their victorious wins.

In Michigan, Democratic candidate Rashida Tlaib became not only one of the first Muslims in Congress, but also the first Palestinian American woman to serve in Congress. Ilhan Omar also represents the Democratic party, and she too is Muslim. She represents Minnesota's fifth Congressional district, and she is the first Somali American woman to serve in Congress (Silverstein, 2018).

There were many more victories for the Democratic party. Sharice Davids and Deb Haaland are the first Native American Congresswomen. Davids won in New Mexico, and Haaland was elected in Kansas. Haaland is also the first lesbian Congresswoman to represent

Kansas (Silverstein, 2018). Kyrsten Sinema, a Democrat, is Arizona's first female senator. She is also the first senator to openly share that she is bisexual (Cooney, 2018). In New York, the youngest woman, Alexandria Ocasio-Cortez, was elected to Congress. At the time of election, Cortez was 29 years old. The state of Maine elected its first female governor, Janet Mills. Mills is a Democrat and was previously the state's attorney general. Voters in Colorado elected Jared Polis, who is the first governor to openly share that he is gay. Ayanna Pressley first made history when she became the first African American woman elected to Boston's City Council, and she made history again when she became the first African American Congresswoman for the state of Massachusetts (Silverstein, 2018).

Tennessee voters elected the state's first female senator, Marsha Blackburn, who is a Republican. Kristi Noem, a Republican, is the first female governor for South Dakota. The state of Iowa also made history, as voters elected Republican candidate Abby Finkenauer. She is the state's first female Congresswoman. History continued to be made on the night of the elections, as more than 100 women won seats in the House of Representatives, which is a fourth of the total number of members (435). This number, by far, exceeds the prior record of 85 women (Watkins, 2018). As each elected official transitions into their role, the nation will be watching to see how each person carries out their term in office. One can only wonder what the cohort from "the night of firsts" will achieve while in their positions.

The Obama Foundation

FORMER PRESIDENT, BARACK OBAMA

In 1983, a 22-year-old Barack Obama decided to become a community organizer. He was determined to organize people and create change for marginalized populations. He left New York and headed to the South Side of Chicago to work with the Developing Communities Project. As a community organizer, Obama would visit people's homes to discuss social issues and concerns. At times, people were hesitant to do the home visit or engage with Obama. There were even instances when people forgot about the home visit and questioned whether they should let Obama enter their home. After he initiated conversation, people eventually became comfortable and shared community concerns. Obama performed many home visits and noticed that many community members shared the same concerns. Residents shared stories about racial tension, White flight from urban areas, and the declines that areas experienced after White residents moved away. People also shared stories of personal success such as home ownership and children graduating from college. Unfortunately, their personal successes did not overshadow the declines in their neighborhood (Obama, 2004).

As an organizer, Obama urged people to look past their individual success and observe the happenings and struggles in their community. He had to motivate people to step outside of their personal surroundings and become engaged in their declining communities. With these early community organizing experiences, Obama learned that individual accomplishments and community decline could coexist in the same space. The goal was to shift people's thinking from focusing solely on investing in individual growth and to encourage them to also invest in community growth (Obama, 2004). Through his community organizing efforts, he helped people understand that community growth would lead to greater economic, social, and political growth for community members.

Community organizing is **grass roots politics** that educated Obama about "the community"; he learned about the community by spending time in it and listening to community members. During his 3 years of community organizing in the South Side of Chicago, Obama developed into an effective community organizer. He learned about the history of the community from community members and understood their concerns. He helped connect and gather community members to reflect on the past, discuss the current state of their community, and encourage people to work toward creating a better future for their community. He motivated and supported community members to take action in their communities rather than be idle residents watching the decline of their neighborhood

FIGURE 10.1 Senator Barack Obama Speaks at an Event in South Carolina.

and waiting for someone to rescue them (Obama, 2004). Through community organizing, Obama was able to empower community members by increasing their cultural and social capital. By obtaining knowledge and investing in community, community members can create a supportive environment that promotes growth and opportunity.

FORMER FIRST LADY, MICHELLE OBAMA

Michelle Robinson was born and raised in the South Side of Chicago. Her father worked for the Chicago Department of Water, and her mother was a stay-at-home mom who managed the home and raised Michelle and her brother, Craig. Michelle completed her primary and secondary studies in Chicago public schools. She attended college at Princeton University and law school at Harvard University. In 1988, she accepted a position at a law firm in Chicago, but after a few years she decided to pursue a career in community development and public service. At the firm, she met the man she would eventually marry, Barack Obama. She continued working in Chicago as the assistant commissioner of planning and development at City Hall, and she was the executive director of public allies in Chicago (White House, n.d.).

Public Allies is an AmeriCorps program that is offered in 25 locations across the United States. The program provides supportive and empowering resources to emerging young leaders. The program helps underrepresented youth become more active in their communities by helping them identify and understand social issues and equip them with the skills to create change in their communities (Public Allies, 2020).

Michelle, like Barack, enjoyed public service and working closely with community members. She continued her community-focused work when she became the associate dean of student services at the University of Chicago. In this role, she created a new program for the university—a community service program. When she transitioned to the University Medical Center, she worked as the vice president of community and external affairs, and under her direction volunteerism increased dramatically (White House, n.d.).

During her time as first lady of the United States, Mrs. Obama continued to dedicate her work efforts toward public service and community. She launched four initiatives while in the White House: Let's Move, Joining Forces, Reach Higher, and Let Girls Learn. Mrs. Obama dedicated her time toward issues that were important to her, and she wanted to create change in areas that needed attention. She urged communities to tackle the issue of childhood obesity so that

FIGURE 10.2 First Lady Michelle Obama Participates in a Roundtable Discussion in Support of the Let Girls Learn Initiative at a High School in Unification Town, Liberia, June 27, 2016.

Source: https://commons.wikimedia.org/wiki/File:Michelle_Obama_participates_in_a_roundtable_discussion_in_support_of_the_Let_Girls_Learn_initiative.jpg.

children could develop into healthy young adults. She worked with Dr. Jill Biden to promote the importance of supporting military families. She also launched an initiative that encouraged youth to pursue a college education by educating youth on the college application process and increasing college preparation services in high schools. Her last initiative focused on girls having access to education. In 2015, she partnered with her husband to get a global commitment for countries to educate and uplift their young girls through the Let Girls Learn initiative (White House, n.d.).

THE FOUNDATION TODAY

The Obamas have a collective history of serving their communities, community organizing, and empowering people to become civically engaged in their communities. Their community efforts have impacted many, and their dedication to community and civic engagement is demonstrated in the mission of the **Obama Foundation**. The foundation encourages and supports civic engagement by inspiring the next generation of civic leaders. The foundation provides resources to anyone who wants to make a positive impact in their community. It supports people who are leaders in their community, as well as those seeking to become more civically engaged in their communities (Obama Foundation, n.d.). In 2018, the foundation shared its first set of projects.

LEADERS, AFRICA

This is a project that connects 200 leaders from across the continent of Africa to address issues in their communities and throughout the countries of Africa. The foundation provides supportive resources to empower and inspire future leaders to become agents of change. During the year-long initiative, the emerging leaders participate in trainings, leadership development, and problem-solving workshops (Obama Foundation, n.d.).

COMMUNITY LEADERSHIP CORPS

The Leadership Corps focuses on providing skills to empower youth, ages 18 to 25, with the skills to become future leaders. The program supports youth as they tackle an issue in their community. The program provides face-to-face and online educational resources for youth to support them through each stage of the project process—from conceptualization to implementation, to assessment. They also receive ongoing support throughout the year; the mentorship aspect of the project is highly important because they can seek guidance at any time during the project. Having access to mentorship is a great asset and resource for becoming an effective, successful leader (Obama Foundation, n.d.).

SCHOLARS

The Obama Foundation Scholars program is offered through the University of Chicago and Columbia University. The 1-year program provides young emerging leaders with educational and supportive resources that help them become effective leaders. Scholars gain valuable forms of social and cultural capital through the program such as experiential experiences, skill-based learning, and community discussions. The program educates, empowers, and brings together the next generation of leaders from different countries around the world. At the end of the program, scholars take newly gained knowledge back to their communities and continue to work toward creating change. As Obama Foundation alumni, the scholars have the opportunity to share their knowledge and experiences with other emerging leaders who attend programs at the foundation (Obama Foundation, n.d.).

MY BROTHER'S KEEPER ALLIANCE

In February 2014, President Obama began the My Brother's Keeper program. The program was designed to support boys and young men of color and decrease the opportunity gaps that this population often experiences in society. The program evolved into My Brother's Keeper Alliance in 2015 and became one of the foundation's programs in 2017. The alliance provides supportive resources for young men of color to help them reach their full potential. In spring 2018, the alliance introduced a national challenge competition for cities that need supportive resources to create opportunity for young men of color in the community. The foundation is building on a body of research that demonstrates how citizens, community, and organizations can provide supportive services to young men of color that reduce barriers such as violence in communities and increase opportunity through services such as mentorship and leadership training. When communities support their boys and young men of color, communities and families also excel (Obama Foundation, n.d.).

FELLOWSHIP

This is a 2-year program that supports civic leaders from around the globe. The fellows have a wide range of diverse backgrounds; the group is comprised of artists, educators, organizers, and more. During the fellowship program, each fellow follows an individualized plan that guides their work and cultivates their leadership abilities. The non-residential, fellowship provides a multitude of resources that support fellows as they address social issues and lead transformative change in their communities (Obama Foundation, n.d.).

SUMMIT

The Obama Foundation hosted 100 civic leaders from all over the world in fall 2017. The two-day summit brought together world leaders to share experiences and discuss innovative solutions. The summit also featured music, technology, and civic art from across the globe. The event included small group sessions to encourage conversation among civic leaders. The summit offered a wealth of resources and provided opportunities for participants to learn from each other (Obama Foundation, n.d.).

TRAINING DAYS

Training days are great events that introduce young people to civic engagement. Some people have low civic engagement and need encouragement to engage in civic activities. These events motivate people to

FIGURE 10.3 President Barack Obama and First Lady Michelle Obama Looking at the Chicago Skyline.

Source: https://commons.wikimedia.org/wiki/File:Barack_and_Michelle_Obama_looking_at_Chicago.jpg.

become civically involved in their communities. The first training day was held in Chicago; there were a 150 young people, ranging in age from 18 to 24. The participants learned how to use personal testimony to stimulate change. They also learned how to identify an issue, organize ideas, and take steps toward creating change. The training days are offered in partnership with various organizations such as churches, universities, and youth-affiliated organizations (Obama Foundation, n.d.).

PUBLIC INVOLVEMENT

The Obama Foundation is still evolving, and there will be more projects to come. One unique aspect of the foundation is that they are involving the public in guiding their projects. The foundation is asking the American people to identify the social issues that are important to them. With input from the public, the foundation can organize and support people as they address social issues and create transformative change in communities throughout the world.

Conclusion

Everyone has a different life story and understanding the context in which people develop is important. Context influences behavior, emotion, language, social practices, and cognition. Developing children are affected by their surroundings—family, community members, the neighborhood, schools, and more. Children across social classes have positive and negative developmental experiences. However, children who grow up in poverty often have greater exposure to adverse childhood experiences because they face personal and neighborhood adversities such as high rates of violence, crime, and drug trafficking.

Poverty research translates the social issue of poverty into qualitative and quantitative data so researchers can study the causes and consequences of poverty. In order to effectively address poverty, practitioners, academics, organizations, and policymakers need to continuously study poverty and its effects. This work is shared by many institutions, as poverty is too big of an issue for one institution to study. By working collectively, universities and the federal government can generate poverty-related research and develop approaches that address many aspects of poverty. However, there are some solutions that can be enacted through community members becoming more civically engaged in their communities.

Our society is at a political, social, and economic crossroads; people are taking a more active stance in politics and their communities. When people in low-income communities organize and become more civically engaged, it helps to strengthen their community and support the healthy development of families and children. A strong community is instrumental in creating social change; effective and sustainable organized movements embody a sense of community. There is strength in numbers, and people can use their collective resources and capital to uplift their communities and community members. They can collectively use their civic voices to inform poverty-related policy and legislation, create access to resources for children and adults, create better schools and educational opportunities for youth, and overall improve the quality of low-income communities.

END-OF-CHAPTER ACTIVITIES

Discussion Questions

1. How does poverty research help to inform poverty-related policy and legislation?

2. What can community organizers do to help increase civic engagement in low-income communities?

3. Why is it important to balance revitalization with community preservation?

4. Why are AmeriCorps members an important resource to nonprofit organizations?

5. How is the Obama Foundation supporting and cultivating emerging leaders?

Interview a Community Organizer

Explore a community organization that promotes and supports creating change in low-income communities through community organizing, organizations that target social issues such as educational justice, homelessness, community improvement, and environmental awareness. Two examples are the Chicago Coalition for the Homeless and the Massachusetts Senior Action Council. To find an organization, it is recommended that you use an Internet search engine or visit idealist.org.

Interview one of the community organizers and find out the following information:

- Describe the organizer's current projects and social issues being targeted.

- What methods do they use to get community members involved in community organizing efforts?

- What are some of the challenges they face in getting community members to organize?

Historic Structures

Identify a low-income community within a 30–50-mile radius of your home. If you need assistance locating an area, information is available through the U.S. Census Bureau, or you can focus on economic opportunity zones such as those listed on the Economic Innovation Group's website: eig.org/opportunityzones. Once you locate an area, research the history of the area and the architectural design of structures in the area. Consider the following questions as you conduct your research:

1. How do individuals and communities get residential and business structures designated as historic landmarks?

2. Why is it beneficial to seek neighborhood designations/ historic districts?

3. Are there any historic structures in the area that you researched? Discuss their historic significance.

4. Are the structures being preserved?

Service-Learning Activity: Use Your Civic Voice

This is an advocacy activity.

Identify a social issue that needs to be addressed in your community or one near you. Find the contact information for your councilperson, senator, or congressperson. Write an e-mail or letter addressing the issue and discuss why the issue is important and how the community will benefit from creating change in regard to the issue. For writing tips, visit the American Psychological Association website (apa.org/index) to view sample e-mails and letters and guidance on how to locate your elected official. Once you are on the site, search "Psychologist's Guide to Advocacy," or access apa.org/advocacy/guide.

References

Bodgas, M. (2017). *16 inspiring working moms who made history by winning 2017 elections.* https://www.workingmother.com/14-inspiring-working-moms-who-made-history-by-winning-2017-elections

Cooney, S. (2018). Here are some of the women who made history in the 2018 midterm elections. *Time.* http://time.com/5323592/2018-elections-women-history-records/

Glasmeier, A. (2018). *New data up: Calculation of the living wage.* http://living-wage.mit.edu/articles/27-new-data-up-calculation-of-the-living-wage

Glatter, H. (2017). Six women of color were elected to Boston City Council. *Boston Magazine.* https://www.bostonmagazine.com/news/2017/11/08/women-election-2017-boston/

Janey, K. (2018). http://kimjaney.org/maiden-speech/

Institute for Research on Poverty, University Wisconsin-Madison. (2020a). *National Poverty Research Center.* https://www.irp.wisc.edu/national-poverty-research-center/

Institute for Research on Poverty, University Wisconsin-Madison. (2020b). *Research networks.* https://www.irp.wisc.edu/research-networks/

Obama, B. (2004). *Dreams from my father: A story of race and inheritance.* Broadway Paperbacks.

Obama Foundation. (n.d.). https://www.obama.org/

Public Allies. (2020). http://publicallies.org/

Silverstein, J. (2018, November 7). *Election 2018: Night of firsts with historic wins for Muslims, Native Americans, Women and LGBT candidates.* CBS News. https://www.cbsnews.com/news/election-2018-night-of-firsts-with-historic-wins-for-muslims-native-americans-women-and-lgbt-candidates/

Watkins, E. (2018, November 9). *Record number of women elected to the house.* CNN Politics. https://www.cnn.com/2018/11/07/politics/women-house-senate/index.html

White House. (n.d.). *Michelle Obama.* https://www.whitehouse.gov/about-the-white-house/first-ladies/michelle-obama/

Afterword

When I was an undergraduate, I remember sitting in my urban studies classes learning about redlining, urban renewal, the birth of suburbia, White flight, and zoning of neighborhoods. I was always very intrigued with the lecture topics and class discussions. I realized that my fascination with the information stemmed from my childhood experiences. I lived in neighborhoods that were examples of topics discussed in my urban studies classes so I could easily relate to the information presented in lectures, slides, discussions, and readings.

During my youth, I grew up in a low-income neighborhood. As a young child, I often wondered, "Why are there differences between neighborhoods? Why doesn't someone fix the differences?" During childhood life is so basic, so you believe that if people know something is not working then they will fix it. However, as I became older, I realized that life was not that simple. With each passing year, the "child blinders" lifted and the "real world" began to filter in.

St. Elmo Village

My family lived in Los Angeles, California, in an area called Vineyard located in mid-city. Vineyard, like many urban communities, experienced periods of development, deterioration, and revitalization. At one time, the neighborhood was home to Wilt Chamberlain, Red Foxx, and Mary Pickford, one of the stars from *The Little Rascals*. Many areas, like ones within mid-city Los Angeles, experienced an economic downturn caused by White flight and the birth of suburbia. By the 1960s, the Vineyard area was in ruins.

Rozzell and Roderick Sykes, uncle and nephew, were visual artists who rented a couple of bungalow-style homes on St. Elmo Drive. Both were talented, thriving artists, but being an African American artist in Los Angeles during the 1960s had many challenges. At that time, many traditional galleries were not interested in displaying Roderick's art (Lieu, 2015). By 1969, Roderick and Rozzell, along with a group of artists, decided to work together to develop an environment to create and display art. They saw the potential to create something amazing in the community, so they created an art space that they called St. Elmo Village. In 1971, the Sykes raised enough money to purchase the property—10 bungalows and 10 garages, which were originally part of Mary Pickford's horse stables. The village became a live, work, and teaching space. The village began to thrive with support from people like City Councilman Tom Bradley, who later became mayor of Los Angeles (Berestein, 1995).

As a young girl, I remember walking with my mom a block and half and entering what seemed like a new world. I do not remember each moment of every visit, but the memories that I do have of St. Elmo Village are magical. Imagine stepping from a black-and-white picture into a world of color; that is what I experienced every time I visited the village. Everything was so vibrant and colorful, and the space encouraged you to be free and create.

Back in the 60s, a 27-year old, Jeff Bridges (a young and upcoming actor), used to visit the village with his girlfriend. His girlfriend and Rozell were friends, and she introduced Bridges to Rozell. Rozell and Bridges became good friends, and he would invite Bridges to play his guitar while he painted. In an article (Stewart, 2017), Bridges cites Rozzell Sykes as a mentor. He says that Sykes taught him that life is not about how many things that you possess, but it's about creating beautiful art with what you have. In 1969, Bridges planted the first two plants in the village's cactus garden. The cactus garden became a wonderful metaphor for the village and surrounding neighborhood, as cacti survive in harsh conditions while retaining their beauty and quiet grace.

As the late 70s transitioned into the 80s many urban areas throughout the United States were once again experiencing declines. In the early 70s, America was still sending tens of thousands of young Americans to fight in the Vietnam War. After the war ended in 1975, many cities and towns across America experienced postwar struggles. Communities and people across America lost many loved ones in the war, and returning veterans often experienced difficulties with transitioning back into civilian life. There were other social problems on the rise as the late 70s transitioned in the 80s: the crack epidemic and an increase in gangs. People were fleeing the cities in droves and moving to suburban communities. These factors affected certain areas within mid-city immensely, and my neighborhood was one that experienced a lot of negative change.

In earlier times, the Vineyard area also underwent zoning changes that permitted the building of multi-family, residential dwellings, which changed the landscape of the neighborhood from single-family houses to a community that was a mixture of houses and apartments. This shift from a stable, single housing community to apartment renters rotating in and out of the neighborhood was another catalyst in the economic and social decline of the community.

As a young child, I remember observing the neighborhood transform. Many of the long-term residents moved away, and new residents moved in. Property owners seemed to lower their renting standards, and the overall care and maintenance of rental properties declined. Homeowners, such as my parents, struggled to sustain the sense of community that once existed because the rental properties created a transient population that was not invested in preserving the community. The neighborhood experienced a slow visual and social deterioration. It was so sad to see how the area changed. I remember when we no longer walked to my art classes at St. Elmo Village, but we started to drive the short distance. Even though I was very young, I knew that the neighborhood was changing rapidly. Toward the end of my time at the village, I remembered that the creative space gave me a break from my decaying neighborhood. The space was a breath of fresh air that provided hope in a community that appeared to be hopeless. My family eventually moved from St. Elmo Drive, but the village continued to be a positive, stable fixture in the mid-city community. Over the years, the village offered free art workshops and art outreach programs, was used as a site for field trips and tours, housed artists in residence, and operated as a voting polling station.

I share the St. Elmo Village story for several reasons. The village has been in the Vineyard area and mid-city Los Angeles for over 50 years. St. Elmo's Village is a safe space where youth and adults can gather, explore the arts, and have a creative outlet. It has survived social, economic, and political changes within the area. When the area suffered massive declines in the 1980s due to crime, gangs, and drugs, the village stood strong and remained a beacon of hope in the community. As the surrounding area deteriorated, the creative space provided resources to its low-income community members, which were mostly African American and Latin American residents.

St. Elmo Village is a great example of how community organizations can provide resources to individuals living in low-income neighborhoods. The village provides low-income community members and schools with access to the arts, which is something that many people across social classes do not experience often, if at all. St. Elmo's Village has not only supported arts; the organization created a space that promoted community gathering, which in turn supports communication among community members, increased civic participation and engagement, and community preservation. The village has functioned as a voting polling station during elections, which provided a historically marginalized population with easy access to cast their votes.

When community organizations provide resources to low-income populations, they invest in the growth of the community and its residents. This can help empower community members, increase their investment in the community, and encourage residents to create positive change in their communities. The story of St. Elmo Village shows how community organizations can create hope and provide resources in communities that face adversity.

References

Berestein, L. (1995, January 1). St. Elmo Village creator lauded at memorial. *LA Times.* http://articles.latimes.com/1995-01-01/news/ci-15472_1_ st-elmo-village

Lieu, K. (2015, March 25). *St. Elmo Village and the importance of art-making in childhood development.* Psychology Tomorrow. http://psychologytomorrowmagazine.com/st-elmo-village-art-child-development/

Stewart, S. (2017, August 10). Jeff Bridges is committed to living the dudeliest life ever. *NY Post.* http://nypost.com/2017/08/10/jeff-bridges-is-committed-to-living-the-dudeliest-life-ever/amp/

Appendix A

Family Health History—Female Version

Question Number	Verbatim Question	Response Categories and Comments
1a	What was the month and year of your birth? Month _____	
	Year _____	
1b	What state were you born in? State _____	enter two letter state code DC = District of Columbia
	I was born outside the U.S.	1 = box checked
2	What is your sex?	1 = male 2 = female
3a	What is your race?	1 = asian 2 = black 3 = white 4 = american indian 5 = other 9 = multiple boxes checked
3b	Are you of Mexican, Latino, or Hispanic origin?	1 = yes 2 = no.
4	Please check how far you've gone in school. ... (Choose one)	1 = Didn't go to high school 2 = Some high school 3 = High school graduate or GED 4 = Some college or technical school 5 = 4 year college graduate 9 = Multiple boxes checked
5	What is your current marital status? Are you now. ...	1 = married 2 = not married, but living together with a partner 3 = widowed 4 = separated 5 = divorced 6 = never married 9 = multiple answers checked

(continued)

Source: CDC, "Family Health History - Female Version."

Question Number	Verbatim Question	Response Categories and Comments
6a	How many times have you been married?	1 = 1 2 = 2 3 = 3 4 = 4 or more 5 = never married 9 = multiple boxes checked
6b	During what month and year were you first married? Month _____	Range: 1–12
	Year _____	Range: 10–96
	Never married	1 = never married
7a	Which of the following best describes your employment status?	1 = full time (35 hours or more) 2 = part-time (1–34 hours) 3 = Not employed outside the home 9 = multiple items checked
	If you are currently employed outside the home:	
7b	How many days of work did you miss in the past 30 days due to stress or feeling depressed?	Range: 0–30
7c	How many days of work did you miss in the past 30 days due to poor physical health?	Range: 0–30
8	For most of your childhood, did your family own their home?	1 = yes 2 = no
9a	During your childhood, how many times did you move residences, even in the same town? # of times _____	Range: 00–99
10	How old was your mother when you were born? Age _____	
11a	How much education does/did your mother have? (Choose one)	1 = Didn't go to high school 2 = Some high school 3 = high school graduate or GED 4 = Some college or technical school 5 = College graduate or higher 9 = Multiple boxes checked
11b	How much education does/did your father have? (Choose one)	1 = Didn't go to high school 2 = Some high school 3 = high school graduate or GED 4 = Some college or technical school 5 = College graduate or higher

Question Number	Verbatim Question	Response Categories and Comments
12	Have you ever been pregnant? *If no skip to question 16*	1 = yes 2 = no
13a	Are you pregnant now?	1 = yes 2 = no 3 = don't know
13b	How many times have you been pregnant? Number _____	Range: 00–99
13c	How many pregnancies resulted in the birth of a child? Number: _____	Range: 00–99
13d	How old were you the first time you became pregnant? age: _____	Range: 00–99
13e	The first time you became pregnant, how old was the person who got you pregnant? age: _____	Range: 00–99
13f	During what month and year did your first pregnancy end? Month _____	Range: 01–12
	Year _____	Range: 00–99
13g	How did your first pregnancy end?	1 = live births 2 = stillbirth/miscarriage 3 = tubal or ectopic pregnancy 4 = elective abortion 5 = other 9 = multiple responses.
13h	When your first pregnancy began, did you intend to get pregnant at that time in your life?	1 = yes 2 = no 3 = didn't care
14	Were you ever pregnant a second time? *If no skip to question 16*	1 = yes 2 = no
15a	What month and year did your second pregnancy end? month _____	Range: 01–12
15a	year _____	Range: 00–99
15b	How did your second pregnancy end?	1 = live birth 2 = stillbirth/miscarriage 3 = tubal or ectopic pregnancy 4 = elective abortion 5 = other 9 = multiple responses
15c	When your second pregnancy began, did you intend to get pregnant at that time in your life?	1 = yes 2 = no 3 = didn't care

(continued)

Question Number	Verbatim Question	Response Categories and Comments
16	*In order to get a more complete picture of the health of our patients, the next three questions are about* <u>voluntary</u> *sexual experiences.* How old were you the first time you had sexual intercourse? Age _____	
	Never had intercourse	1 = box checked
17	With how many different partners have you ever had sexual intercourse? # of partners_____	number of intercourse partners, lifetime Range: 0–999
18	During the past year, with how many different partners have you ever had sexual intercourse? # of partners _____	number of intercourse partners, past year Range: 0–999
19a	Have you smoked at least 100 cigarettes in your entire life?	1 = yes 2 = no
19b	How old were you when you began to smoke cigarettes fairly regularly? age: _____	Range: 0–99
20c	Do you smoke cigarettes now?	1 = yes 2 = no
20d	If yes, on average, about how many cigarettes a day do you smoke? # cigarettes: _____	Range: 0–99
21a	If you used to smoke cigarettes but don't smoke now, about how many cigarettes a day did you smoke? # cigarettes: _____	Range: 00–99
21b	How old were you when you quit? Age _____	Range: 00–99
22a	During your first 18 years of life did your father smoke?	1 = yes 2 = no
22b	During your first 18 years of life did your mother smoke?	1 = yes 2 = no
23a	During the past month, about how many days per week did you exercise for recreation or to keep in shape?	Range: 0–7
23b	During the past month, when you exercised for recreation or to keep in shape, how long did you usually exercise (minutes)? _____ minutes	0 = 0 1 = 1–19 2 = 20–29 3 = 30–39 4 = 40–49 5 = 50–59 6 = 60 or more 9 = multiple responses

Question Number	Verbatim Question	Response Categories and Comments
24a	What is the most you have ever weighed? Weight in pounds _____	Range: 60–500
24b	How old were you then? age: _____	Range: 18–99
25a	How old were you when you had your first drink of alcohol other than a few sips? age: _____	Range: 00–99
	Never drank alcohol	1 = Yes
	During each of the following age intervals, what was your usual number of drinks of alcohol per week?	
25b1	Age 19–29	1 = None 2 = Less than 6 per wk 3 = 7–13 per wk 4 = 14 or more per wk 9 = multiple responses
25b2	Age 30–39	1 = None 2 = Less than 6 per wk 3 = 7–13 per wk 4 = 14 or more per wk 9 = multiple responses
25b3	Age 40–49	1 = None 2 = Less than 6 per wk 3 = 7–13 per wk 4 = 14 or more per wk 9 = multiple responses
25b4	Age 50 and older	1 = None 2 = Less than 6 per wk 3 = 7–13 per wk 4 = 14 or more per wk 9 = multiple responses
25c	During the past month, have you had any beer, wine, wine coolers, cocktails or liquor?	1 = yes 2 = no
25d	During the past month, how many <u>days per week</u> did you drink any alcoholic beverages on average?	Range: - 0–7
25e	On the days when you drank, about how many <u>drinks per day</u> did you have on average?	1 = 1 2 = 2 3 = 3 4 = 4 or more 5 = didn't drink in past month 9 = multiple responses

(continued)

Question Number	Verbatim Question	Response Categories and Comments
25f	Considering all types of alcoholic beverages, how many times during the past month did you have 5 or more drinks on an occasion? Number of times _____	Range: 0–999
25g	During the past month, how many times have you driven when you've had perhaps too much to drink? Number of times _____	Range: 0–999
25h	During the past 30 days, how many times did you ride in a car or other vehicle driven by someone who had been drinking alcohol? Number of times _____	Range: 0–999
26	Have you ever had a problem with your use of alcohol?	1 = yes 2 = no
27	Have you ever considered yourself to be an alcoholic?	1 = yes 2 = no
28a	During your first 18 years of life did you live with anyone who was a problem drinker or alcoholic?	1 = yes 2 = no
28b	If "yes" check all who were:	
	father	1 = if box checked
	mother	1 = if box checked
	brothers	1 = if boxed checked
	other relatives	1 = if box checked
	other non-relative	1 = if box checked
	sisters	1 = if box checked
29	Have you ever been married to someone (or lived with someone as if you were married) who was a problem drinker or alcoholic?	1 = yes 2 = no
30a	Have you ever used street drugs?	1 = yes 2 = no
30b	If "yes" how old were you the first time you used them? Age _____	Range: 0–99
30c	About how many times have you used street drugs?	0 = 0 1 = 1–2 2 = 3–10 3 = 11–25 4 = 26–99 5 = 100+ 9 = multiple responses

Question Number	Verbatim Question	Response Categories and Comments
30d	Have you ever had a problem with street drugs?	1 = yes 2 = no
30e	Have you ever considered yourself to be addicted to street drugs?	1 = yes 2 = no
30f	Have you ever injected street drugs?	1 = yes 2 = no
31	Have you ever been under the care of a psychologist, psychiatrist, or therapist?	1 = yes 2 = no
32a	Has a doctor, nurse, or health professional ever asked you about family or household problems during your childhood?	1 = yes 2 = no . = no entry by respondent
32b	How many close friends or relatives would help you with your emotional problems or feelings if you needed it?	1 = none 2 = 1 3 = 2 4 = 3 or more
	During your first 18 years of life, was anyone in your household. ...	
33	Did you live with anyone who used street drugs?	1 = yes 2 = no
34a	Were your parents ever separated or divorced?	1 = yes 2 = no
34b	Did you ever live with a stepfather?	1 = yes 2 = no
34c	Did you ever live with a stepmother?	1 = yes 2 = no
35	Did you ever live in a foster home?	1 = yes 2 = no
36a	Did you ever run away from home for more than one day?	1 = yes 2 = no
36b	Did your brothers or sisters run away from home for more than one day?	1 = yes 2 = no
37	Was anyone in your household depressed or mentally ill?	1 = yes 2 = no
38	Did anyone in your household attempt to commit suicide?	1 = yes 2 = no
39a	Did anyone in your household go to prison?	1 = yes 2 = no
39b	Did anyone in your household ever commit a serious crime?	1 = yes 2 = no
40a	Have you ever attempted to commit suicide?	1 = yes 2 = no

(continued)

Question Number	Verbatim Question	Response Categories and Comments
40b	If "yes", how old were you the first time you attempted suicide? Age _____	Range: 1–99
40c	If "yes", how old were you the last time you attempted suicide? Age _____	Range: 1–99
40d	How many times have you attempted suicide? # of times _____	Range: 01–99,
40e	Did any suicide attempt ever result in an injury, poisoning, or overdose that had to be treated by a doctor or nurse?	1 = yes 2 = no
	Sometimes physical blows occur between parents. While you were growing up in your first 18 years of life, how often did your father (or stepfather) or mother's boyfriend do any to these things to your mother (or stepmother)?	
41a	Push, grab, slap or throw something at her?	1 = never 2 = once, twice 3 = sometimes 4 = often 5 = very often 9 = multiple responses
41b	Kick, bite, hit her with a fist, or hit her with something hard?	1 = never 2 = once, twice 3 = sometimes 4 = often 5 = very often 9 = multiple responses
41c	Repeatedly hit her over at least a few minutes?	1 = never 2 = once, twice 3 = sometimes 4 = often 5 = very often 9 = multiple responses
41d	Threaten her with a knife or gun, or use a knife or gun to hurt her?	1 = never 2 = once, twice 3 = sometimes 4 = often 5 = very often 9 = multiple responses
	Sometimes parents spank their children as a form of discipline. While you were growing up during your first 18 years of life:	

Question Number	Verbatim Question	Response Categories and Comments
42a	How often were you spanked?	1 = never 2 = once or twice 3 = a few times a year 4 = many times a year 5 = weekly or more 9 = multiple responses
42b	How severely were you spanked?	1 = not hard 2 = a little hard 3 = medium 4 = quite hard 5 = very hard 9 = multiple responses
42c	How old were you the last time you remember being spanked? age: _____	Range: 1–99
	While you were growing up, during your first 18 years of life, how true were each of the following statements?.	
43	You didn't have enough to eat?	1 = never true 2 = rarely true 3 = sometimes true 4 = often true 5 = very often true 9 = multiple responses
44	You knew there was someone to take care of you and protect you?	1 = never true 2 = rarely true 3 = sometimes true 4 = often true 5 = very often true 9 = multiple responses
45	People in your family called you things like "lazy" or "ugly"?	1 = never true 2 = rarely true 3 = sometimes true 4 = often true 5 = very often true 9 = multiple responses
46	Your parents were too drunk or high to take care of the family?	1 = never true 2 = rarely true 3 = sometimes true 4 = often true 5 = very often true 9 = multiple responses
47	There was someone in your family who helped you feel important or special?	1 = never true 2 = rarely true 3 = sometimes true 4 = often true 5 = very often true 9 = multiple responses

(continued)

Question Number	Verbatim Question	Response Categories and Comments
48	You had to wear dirty clothes?	1 = never true 2 = rarely true 3 = sometimes true 4 = often true 5 = very often true 9 = multiple responses
49	You felt loved?	1 = never true 2 = rarely true 3 = sometimes true 4 = often true 5 = very often true 9 = multiple responses
50	You thought your parents wished you had never been born?	1 = never true 2 = rarely true 3 = sometimes true 4 = often true 5 = very often true 9 = multiple responses
51	People in your family looked out for each other?	1 = never true 2 = rarely true 3 = sometimes true 4 = often true 5 = very often true 9 = multiple responses
52	You felt that someone in your family hated you?	1 = never true 2 = rarely true 3 = sometimes true 4 = often true 5 = very often true 9 = multiple responses
53	People in your family said hurtful or insulting things to you?	1 = never true 2 = rarely true 3 = sometimes true 4 = often true 5 = very often true 9 = multiple responses
54	People in your family felt close to each other?	1 = never true 2 = rarely true 3 = sometimes true 4 = often true 5 = very often true 9 = multiple responses
55	You believe that you were emotionally abused?	1 = never true 2 = rarely true 3 = sometimes true 4 = often true 5 = very often true 9 = multiple responses

Question Number	Verbatim Question	Response Categories and Comments
56	There was someone to take you to the doctor if you needed it?	1 = never true 2 = rarely true 3 = sometimes true 4 = often true 5 = very often true 9 = multiple responses
57	Your family was a source of strength and support?	1 = never true 2 = rarely true 3 = sometimes true 4 = often true 5 = very often true 9 = multiple responses
	Sometimes parents or other adults hurt children. While you were growing up, that is, during your first 18 years of life, how often did a parent, step-parent, or adult living in your home:	
58a	Swear at you, insult you, or put you down?	1 = never 2 = once, twice 3 = sometimes 4 = often 5 = very often 9 = multiple responses
58b	Threaten to hit you or throw something at you, but didn't do it?	1 = never 2 = once, twice 3 = sometimes 4 = often 5 = very often 9 = multiple responses
58c	Actually push, grab, shove, slap you, or throw something at you?	1 = never 2 = once, twice 3 = sometimes 4 = often 5 = very often 9 = multiple responses
58d	Hit you so hard that you had marks or were injured?	1 = never 2 = once, twice 3 = sometimes 4 = often 5 = very often 9 = multiple responses
58e	Act in a way that made you afraid that you might be physically hurt?	1 = never 2 = once, twice 3 = sometimes 4 = often 5 = very often 9 = multiple responses

(continued)

Question Number	Verbatim Question	Response Categories and Comments
	Some people, while growing up in their first 18 years of life, had a sexual experience with an <u>adult or someone at least five years older than themselves</u>. These experiences may have involved a relative family friend or stranger. During the first 18 years of life, did an adult or older relative, family friend or stranger ever:	
59a	Touch or fondle your body in a sexual way? If "Yes"	1 = yes 2 = no
	The first time this happened, how old were you? age: _____	Range: 00–99
	The first time, did this happen against your wishes?	1 = yes 2 = no
	The last time this happened, how old were you? age: _____	Range: 00–99
	About how many times did this happen to you? # times: _____	Range: 00–99
	How many different people did this to you? # people: _____	Range: 00–99
	What was the sex of the person(s) who did this?	1 = male 2 = female 3 = both 9 = multiple responses
60a	Have you touch their body in a sexual way? If "Yes":	1 = yes 2 = no
	The first time this happened, how old were you? age: _____	Range: 00–99
	The first time, did this happen against your wishes?	1 = yes 2 = no
	The last time this happened, how old were you? age: _____	Range: 00–99
	About how many times did this happen to you? # times: _____	Range: 00–99

Question Number	Verbatim Question	Response Categories and Comments
	How many different people did this to you? # people: _____	Range: 00–99
	What was the sex of the person(s) who did this?	1 = male 2 = female 3 = both 9 = multiple responses
61a	**Attempt** to have any type of sexual intercourse (oral, anal, or vaginal) with you? If "Yes":	1 = yes 2 = no
	The first time this happened, how old were you? age: _____	Range: 00–99
	The first time, did this happen against your wishes?	1 = yes 2 = no
	The last time this happened, how old were you? age: _____	Range: 00–99
	About how many times did this happen to you? # times: _____	Range: 00–99
	How many different people did this to you? # people: _____	Range: 00–99
	What was the sex of the person(s) who did this?	1 = male 2 = female 3 = both 9 = multiple responses
62a	**Actually have** any type of sexual intercourse with you (oral, anal, or vaginal) with you? If "Yes":	1 = yes 2 = no
	The first time this happened, how old were you? age: _____	Range: 00–99
	The first time, did this happen against your wishes?	1 = yes 2 = no
	The last time this happened, how old were you? age: _____	Range: 00–99
	About how many times did this happen to you? # times: _____	Range: 00–99

(continued)

Question Number	Verbatim Question	Response Categories and Comments
	How many different people did this to you? \# people: _____	Range: 00–99
	What was the sex of the person(s) who did this?	1 = male 2 = female 3 = both 9 = multiple responses
	If you answered "No" to each of the last 4 questions (59a–62a) about sexual experiences with older persons, please skip to question 67a. *Mark all that apply. Did any of these sexual experiences with an adult or person at least 5 years older than you involve:*	
63a	A relative who lived in your home?	1 = yes 2 = no
63b	A non-relative who lived in your home?	1 = yes 2 = no
63c	A relative who didn't live in your home?	1 = yes 2 = no
63d	A family friend or person who you knew and who didn't live in your household?	1 = yes 2 = no
63e	A stranger?	1 = yes 2 = no 9
63f	Someone who was supposed to be taking care of you?	1 = yes 2 = no
63g	Someone you trusted?	1 = yes 2 = no
	Did any of these sexual experiences involve:	
64a	Trickery, verbal persuasion, or pressure to get you to participate?	1 = yes 2 = no
64b	Being given alcohol or drugs?	1 = yes 2 = no
64c	Threats to harm you if you didn't participate?	1 = yes 2 = no
64d	Being physically forced or overpowered to make you participate?	1 = yes 2 = no
65a	Have you ever told a doctor, nurse, or other health professional about these sexual experiences?	1 = yes 2 = no

Question Number	Verbatim Question	Response Categories and Comments
65b	Has a therapist or counselor ever suggested to you that you were sexually abused as a child?	1 = yes 2 = no
66	Do you think that you were sexually abused as a child?	1 = yes 2 = no
	Apart from other sexual experiences you have already told us about, while you were growing up during your first 18 years of life	
67a	Did a boy or group of boys about your own age ever force or threaten to harm you in order to have sexual contact?	1 = yes 2 = no
67b	If yes did the contact involve someone touching your sexual parts or trying to have intercourse with you (oral, anal, vaginal)?	1 = yes 2 = no
67c	If yes how many times did someone do this to you?	1 = once 2 = twice 3 = 3–5 times 4 = 6–10 times 5 = more than 10 times 9 = multiple responses
67d	Did the contact involve a person actually having intercourse with you (oral, anal, vaginal)?	1 = yes 2 = no
67e	If yes how many times did someone do this to you?	1 = once 2 = twice 3 = 3–5 times 4 = 6–10 times 5 = more than 10 times 9 = multiple responses
68a	***As an adult,*** *(age 19 or older) did anyone ever force or threaten you with harm in order to have sexual contact?*	1 = yes 2 = no
68b	If yes did the contact involve someone touching your sexual parts or trying to have intercourse with you (oral, anal, vaginal)?	1 = yes 2 = no
68c	If yes how many times did someone do this to you?	1 = once 2 = twice 3 = 3–5 times 4 = 6–10 times 5 = more than 10 times 9 = multiple responses

(continued)

Question Number	Verbatim Question	Response Categories and Comments
68d	Did the contact involve a person actually having intercourse with you (oral, anal, vaginal)?	1 = yes 2 = no
68e	If yes how many times did someone do this to you?	1 = once 2 = twice 3 = 3–5 times 4 = 6–10 times 5 = more than 10 times 9 = multiple responses

Appendix B

Family Health History—Male Version

Question Number	Verbatim Question	Response categories and comments
1	What is your birthrate? Month _____	
	Year _____	
1b	What state were you born in? State _____	enter two letter state code DC = District of Columbia
	I was born outside the U.S.	1 = box checked
2	What is your sex?	1 = male 2 = female
3a	What is your race?	1 = asian 2 = black 3 = white 4 = american indian 5 = other 9 = multiple boxes checked
3b	Are you of Mexican, Latino, or Hispanic origin?	1 = yes 2 = no
4	Please check how far you've gone in school. ... (Choose one)	1 = Didn't go to high school 2 = Some high school 3 = High school graduate or GED 4 = Some college or technical school 5 = 4 year college graduate 9 = Multiple boxes checked
5	What is your current marital status? Are you now ...	1 = married 2 = not married, but living together with a partner 3 = widowed 4 = separated 5 = divorced 6 = never married 9 = multiple answers checked

Source: CDC, "Family Health History - Male Version." *(continued)*

Question Number	Verbatim Question	Response categories and comments
6a	How many times have you been married?	1 = 1 2 = 2 3 = 3 4 = 4 or more 5 = never married 9 = multiple boxes checked
6b	During what month and year were you first married? Month _____	Range: 1–12
	Year _____	Range: 10–96
	Never married	1 = never married
7a	Which of the following best describes your employment status?	1 = full time (35 hours or more) 2 = part-time (1–34 hours) 3 = Not employed outside the home 9 = multiple items checked
7b	*If you are employed full time (35 hours per week or more):* How many days of work did you miss in the past 30 days due to stress or feeling depressed?	Range: 0–30
7c	How many days of work did you miss in the past 30 days due to poor physical health?	Range: 0–30
8	For most of your childhood, did your family own their home?	1 = yes 2 = no
9a	During your childhood, how many times did you move residences, even in the same town? # of times _____	Range: 0–999
9b	How long have you lived at your current residence?	1 = Less than 6 months 2 = Less than 1 year 3 = Less than 2 years 4 = 2 or more years 9 = Multiple boxes checked
10	How old was your mother when you were born? Age _____	Range: 0–99
11a	How much education does/did your mother have? (Choose one)	1 = Didn't go to high school 2 = Some high school 3 = High school graduate or GED 4 = Some college or technical school 5 = 4 year college degree graduate or higher 9 = Multiple boxes checked

Question Number	Verbatim Question	Response categories and comments
11b	How much education does/did your father have? (Choose one)	1 = Didn't go to high school 2 = Some high school 3 = High school graduate or GED 4 = Some college or technical school 5 = 4 year college graduate or higher 9 = Multiple boxes checked
12a	Have you smoked at least 100 cigarettes in your entire life?	1 = yes 2 = no
12b	How old were you when you began to smoke cigarettes fairly regularly? Age _____	Range: 0–99
12c	Do you smoke cigarettes now?	1 = yes 2 = no
12d	If yes, on average, about how many cigarettes a day do you smoke? Number of cigarettes _____	Range: 0–99
13a	If you used to smoke cigarettes but don't smoke now, about how many cigarettes a day did you smoke?	Range: 00–99
13b	How old were you when you quit? Age _____	Range: 00–99
14a	During your first 18 years of life did your father smoke?	1 = yes 2 = no
14b	During your first 18 years of life did your mother smoke?	1 = yes 2 = no
15a	During the past month, about how many days per week did you exercise for recreation or to keep in shape? _____ days per week	Range: 0–7
15b	During the past month, when you exercised for recreation or to keep in shape, how long did you usually exercise (minutes)? _____ minutes	0 = 0 1 = 1–19 2 = 20–29 3 = 30–39 4 = 40–49 5 = 50–59 6 = 60 or more
16a	How old were you when you had your first drink of alcohol other than a few sips? Age _____	Range: 00–99
	Never drank alcohol	1 = Box Checked
	During each of the following age intervals, what was your usual number of drinks of alcohol per week?	

(continued)

Question Number	Verbatim Question	Response categories and comments
16b1	Age 19–29	1 = None 2 = Less than 6 per wk 3 = 7–13 per wk 4 = 14 or more per wk 9 = multiple responses
16b2	Age 30–39	1 = None 2 = Less than 6 per wk 3 = 7–13 per wk 4 = 14 or more per wk 9 = multiple responses
16b3	Age 40–49	1 = None 2 = Less than 6 per wk 3 = 7–13 per wk 4 = 14 or more per wk 9 = multiple responses
16b4	Age 50 and older	1 = None 2 = Less than 6 per wk 3 = 7–13 per wk 4 = 14 or more per wk 9 = multiple responses
16c	During the past month, have you had any beer, wine, wine coolers, cocktails or liquor?	1 = yes 2 = no
16d	During the past month, how many days per week did you drink any alcoholic beverages on average?	Range: 0–7
16e	On the days when you drank, about how many drinks per day did you have on average?	1 = 1 2 = 2 3 = 3 4 = 4 or more 5 = didn't drink in past month
16f	Considering all types of alcoholic beverages, how many times during the past month did you have 5 or more drinks on an occasion? Number of times _____	Range: 0–999
16g	During the past month, how many times have you driven when you've had perhaps too much to drink? Number of times _____	Range: 0–999
16h	During the past 30 days, how many times did you ride in a car or other vehicle driven by someone who had been drinking alcohol? Number of times _____	Range: 0–999
17	Have you ever had a problem with your use of alcohol?	1 = yes 2 = no

Question Number	Verbatim Question	Response categories and comments
18	Have you ever considered yourself to be an alcoholic?	1 = yes 2 = no
19a	During your first 18 years of life did you live with anyone who was a problem drinker or alcoholic?	1 = yes 2 = no
19b	*If "yes" check all who were:*	
	father	1 = if boxed checked
	mother	1 = if boxed checked
	brothers	1 = if boxed checked
	other relative	1 = if boxed checked
	other non-relative	1 = if boxed checked
	sisters	1 = if boxed checked
20	Have you ever been married to someone (or lived with someone as if you were married) who was a problem drinker or alcoholic?	1 = yes 2 = no
21a	Have you ever used street drugs?	1 = yes 2 = no
21b	If "yes" how old were you the first time you used them? Age _____	Range: 0–99
21c	About how many times have you used street drugs?	0 = 0 1 = 1–2 2 = 3–10 3 = 11–25 4 = 26–99 5 = 100+ 9 = multiple responses
21d	Have you ever had a problem with street drugs?	1 = yes 2 = no
21e	Have you ever considered yourself to be addicted to street drugs?	1 = yes 2 = no
21f	Have you ever injected street drugs?	1 = yes 2 = no
22	Have you ever been under the care of a psychologist, psychiatrist, or therapist?	1 = yes 2 = no
23a	Has a doctor, nurse, or health professional ever asked you about family or household problems during your childhood?	1 = yes 2 = no
23b	How many close friends or relatives would help you with your emotional problems or feelings if you needed it?	1 = none 2 = one 3 = two 4 = 3 or more 9 = multiple responses

(continued)

Question Number	Verbatim Question	Response categories and comments
	During your first 18 years of life, was anyone in your household. …	
24	Did you live with anyone who used street drugs?	1 = yes 2 = no
25a	Were your parents ever separated or divorced?	1 = yes 2 = no
25b	Did you ever live with a stepfather?	1 = yes 2 = no
25c	Did you ever live with a stepmother?	1 = yes 2 = no
26	Were you a foster child?	1 = yes 2 = no
27a	Did you ever run away from home for more than one day?	1 = yes 2 = no
27b	Did your brothers or sisters run away from home for more than one day?	1 = yes 2 = no
28	Was anyone in your household depressed or mentally ill?	1 = yes 2 = no
29	Did anyone in your household attempt to commit suicide?	1 = yes 2 = no
30a	Did anyone in your household go to prison?	1 = yes 2 = no
30b	Did anyone in your household ever commit a serious crime?	1 = yes 2 = no
31a	What is the most you have ever weighed? Weight in pounds _____	Range: 000–999
31b	How old were you then? age: _____	Range: 18–99
32a	Have you ever attempted to commit suicide?	1 = yes 2 = no
32b	If "yes", how old were you the first time you attempted suicide? Age _____	Range: 1–99
32c	If "yes", how old were you the last time you attempted suicide? Age _____	Range: 1–99
32d	How many times have you attempted suicide? # of times _____	Range: 01–99,
32e	Did any suicide attempt ever result in an injury, poisoning, or overdose that had to be treated by a doctor or nurse?	1 = yes 2 = no

Question Number	Verbatim Question	Response categories and comments
	In order to get a more complete picture of the health of our patients, the next three questions are about <u>voluntary</u> sexual experiences.	
33a	How old were you the first time you had sexual intercourse? Years _____	
	Never had intercourse	1 = box checked
33b	With how many different partners have you ever had sexual intercourse? Number of partners _____	number of intercourse partners, lifetime Range: 0–999
33c	During the past year, with how many different partners have you ever had sexual intercourse? # of partners _____	number of intercourse partners, past year Range: 0–999
34a	Have you ever gotten someone pregnant? *If "Yes":*	1 = yes 2 = no
34b	How old were you the first time you got someone pregnant? age: _____	Range: 00–99
	Never got someone pregnant	1 = box checked
34c	What was the age of the youngest woman you ever got pregnant?	Range: 00–99
	Never got someone pregnant	1 = box checked
34d	How old were you then?	Range: 00–99
	Sometimes physical blows occur between parents. While you were growing up in your first 18 years of life, how often did your father (or stepfather) or mother's boyfriend do any to these things to your mother (or stepmother)?	
35a	Push, grab, slap or throw something at her?	1 = never 2 = once, twice 3 = sometimes 4 = often 5 = very often 9 = multiple responses
35b	Kick, bite, hit her with a fist, or hit her with something hard?	1 = never 2 = once, twice 3 = sometimes 4 = often 5 = very often 9 = multiple responses

(continued)

Question Number	Verbatim Question	Response categories and comments
35c	Repeatedly hit her over at least a few minutes?	1 = never 2 = once, twice 3 = sometimes 4 = often 5 = very often 9 = multiple responses
35d	Threaten her with a knife or gun, or use a knife or gun to hurt her?	1 = never 2 = once, twice 3 = sometimes 4 = often 5 = very often 9 = multiple responses
	Sometimes parents spank their children as a form of discipline. While you were growing up during your first 18 years of life:	
36a	How often were you spanked?	1 = never 2 = once or twice 3 = a few times a year 4 = many times a year 5 = weekly or more 9 = multiple responses
36b	How severely were you spanked?	1 = not hard 2 = a little hard 3 = medium 4 = quite hard 5 = very hard 9 = multiple responses
36c	How old were you the last time you remember being spanked? age: _____	Range: 18–99
	While you were growing up, during your first 18 years of life, how true were each of the following statements:	
37	You didn't have enough to eat?	1 = never true 2 = rarely true 3 = sometimes true 4 = often true 5 = very often true 9 = multiple responses
38	You knew there was someone to take care of you and protect you?	1 = never true 2 = rarely true 3 = sometimes true 4 = often true 5 = very often true 9 = multiple responses

Question Number	Verbatim Question	Response categories and comments
39	People in your family called you things like "lazy" or "ugly"?	1 = never true 2 = rarely true 3 = sometimes true 4 = often true 5 = very often true 9 = multiple responses
40	Your parents were too drunk or high to take care of the family?	1 = never true 2 = rarely true 3 = sometimes true 4 = often true 5 = very often true 9 = multiple responses
41	There was someone in your family who helped you feel important or special?	1 = never true 2 = rarely true 3 = sometimes true 4 = often true 5 = very often true 9 = multiple responses
42	You had to wear dirty clothes?	1 = never true 2 = rarely true 3 = sometimes true 4 = often true 5 = very often true 9 = multiple responses
43	You felt loved?	1 = never true 2 = rarely true 3 = sometimes true 4 = often true 5 = very often true 9 = multiple responses
44	You thought your parents wished you had never been born?	1 = never true 2 = rarely true 3 = sometimes true 4 = often true 5 = very often true 9 = multiple responses
45	People in your family looked out for each other?	1 = never true 2 = rarely true 3 = sometimes true 4 = often true 5 = very often true 9 = multiple responses
46	You felt that someone in your family hated you?	1 = never true 2 = rarely true 3 = sometimes true 4 = often true 5 = very often true 9 = multiple responses

(continued)

Question Number	Verbatim Question	Response categories and comments
47	People in your family said hurtful or insulting things to you?	1 = never true 2 = rarely true 3 = sometimes true 4 = often true 5 = very often true 9 = multiple responses
48	People in your family felt close to each other?	1 = never true 2 = rarely true 3 = sometimes true 4 = often true 5 = very often true 9 = multiple responses
49	You believe that you were emotionally abused?	1 = never true 2 = rarely true 3 = sometimes true 4 = often true 5 = very often true 9 = multiple responses
50	There was someone to take you to the doctor if you needed it?	1 = never true 2 = rarely true 3 = sometimes true 4 = often true 5 = very often true 9 = multiple responses
51	Your family was a source of strength and support?	1 = never true 2 = rarely true 3 = sometimes true 4 = often true 5 = very often true 9 = multiple responses
	Sometimes parents or other adults hurt children. While you were growing up, that is, during your first 18 years of life, how often did a parent, step-parent, or adult living in your home:	
52a	Swear at you, insult you, or put you down?	1 = never 2 = once, twice 3 = sometimes 4 = often 5 = very often 9 = multiple responses
52b	Threaten to hit you or throw something at you, but didn't do it?	1 = never 2 = once, twice 3 = sometimes 4 = often 5 = very often 9 = multiple responses

Question Number	Verbatim Question	Response categories and comments
52c	Actually push, grab, shove, slap you, or throw something at you?	1 = never 2 = once, twice 3 = sometimes 4 = often 5 = very often 9 = multiple responses
52d	Hit you so hard that you had marks or were injured?	1 = never 2 = once, twice 3 = sometimes 4 = often 5 = very often 9 = multiple responses
52e	Act in a way that made you afraid that you might be physically hurt?	1 = never 2 = once, twice 3 = sometimes 4 = often 5 = very often 9 = multiple responses
	Some people, while growing up in their first 18 years of life, had a sexual experience with <u>an adult or</u> <u>someone at least five years older than themselves.</u> These experiences may have involved a relative family friend or stranger. During the first 18 years of life, did an adult or older relative, family friend or stranger ever:	
53a	Touch or fondle your body in a sexual way? *If "Yes":*	1 = yes 2 = no
	The first time this happened, how old were you? age: _____	Range: 00–99
	The first time, did this happen against your wishes?	1 = yes 2 = no
	The last time this happened, how old were you? age: _____	Range: 00–99
	About how many times did this happen to you? # times: _____	Range: 00–99
	How many different people did this to you? # people _____	Range: 00–99

(continued)

Question Number	Verbatim Question	Response categories and comments
	What was the sex of the person(s) who did this?	1 = male 2 = female 3 = both 9 = multiple responses
54a	Have you touch their body in a sexual way? *If "Yes":*	1 = yes 2 = no
	The first time this happened, how old were you? age: _____	Range: 00–99
	The first time, did this happen against your wishes?	1 = yes 2 = no
	The last time this happened, how old were you? age: _____	Range: 00–99
	About how many times did this happen to you? # times: _____	Range: 00–99
	How many different people did this to you? # people: _____	Range: 00–99
	What was the sex of the person(s) who did this?	1 = male 2 = female 3 = both 9 = multiple responses
55a	**Attempt** to have any type of sexual intercourse (oral, anal, or vaginal) with you? *If "Yes":*	1 = yes 2 = no
	The first time this happened, how old were you? age: _____	Range: 00–99
	The first time, did this happen against your wishes?	1 = yes 2 = no
	The last time this happened, how old were you? age: _____	Range: 00–99
	About how many times did this happen to you? # times: _____	Range: 00–99
	How many different people did this to you? # people: _____	Range: 00–99
	What was the sex of the person(s) who did this?	1 = male 2 = female 3 = both 9 = multiple responses

Question Number	Verbatim Question	Response categories and comments
56a	**Actually have** any type of sexual intercourse with you (oral, anal, or vaginal) with you? *If "Yes":*	1 = yes 2 = no
	The first time this happened, how old were you? age: _____	Range: 00–99
	The first time, did this happen against your wishes?	1 = yes 2 = no
	The last time this happened, how old were you? age: _____	Range: 00–99
	About how many times did this happen to you? # times: _____	Range: 00–99
	How many different people did this to you? # people: _____	Range: 00–99
	What was the sex of the person(s) who did this?	1 = male 2 = female 3 = both 9 = multiple responses
	If you answered "No" to each of the last 4 questions (54a–57a) about sexual experiences with older people, please skip to question 62a. *Did any of these sexual experiences with an adult or person at least 5 years older than you involve:*	
57a	A relative who lived in your home?	1 = yes 2 = no
57b	A non-relative who lived in your home?	1 = yes 2 = no
57c	A relative who didn't live in your home?	1 = yes 2 = no
57d	A family friend or person who you knew, and who didn't live in your home?	1 = yes 2 = no
57e	A stranger?	1 = yes 2 = no
57f	Someone who was supposed to be taking care of you?	1 = yes 2 = no
57g	Someone you trusted?	1 = yes 2 = no

(continued)

Question Number	Verbatim Question	Response categories and comments
	Did any of these sexual experiences involve:	
58a	Trickery, verbal persuasion, or pressure to get you to participate?	1 = yes 2 = no
58b	Being given alcohol or drugs?	1 = yes 2 = no
58c	Threats to harm you if you didn't participate?	1 = yes 2 = no
58d	Being physically forced or overpowered to make you participate?	1 = yes 2 = no
59a	Have you ever told a doctor, nurse, or other health professional about these sexual experiences?	1 = yes 2 = no
59b	Has a therapist of counselor ever suggested to you that you were sexually abused as a child?	1 = yes 2 = no
60	Do you think that you were sexually abused as a child?	1 = yes 2 = no
	Apart from the other experiences you have already told us about, while you were growing up during your first 18 years of life:	
61a	Did a boy or group of boys about your own age, ever force or threaten you with harm in order have sexual contact?	1 = yes 2 = no
61b	If yes did the contact involve someone touching your sexual parts or trying to have intercourse with you (oral or anal)?	1 = yes 2 = no
61c	If yes how many times did someone do this to you?	1 = once 2 = twice 3 = 3–5 times 4 = 6–10 times 5 = more than 10 times 9 = multiple responses
61d	Did the contact involve a person actually having intercourse with you (vaginal, oral or anal)?	1 = yes 2 = no
61e	If yes how many times did someone do this to you?	1 = once 2 = twice 3 = 3–5 times 4 = 6–10 times 5 = more than 10 times 9 = multiple responses

Question Number	Verbatim Question	Response categories and comments
62a	**As an adult**, *(age 19 or older) has any-one ever physically forced or threaten you to have sexual contact?*	1 = yes 2 = no
62b	If yes did the contact involve someone touching your sexual parts or trying to have intercourse with you (vaginal, oral or anal)?	1 = yes 2 = no
62c	If yes how many times has someone done this to you?	1 = once 2 = twice 3 = 3–5 times 4 = 6–10 times 5 = more than 10 times 9 = multiple responses
62d	Did the contact involve a person actually having intercourse with you (vaginal, oral or anal)?	1 = yes 2 = no
62e	If yes how many times did someone do this to you?	1 = once 2 = twice 3 = 3–5 times 4 = 6–10 times 5 = more than 10 times 9 = multiple responses

Appendix C

Health Appraisal Questionnaire
Female Version

Do you have:	
Frequent stuffy or watery nose, sneezing	1 = yes 2 = no
An allergy to any medications	1 = yes 2 = no
Asthma or notice yourself wheezing	1 = yes 2 = no
Chronic bronchitis or emphysema	1 = yes 2 = no
A frequent cough for any reason	1 = yes 2 = no
Shortness of breath	1 = yes 2 = no
Have you ever:	
Coughed up blood (coughed not vomited)	1 = yes 2 = no
Been treated for TB or Coccidomycosis (Valley Fever)	1 = yes 2 = no
Had a positive TB test	1 = yes 2 = no
Been a smoker	1 = yes 2 = no
If now a smoker how many cigarettes a day _____	
Had lung cancer	1 = yes 2 = no
Do you chew tobacco	1 = yes 2 = no

(continued)

Source: CDC, "Health Appraisal Questionnaire - Female Version."

Have you ever had, or ever been told you have:	
High blood pressure	1 = yes 2 = no
To take blood pressure medicine	1 = yes 2 = no
A heart attack (coronary)	1 = yes 2 = no
To take medicine to lower your cholesterol	1 = yes 2 = no
Do you get:	
Pains or heavy pressure in your chest with exertion	1 = yes 2 = no
Do you use nitroglycerin	1 = yes 2 = no
Episodes of fast heart beats or skipped beats	1 = yes 2 = no
Other heart problems	1 = yes 2 = no
Nocturnal leg cramps	1 = yes 2 = no
Leg pains from rapid or uphill walking, stairs	1 = yes 2 = no
Do you have:	
Varicose veins	1 = yes 2 = no
Any skin problems	1 = yes 2 = no
Are you troubled by:	
Abdominal (stomach) pains	1 = yes 2 = no
Frequent indigestion or heartburn	1 = yes 2 = no
Constipation	1 = yes 2 = no
Frequent diarrhea, loose bowels	1 = yes 2 = no
Has there been a definite change:	
In the pattern or regularity of your bowel movements in the last year	1 = yes 2 = no
Are you a vegetarian	1 = yes 2 = no

Have you ever had, or been told you have:	
An ulcer	1 = yes 2 = no
Vomited blood	1 = yes 2 = no
Black tar-like bowel movements	1 = yes 2 = no
Gallstones, gallbladder problems	1 = yes 2 = no
Yellow jaundice, hepatitis, or any liver trouble	1 = yes 2 = no
Definite change in your weight in recent months	1 = yes 2 = no
Are you troubled by:	
Frequent headaches	1 = yes 2 = no
Attacks of dizziness	1 = yes 2 = no
Have you ever	
Had seizures, convulsions, fits	1 = yes 2 = no
Fainted or lost consciousness for no obvious reason	1 = yes 2 = no
Temporarily lost control of a hand or foot (paralysis)	1 = yes 2 = no
Had a stroke or "small stroke"	1 = yes 2 = no
Been temporarily unable to speak	1 = yes 2 = no
Are you troubled by:	
Frequent back pain	1 = yes 2 = no
Pain or swelling in your joints	1 = yes 2 = no
Have you ever:	
Broken any bones	1 = yes 2 = no
Frequently worried about being ill	1 = yes 2 = no
Been troubled as a result of being more sensitive than most people	1 = yes 2 = no
Had special circumstances in which you find yourself panicked	1 = yes 2 = no
Had reason to fear your anger getting out of control	1 = yes 2 = no

(continued)

Have you had, or do you have:	
Any problems with your urinary tract (kidney, bladder)	1 = yes 2 = no
Loss of control of your urine	1 = yes 2 = no
Pain or burning when you urinate	1 = yes 2 = no
Blood in your urine	1 = yes 2 = no
Trouble starting the flow of urine	1 = yes 2 = no
To get up repeatedly at night to urinate	1 = yes 2 = no
Vaginal bleeding between periods	1 = yes 2 = no
After menopause, any vaginal bleeding whatsoever	1 = yes 2 = no
A noticable lump in your breast	1 = yes 2 = no
Do breast self-exams regularly	1 = yes 2 = no
Discharge from your nipples	1 = yes 2 = no
Have you ever been treated for or told you had:	
Any venereal disease	1 = yes 2 = no
Diabetes	1 = yes 2 = no
To take *medicine* for diabetes	1 = yes 2 = no
Thyroid disease	1 = yes 2 = no
Cancer	1 = yes 2 = no
Have you ever had or do you now have:	
Radiation therapy	1 = yes 2 = no
Trouble refusing requests or saying "No"	1 = yes 2 = no
Hallucinations (seen, smelled, or heard things that were not really there)	1 = yes 2 = no
Trouble falling asleep or staying asleep	1 = yes 2 = no

Tiredness, even after a good night's sleep	1 = yes 2 = no
Crying spells	1 = yes 2 = no
Depression or "feel down in the dumps"	1 = yes 2 = no
Much trouble with nervousness	1 = yes 2 = no
Do you:	
Sometimes drink more than is good for you	1 = yes 2 = no
Use street drugs	1 = yes 2 = no
Have you ever:	
Been raped, or sexually molested as a child	1 = yes 2 = no
Are you:	
Currently sexually active with a partner	1 = yes 2 = no
Satisfied with your sex life	1 = yes 2 = no
Concerned you are at risk for AIDS	1 = yes 2 = no
Please tell us:	
In the past year, about how many visits to a doctor have you made _____	.
How far have you gone in school	.
Are you married	1 = yes 2 = no
How many times have you been married _____	.
Are you now having serious or disturbing problems with your:	
Marriage	1 = yes 2 = no
Family	1 = yes 2 = no
Drug usage	1 = yes 2 = no
Job	1 = yes 2 = no
Financial matters	1 = yes 2 = no

(continued)

Have you ever had coronary artery surgery	1 = yes 2 = no
Approximate year	.
Did you have a blood transfusion between 1978 and 1985	1 = yes 2 = no
Do you feel you need any immunizations	1,2, .
Are you retired	1 = yes 2 = no
Have members of your family died before the age of 65?	1 = yes 2 = no
Are there diseases which a number of family members have had?	1 = yes 2 = no
Are there any unusual illnesses in your family you didn't list previously?	1 = yes 2 = no
Has a parent, brother, or sister developed coronary (heart) disease before age 60?	1 = yes 2 = no
Do you have an identical twin?	1 = yes 2 = no
Please fill in the circle that you think best describes your current state of health	1 = excellent 2 = good 3 = fair 4 = poor
Do you regularly use seat belts in a car?	1 = yes 2 = no
Please fill in the circle that best describes your stress level:	1 = high 2 = medium 3 = low
Year of last mammogram	
EXAMINATION DATA	

Appendix D

Health Appraisal Questionnaire

Male Version

Verbatim Question	Coding and Comments
Do you have:	
Frequent stuffy or watery nose, sneezing	1 = yes 2 = no
An allergy to any medications	1 = yes 2 = no
Asthma or notice yourself wheezing	1 = yes 2 = no
Chronic bronchitis or emphysema	1 = yes 2 = no
A frequent cough for any reason	1 = yes 2 = no
Shortness of breath	1 = yes 2 = no
Have you ever:	
Coughed up blood (coughed not vomited)	1 = yes 2 = no
Been treated for TB or Coccidomycosis (Valley Fever)	1 = yes 2 = no
Had a positive TB test	1 = yes 2 = no
Been a smoker	1 = yes 2 = no
If now a smoker how many cigarettes a day _____	
Had lung cancer	1 = yes 2 = no
Do you chew tobacco	1 = yes 2 = no

(continued)

Verbatim Question	Coding and Comments
Have you ever had, or ever been told you have:	
High blood pressure	1 = yes 2 = no
To take blood pressure medicine	1 = yes 2 = no
A heart attack (coronary)	1 = yes 2 = no
To take medicine to lower your cholesterol	1 = yes 2 = no
Do you get:	
Pains or heavy pressure in your chest with exertion	1 = yes 2 = no
Do you use nitroglycerin	1 = yes 2 = no
Episodes of fast heart beats or skipped beats	1 = yes 2 = no
Other heart problems	1 = yes 2 = no
Nocturnal leg cramps	1 = yes 2 = no
Leg pains from rapid or uphill walking, stairs	1 = yes 2 = no
Do you have:	
Varicose veins	1 = yes 2 = no
Any skin problems	1 = yes 2 = no
Are you troubled by:	
Abdominal (stomach) Pains	1 = yes 2 = no
Frequent indigestion or heartburn	1 = yes 2 = no
Constipation	1 = yes 2 = no
Frequent diarrhea, loose bowels	1 = yes 2 = no
Has there been a definite change:	
In the pattern or regularity of your bowel movements in the last year	1 = yes 2 = no
Are you a vegetarian	1 = yes 2 = no

Verbatim Question	Coding and Comments
Have you ever had, or been told you have:	
An ulcer	1 = yes 2 = no
Vomited blood	1 = yes 2 = no
Black tar-like bowel movements	1 = yes 2 = no
Gallstones, gallbladder problems	1 = yes 2 = no
Yellow jaundice, hepatitis, or any liver trouble	1 = yes 2 = no
Definite change in your weight in recent months	1 = yes 2 = no
Are you troubled by:	
Frequent headaches	1 = yes 2 = no
Attacks of dizziness	1 = yes 2 = no
Have you ever	
Had seizures, convulsions, fits	1 = yes 2 = no
Fainted or lost consciousness for no obvious reason	1 = yes 2 = no
Temporarily lost control of a hand or foot (paralysis)	1 = yes 2 = no
Had a stroke or "small stroke"	1 = yes 2 = no
Been temporarily unable to speak	1 = yes 2 = no
Are you troubled by:	
Frequent back pain	1 = yes 2 = no
Pain or swelling in your joints	1 = yes 2 = no
Have you ever:	
Broken any bones	1 = yes 2 = no
Frequently worried about being ill	1 = yes 2 = no
Been troubled as a result of being more sensitive than most people	1 = yes 2 = no

(continued)

Verbatim Question	Coding and Comments
Had special circumstances in which you find yourself panicked	1 = yes 2 = no
Had reason to fear your anger getting out of control	1 = yes 2 = no
Have you had, or do you have:	
Any problems with your urinary tract (kidney, bladder)	1 = yes 2 = no
Loss of control of your urine	1 = yes 2 = no
Pain or burning when you urinate	1 = yes 2 = no
Blood in your urine	1 = yes 2 = no
Trouble starting the flow of urine	1 = yes 2 = no
To get up repeatedly at night to urinate	1 = yes 2 = no
Discharge from your nipples	1 = yes 2 = no
Have you ever been treated for or told you had:	
Any venereal disease	1 = yes 2 = no
Diabetes	1 = yes 2 = no
To take *medicine* for diabetes	1 = yes 2 = no
Thyroid disease	1 = yes 2 = no
Cancer	1 = yes 2 = no
Have you ever had or do you now have:	
Radiation therapy	1 = yes 2 = no
Trouble refusing requests or saying "No"	1 = yes 2 = no
Hallucinations (seen, smelled, or heard things that were not really there)	1 = yes 2 = no
Trouble falling asleep or staying asleep	1 = yes 2 = no
Tiredness, even after a good night's sleep	1 = yes 2 = no

Verbatim Question	Coding and Comments
Crying spells	1 = yes 2 = no
Depression or "feel down in the dumps"	1 = yes 2 = no
Much trouble with nervousness	1 = yes 2 = no
Do you:	
Sometimes drink more than is good for you	1 = yes 2 = no
Use street drugs	1 = yes 2 = no
Have you ever:	
Been raped, or sexually molested as a child	1 = yes 2 = no
Are you:	
Currently sexually active with a partner	1 = yes 2 = no
Satisfied with your sex life	1 = yes 2 = no
Concerned you are at risk for AIDS	1 = yes 2 = no
Please tell us:	
In the past year, about how many visits to a doctor have you made _____	.
How far have you gone in school	.
Are you married	1 = yes 2 = no
How many times have you been married _____	.
Are you now having serious or disturbing problems with your:	
Marriage	1 = yes 2 = no
Family	1 = yes 2 = no
Drug usage	1 = yes 2 = no
Job	1 = yes 2 = no
Financial matters	1 = yes 2 = no
Have you ever had coronary artery surgery	1 = yes 2 = no

(continued)

Verbatim Question	Coding and Comments
Approximate year	Range: 1–96.
Did you have a blood transfusion between 1978 and 1985	1,2.
Do you feel you need any immunizations	1,2.
Are you retired	1 = yes 2 = no
Have members of your family died before the age of 65?	1 = yes 2 = no
Are there diseases which a number of family members have had?	1 = yes 2 = no
Are there any unusual illnesses in your family you didn't list previously?	1 = yes 2 = no
Has a parent, brother, or sister developed coronary (heart) disease before age 60?	1 = yes 2 = no
Do you have an identical twin?	1 = yes 2 = no
Please fill in the circle that you think best describes your current state of health	1 = excellent 2 = good 3 = fair 4 = poor
Do you regularly use seat belts in a car?	1 = yes 2 = no
Please fill in the circle that best describes your stress level:	1 = high 2 = medium 3 = low

Appendix E

BRFSS Adverse Childhood Experience (ACE) Module

Prologue: I'd like to ask you some questions about events that happened during your childhood. This information will allow us to better understand problems that may occur early in life, and may help others in the future. This is a sensitive topic and some people may feel uncomfortable with these questions. At the end of this section, I will give you a phone number for an organization that can provide information and referral for these issues. Please keep in mind that you can ask me to skip any question you do not want to answer. All questions refer to the time period before you were 18 years of age. Now, looking back before you were 18 years of age.

1. Did you live with anyone who was depressed, mentally ill, or suicidal?

2. Did you live with anyone who was a problem drinker or alcoholic?

3. Did you live with anyone who used illegal street drugs or who abused prescription medications?

Source: CDC, "BRFSS Adverse Childhood Experience (ACE) Module."

4. Did you live with anyone who served time or was sentenced to serve time in a prison, jail, or other correctional facility?

5. Were your parents separated or divorced?

6. How often did your parents or adults in your home ever slap, hit, kick, punch or beat each other up?

7. Before age 18, how often did a parent or adult in your home ever hit, beat, kick, or physically hurt you in any way? Do not include spanking. Would you say—

8. How often did a parent or adult in your home ever swear at you, insult you, or put you down?

9. How often did anyone at least 5 years older than you or an adult, ever touch you sexually?

10. How often did anyone at least 5 years older than you or an adult, try to make you touch sexually?

11. How often did anyone at least 5 years older than you or an adult, force you to have sex?

Response Options

Questions 1–4	Question 5	Questions 6–11
1 = Yes	1 = Yes	1 = Never
2 = No	2 = No	2 = Once
7 = DK/NS	8 = Parents not married	3 = More than once
9 = Refused	7 = DK/NS	7 = DK/NS
	9 = Refused	9 = Refused

Index

About the Author

Monica Miller-Smith, EdD, has been a professor for 12 years. She has instructed human development and family studies courses at the University of Connecticut, University of Bridgeport, and Central Michigan University. She has expertise in service-learning and distance education. In 2011, she partnered with Stamford Public Education Foundation to develop a service-learning mentoring program for elementary schools in Stamford, Connecticut. The program was offered for eight years  and provided service-learning experiences to thousands of elementary students and hundreds of University of Connecticut students. She has presented at national and international conferences on topics such as economic inequality, service-learning, and distance education. She is an avid traveler and has lived in California, Connecticut, Massachusetts, New York, Puerto Rico, and Nevis, West Indies. She currently lives in Georgia with her husband and two daughters.

CPSIA information can be obtained
at www.ICGtesting.com
Printed in the USA
LVHW081953211221
706856LV00002B/14